BELFAST

By the same author

Breakfast in a Bright Room (poetry)
Images of Belfast
All Shy Wildness as editor
Eden to Edenderry (poetry)

BELFAST

PORTRAITS OF A CITY

ROBERT JOHNSTONE

BARRIE & JENKINS

LONDON

First published in Great Britain in 1990 by
Barrie & Jenkins Ltd
20 Vauxhall Bridge Road, London SW1V 2SA

British Library Cataloguing in Publication Data
Johnstone, Robert, 1951–
    Belfast : portraits of a city. — (Cities).
    1. Belfast, history
    I. Title   II. Series
    941.67

ISBN 0–7126–3744–3

Typeset by 🅐 Tek Art Limited, Addiscombe, Croydon, Surrey
Printed in Great Britain by Butler and Tanner, London and Frome

CONTENTS

LIST OF ILLUSTRATIONS

1   *Captain Thomas Lee*, 1594 by Marcus Gheeraedts the Younger
2   The Giant's Ring
3a   Dolmens in the Giant's Ring
3b   Carrickfergus Castle
4a   Sir Arthur Chichester
4b   Plate III from *The Image of Irelande* by John Derricke, 1581
5   *William III*, by an unknown artist, 1690–1700
6   Ground Plan of Belfast, 1685 (with south at the top)
7a   High Street in 1786
7b   *William Drennan* by Robert Home
8   A Map of the Town and Environs of Belfast Surveyed in 1791
     by James Williamson
9   Henry Cooke.
10   The 'Black Squad'
11a   *Titanic* leaving Belfast
11b   The Partners of Harland & Wolff
12   Viscount and Lady Pirrie
13a   York Street Mill: warping
13b   A Beetling engine
14a   Prime Minister Terence O'Neill meets Taoiseach Jack Lynch
14b   City Hall, November 1985. Rally against the Anglo–Irish agreement
15   Bomb at Smithfield
16a   Cave Hill Road
16b   McArt's Fort

Endpapers: J.H. Connop's Bird's Eye View of Belfast, 1863

PICTURE CREDITS

Linen Hall Library: 6,8, Endpapers; National Portrait Gallery: 5; Northern Ireland Tourist Board: 3a,3b,16b; Pacemaker: 14a,14b,15; Department of Archaeology, Queen's University: 2; The Tate Gallery: 1; Ulster Folk and Transport Museum: 13a,13b,16a in the W.A. Green Collection, and 10,11a,11b,12 in the Harland & Wolff Collection; Ulster Museum: 4a,7a,7b.

PREFACE

It needs but a glance at Belfast and the surrounding country to perceive that the town and its neighbouring districts have nothing in common with the rest of Ireland.

Events since 1834 have made H.D. Inglis's observation more applicable than ever. Constantly filmed, reported from and travelled to by explorers like Inglis, Belfast is self-aware, conscious of how special it is. This book considers some causes of that difference.

It is not an exhaustive academic or scholarly history but a look at some of the more colourful individuals and events that have helped to create Belfast. It is a reading of origins, biased towards beginnings rather than outcomes. The nature of the place and of its past means that names and themes keep reappearing, still influential when they seemed done with. To pull one thread in what the critic Edna Longley has called the 'Belfast tangle' is to be aware of contending threads pulling back.

There are numerous straightforward historical, geographical, sociological and literary works, many of them excellent, about Belfast or relevant to it. Some have been relied on in the writing of this book and are usually referred to in the text by the author's name. Full details are given in the bibliography.

The author warmly thanks the following for their generous help: Jonathan Bardon, Patricia Craig, John Gray, Librarian at the Linen Hall Library, Barry Hartwell of the Archaeology Department, Queen's University, Edna Longley, Steve McBride, Perry Morrison, John Morrow, and Anne Tannahill of the Blackstaff Press.

CHAPTER ONE

BLAME FALL
ON THE BUILDERS

The playwright Martin Lynch tells a story about the premiere of *The Interrogation of Ambrose Fogarty*. The play is remarkable for its authentic portrayal of police interrogations, written by someone who himself was picked up and questioned several times, though never charged with any offence. Lynch, using one of the techniques of community drama which he had developed in Turf Lodge, had written into the play a comic figure, Willie Lagan, based on an actual local character famous for his eccentricities. He invited this man to the premiere at the Lyric Theatre, and when Willie Lagan appeared on the stage, the original cried out with delight, 'That's me!', exhibiting the antics faithfully recreated by playwright and actor.

Such self-absorption may be ambiguous, both valuable socially and inward in a limiting way, but it is potent. That foreign country in which they do things differently is, for the backward-looking narrator of L.P. Hartley's *The Go-Between*, the past. And the past is not history, especially in Belfast. There, history is more familiar, more amenable, more fascinating, and not at all foreign. It is certainly not over and done with. The citizens have a hunger to hear the story of themselves retold and reinterpreted. They consume large numbers of general and particular histories, reprints of biographies, newspaper columns, memoirs, street directories. They form passionate local studies groups, which produce pamphlets and articles. In a place in which, twenty-five years ago, there were no book publishers at all, there are now two busy general publishing houses and at least two small but very successful companies recently established expressly for the purpose of studying locales and reissuing photographs, stories and novels of local interest. Academics compile oral reminiscences about neighbourhoods, economic eras, factory work, and find themselves responsible for bestsellers. Playwrights re-enact the events of a year or twenty years ago, and the people outside whose front doors those events took place, and occasionally even those who supplied the originals of the characters, come to the theatre and watch what has been made of their story.

Such an appetite for reappraisal may be in part a very human and healthy reaction to the years of relative undernourishment which preceded it. In the half-century during which Belfast was a capital with a devolved parliament, reappraisal was not on the official agenda, however necessary. Martin Lynch might acknowledge Sam Thompson as a predecessor: Thompson's play about sectarianism in the shipyard, *Over the Bridge*, was thought too hot to handle by the forerunner of the Arts Council in Belfast. But when one's home town features as a trouble spot on the world's news, when populations shift and whole urban villages are destroyed, by planners or by political violence, when streets of houses are appropriated by one armed group or another, when one's beer money goes not to a landlord but to racketeers, when public transport is replaced by 'people's taxis' run by retired revolutionaries, when so much changes so quickly and so violently, and a community is repeatedly being surprised at renewed evidence of how degraded and how admirable people can be, when old certainties about who we are, what we are like, where we are, get challenged, it is understandable if mirror-gazing becomes compulsive. Does that look in the eyes denote some fatal flaw of character, does it mean stubbornness, naivety or bewilderment? Is that smile sincere, an expression of fortitude or callous indifference?

But there are other uses for history. In the several simultaneous wars being waged within and on the fringes of society, it can be a weapon against one's enemies, a certificate of identity, and a justification of injustice. One would not expect a sport which invited enthusiastic spectators to be discussed coolly. But in this game one can contest not only the referee's decisions and the tactics of both sides, one can argue about who the referee should be and under which rules the match should be played. There is considerable doubt about the score. When the street artists commemorate the latest atrocity ('IRA 1 BRITS 0', sprayed on a gable wall), its significance to all but the victim's loved ones fades faster than the paint. Besides, how would we recognize the final whistle?

In *The Peoples of Ireland* Liam de Paor says of the island, 'Its landscapes are fragmented and variegated: a country difficult to grasp.' The distinguished historians of Belfast – like George Benn in the last century, or Jonathan Bardon in this – are aware that the true landscape of the city's past is equally fragmented and variegated, even though the population of bar-stool historians finds it a lot easier to grasp. Arguably, the wish-fulfilment versions of history current in the bar or on the street are of more immediate import, since they are more likely to be called upon to excuse present actions. Like other art forms, history, crude or conscientious, has to do with making models of the world: the effectiveness of a Henry Moore sculpture is not entirely to do with anatomical accuracy. The origins of everything in Ireland, more so than in most places and if we go back far enough, are gratifyingly misty, and allow for all manner of pointed interpretations. The origins of Belfast itself are absolutely typical in this respect.

To begin as uncontentiously as possible, one might say that until 50,000 years ago Ireland could not be distinguished from Britain or the continent of Europe. But even here we immediately have problems, for fundamentalists, who believe in the literal truth of the Bible and especially of the book of Genesis, and who are uncommonly thick on the ground in Belfast, would object that nothing in creation is 50,000 years old, not even the link with Britain. Nevertheless, ice receded and the waters rose and first Ireland, and then, four millennia later, Britain, were lopped off, only just, from the continent of Europe. The intervening period was crucial to Ireland's natural history for, as the world warmed up, plants and animals spread northwards until they reached the barrier of the sea. As a result the variety of flora and fauna in Ireland is about one third smaller than that in the larger island, although Ireland has some plants which may have been indigenous to the lands that once existed to the west, and some plants which are found elsewhere only in Spain.

The topography of the island has been likened to that of a saucer or bowl – mountains round the rim, low-lying in the middle. The bedrock of the central plain is of fertile carboniferous limestone. It is a wet land, with many rivers. Glaciers left behind the extraordinary landscape south of Belfast, the drumlins of County Down, like bubble-packaging, regular grassy dunes of soil, or, when drowned in Strangford Lough, a series of islands which look exquisite from the air. They are elongated hummocks of boulder clay whose long axes run parallel to the direction of movement of the ice. Dunmurry Esker, a finger pointing at the city from the southwest, marks the path of a stream of glacial meltwater that shed its load of coarse sand and gravel as the ice sheet retreated. It lies at right angles to the edge of the ice. A readvance of the ice formed Belfast Lough and left deposits and lake silts 200 feet thick.

Seamus Heaney's haunting image of the bog as a way of talking about Ireland's malady – most acute now in the North – is powerful partly because of its geological accuracy. In the poem 'Bogland', Ireland pickles its past and will not let it go: the bottomless 'wet centre' could be the great gap in the middle of Northern Ireland, Lough Neagh, which is such a presence throughout the collection of poems *Door Into the Dark*: for the city, it is like an empty presence.

Glacial drifts and moraines cover much of the island, and it is tempting to emulate Heaney by interpreting this prevalence of superficial deposits as some sort of emblem – a bedrock that is, in everyday terms, unconsidered, overlaid by a veneer of minor features which we know and live amongst. But that is not the whole story. Further north of the city is the volcanic Antrim Plateau, composed of fine-grained, silica-rich dark basalt, which flowed from a pipe or fissure in the earth's crust into a sheet. When it solidified in the north it formed hexagonal columns at the Giant's Causeway. At Lough Neagh it is only fifty feet above sea level, but it is tilted upwards on the east, and it juts out over Belfast and forms, according to the weather, by turns a pretty or brooding or spectacular escarpment which hangs over the city. Divis is 1,374 feet high. The basalt overlays cretaceous rock and on some hill paths overlooking the city, walkers can see the sandwich of white skeletal remains exposed at waist level.

Between the gentle, glaciated features of Down and the abrupt, upland, volcanic features of Antrim, the area where the centre of the city now stands would have been more of a barrier than a place for settlement for the first people. The six-mile-wide basin from Cave Hill on the west to Dundonald Gap on the east marks the uncertain and unsatisfactory union of the River Lagan with the Irish Sea.

The river rises near the top of Slieve Croob, 1,755 feet above sea level. By the time it reaches Lisburn it is in a broad rolling plain. From this it derives its name, from the Irish *Abhainn an Lagáinn*, 'the water of the plain'. Here it is sluggish and liable to flooding, having a fall of only four feet per mile. It approaches Belfast Lough from the southwest. Before glaciation it flowed through the Bog Meadows, to the west of its present course. The light soils of the valley floor are easily tilled and fertile, but the boulder clays of the Antrim Plateau, which averages a height of 1,200 feet, are heavy and suitable only for grazing.

The river lies closer to the Down Plateau, with its gentler green hillsides notched by many streams. Geographers and geologists like to make puns with the landscape: it may be true that where there are drumlins there are drums, or that the north of Ireland is volcanic, but there are drums throughout Northern Ireland, and all sorts of processes have shaped the landscape as well as vulcanism. Possibly the contrast in landscapes north and south of the Lagan was reflected by contrasts in early human activities too. E. Estyn Evans is very fond of the physical setting: 'Few cities can show an environment so varied and picturesque as Belfast.'

The Mesolithic people of the Middle Stone Age were probably few in number, and we know little about them. They favoured the valley of the River Bann, where they could obtain flint for their tools. But flint tools are easily picked up in ploughed fields all around Belfast. In *'The Most Unpretending of Places'* Peter Carr maps finds on the east of the city, for example. Deer and smaller animals were hunted, and berries, nuts and seeds gathered from the forest. There were wolves and bears. As the forest was cleared, ring forts were built for protection: there are twenty below the 600-foot contour ringing the valley floor. The introduction of farming is associated with the Neolithic people. It was a technique which spread overland, at a regular rate of about forty-five miles every one hundred years, from its origin in the Balkans, though it would have spread less predictably along coastlines and across straits. About 6,000 or 7,000 years ago domestic species of animals and cultivated plants arrived in Ireland. From the evidence of excavations, it seems that modern breeds of cattle were already established on the island by 5,000 years ago. Rectangular houses were built of wooden posts, with rafters and thatch, as elsewhere in Europe, and variations on this theme could be found into modern times. Liam de Paor points out that 'in Ireland as elsewhere, up to 100 or 200 years ago, large numbers of people lived working lives not very different from those of their distant neolithic ancestors'.

Cultivation and grazing would have been easier on high ground, away from flooding, or on light soils, away from the forest. The trees would have been cleared by stone axes and by livestock grazing and, although it is possible that early assarted land could have given way to bog, some of these earliest clearances probably gave rise to the townland divisions that are still referred to today. It is tempting to imagine the Neolithic farmers on the crest of the Castlereagh Hills or on the Antrim Plateau, looking at the view across forest and estuary. Let the first imaginary person to do so be a woman, for it was probably women who did the bulk of the cultivation.

Her people might have used the exposed layer of white chalk on the Antrim Plateau for flint tools. The new red sandstone underlying the glacial deposits would have provided pure water, if she had been able to sink wells into it. (It was not until the nineteenth century that Belfast's ginger ale conquered the world.) After the ice retreated and until about 2,500 BC, the post-glacial sea was up to twenty feet higher than now, its shore being at Balmoral and Stranmillis. The old seacliff, fifty feet high, can still be seen at Sydenham and Skegoneill.

Early people used the Dunmurry Esker and the Malone Ridge, the tongue of fine sands which lies between the former and present courses of the Lagan, as dry routes; many pieces of pottery, flints and polished axes have been found there. Evans provides an irresistible picture of an ancient fisherman: fishing spears dating from 2,000 BC have been found on a site near the present Ormeau Bridge where there may have been a squatting place where salmon were speared. Up to the last century, Belfast Lough was famous for salmon, shellfish and shrimps, as well as for its wildfowl. It was still a famous beauty spot when William Makepeace Thackeray visited in 1842, so he was disappointed that it was obscured by an 'envious mist' as he left for Larne: the fog extended to the interior of the coach, where he became involved in a theological controversy with 'two grave gentlemen' all the way to Carrickfergus.

Evans locates Belfast's earliest 'metropolis' three miles upstream from Belfast Lough, at Ballynahatty. The Giant's Ring is a Neolithic or Bronze Age construction on a little platform of gravelly sand that is naturally set apart from its surroundings, being bordered on three sides by the Lagan and Purdysburn rivers, and by a steep slope on the east. Cathal O'Byrne records in As I Roved Out a visit one still evening to look again at the place he had seen as a child, but 'the height of the huge boulders we no longer find impressive', he says, for the world had changed scale as he grew up. For those without preconceptions, the Giant's Ring is awe-inspiring for all sorts of reasons, from our agreeably vague fantasies of the ancient past to personal memories of teenage romance.

The Giant's Ring is a huge circle made up of a grassy rampart built of earth and boulders fifteen feet high. It is divided into seven unequal segments by depressions, but at least two of these are not original. Tall trees grow in some of the gaps. The ring is 590 feet in diameter and encloses an area of seven acres. There is a slight crown in the enclosure, at the centre of which is a megalith or dolmen. This has a capstone seven feet across which rests on the three upright stones two to three feet high. Other stones have been dislodged and lie nearby.

They originally formed a circular chamber five feet across with a small entrance passage. Perhaps it was an altar, as O'Byrne says, but it seems more likely that it was a grave. The enclosure has also been used as a racecourse and for grazing cattle, and the circuit is a handy length for walking the dog. Evans says that its nearest parallels are in northern England, but in this he may reflect the attitude of his time, which tended to regard any ancient circle as a 'henge'. The current view is that the Ring may be the product of a thriving Neolithic population which shared a culture with other parts of Ireland and Britain, and that its position in the Lagan Valley provokes comparison with the ancient features of the River Boyne.

We are remarkably lucky that the Ring has survived almost unscathed: it has also, until now, avoided detailed archaeological investigation. The latest chemical analysis of the soil suggests that the whole area of the platform within the river bend was 'set aside' for some sort of religious or 'ritual' purpose, for it was not settled, and it is almost completely bare of flint tools, so commonplace elsewhere. The archaeologists who are currently studying it, when they set about photographing the Ring, realised that it was intended to be seen from above: but while aerial photography may provide the most effective view, the site is still impressive from the surrounding hills.

The view from within the Ring, around 360 degrees, is spectacular. On a blustery day the line of hills formed by the Antrim escarpment can seem like a low black curtain drawn across the north and west, with clouds scudding above them. Turning around, one can view the soothing slopes of the Lagan Valley and County Down. Apart from the few modern buildings, the look of the countryside may not be that different from what it was thousands of years ago: the lucky presence of a boggy patch on the site is allowing archaeologists to determine the history of the vegetation and the extent of tree cover. The feeling that one is somehow at the centre of everything is insidious. If the navel of Seamus Heaney's world is located on a farm in south Derry, the omphalos of the Belfast perspective could be the Giant's Ring.

There have been numerous finds nearby suggesting prehistoric burials in the fields to the northwest. In the middle of the last century an underground chamber was discovered 250 yards away. It was paved, and seven feet in diameter. At the centre, three feet high, was an upright stone pillar. Around it were six adjoining cists, or chest-like tombs. Four cinerary urns were found as well as bones, burnt and unburnt, human and animal.

Like certain other ancient sites that have been absorbed into nature, and like some wholly natural places, the Giant's Ring has a magic, for its configuration implies that it vouchsafes an insight of some kind. It is still a very rural place, although the eerie industrial village of Edenderry, a literal dead end, nestles in the same crook of the Lagan. On the Twelfth of July the Orangemen now march from the city centre up the ancient pathway that has become the Malone Road to their meeting at 'The Field' in Edenderry. 'The Field' used to be the Hatchet

Field, then it moved to the outskirts of Andersonstown, until shifts in the demographic map meant it had to move again: the stronghold of Sinn Féin was just over the M1 motorway, and somewhere better insulated from potential trouble was needed. So now the Orangemen process to a site that has mystical associations as irrational as those of their own possessed and bacchanalian drums. Until recently the Orangemen's popular history began only when their ancestors stepped off the boat from Scotland, but perhaps they are no less, and no more, entitled to regard the Ring as their own than the people represented by Cathal O'Byrne, who never let an opportunity slip by for reminding his readers who rightfully owned the city he loved and chronicled. It would be foolish to use the remains of a past we only dimly understand as an argument for anything.

The ineffable impression of significance that the Giant's Ring suggests to us is assisted by the fact that countryside appears to stretch away in every direction. The farms, villages and housing estates that can be seen are few, small or far away. E.R.R. Green remarks that the region as a whole is more rural than might be expected in the environs of an industrial city. Agriculture is practised right up to the suburbs, and local farmers have been tenacious of their way of life. The suburbs have spread enormously since Green wrote in 1944, but the point still appears valid.

The River Lagan itself is in a green corridor that reaches almost uninterrupted to the city centre. From Edenderry it runs through Dixon Park, Barnett's Park, Clement Wilson Park and Belvoir Park. All along here it would be churlish to wish for a more pleasant, secluded and non-urban walk. Swans, moorhens and kingfishers are visible from the towpath, which is a relic of the time when barges used the Lagan. The canal was started in 1756, and at one time it was possible to travel by inland waterway to Lough Neagh, Newry, the Shannon, Limerick and Dublin. Shaw's Bridge commemorates Captain Shaw, who built an oak bridge there in 1655 so that Oliver Cromwell's cannon could cross. Beside the new road bridge is a stone bridge that has lasted since 1711. The Duke of Wellington spent his school holidays at Belvoir, where his grandfather had a house. Along the way there are plantations of trees, courses for canoe races, and at one point even a tastefully concealed car park, but it is only after the tennis courts and boathouses at Stranmillis that everyday urban life intrudes and the phenomenon of embankments appear. These are relieved by the lower part of Botanic Gardens on one side and then Ormeau Park on the other, and already we have reached the gasworks. Or rather, where the gasworks used to be. Victorian town gas is out of fashion and, despite hopes of a pipeline from Scotland or the South, Belfast is now a city of yellow butane bottles, and the Belfast City Council is threatening to redevelop the gasworks riverside site in the style of London's Isle of Dogs or Chelsea Harbour.

About the same time as salmon were being harpooned down by Ormeau Bridge, people were beginning to settle on the Antrim Plateau, where they were away from the forest and they could mine flints. Perhaps they bartered them with the people down below. They left evidence of their presence in Megalithic burials, cairns, standing stones and earthworks. Across Northern Ireland the Megalithic culture of about 2,000 to 1,500 BC is mostly associated with uplands.

Four lines of sandy deposits radiate from the Giant's Ring, and were probably used as lines of communication across the difficult, swampy and wooded lowland. One runs along the present Dunmurry Lane, at what was once the first easy crossing of the river. But as the climate became drier it became easier to cross further downstream. The ford which is supposed to have given Belfast its name was probably a spit of sand between the mouths of the Farset and Blackstaff rivers on the northwest of the Lagan. (The Farset, half hidden now, still forms the boundary between the Shankill and Falls roads.) Estyn Evans decides that this sandspit is the origin of the 'ford of the sandbank' from which we get *Béal Feirste*, Belfast, and hopes thereby to put an end to the controversy that exercised local historians, antiquarians, guidebook compilers and contributors to the *Ulster Journal of Archaeology* for over a century. There was scope for endless argument about where exactly the ford was and, one step further back, what the name meant.

In his magnificently rich, learned and humorous book *Belfast Confetti*, Ciarán Carson tackles the problem of the name as it has been glossed by everyone from Dubourdieu to the comedian who invented the city's coat of arms (we can at least be sure that *Bel* does not refer to a bell). Carson quotes from George Benn, writing in the 1820s:

> The utmost obscurity and perplexity, however, attend the derivation of the name . . . of Bealafarsad, which means, according to some, hurdleford town, while others have translated it, the mouth of the pool.

In an appendix to a later edition, Benn is no more certain:

> The meaning of the name Belfast is still rather unsettled. Mr. Hennessy, of the Record Office, adheres to the old translation, 'the mouth of the ford'. Dr. Joyce (Irish Names of Places, p. 331) says, 'Belfast, which is called in Irish authorities Belfeirsde, "the town of the Farset".' Other persons, not so familiar with the derivation of place names as these two eminent Irish scholars, have alleged that the term 'mouth of the ford' is in some sense a misnomer, insomuch as a ford cannot properly be said to have a mouth, and that the true meaning is the 'mouth or entrance of the Fearsaid'. Some other meanings have been offered, but devoid of any authority.

Sometimes the syllable *Bel*, 'mouth or opening', has been mistaken for *baile*, which means 'town', and Carson, in his characteristically anfractuous manner, manages to demonstrate that Belfast was mistaken by Benn's 'other persons' for Dublin, which really is 'hurdleford town'. *Feirste* is the genitive of *fearsad*, which means a great many things, including 'shaft', 'ulna', 'club', 'sandbar', 'tidal channel', 'pool', 'verse' and 'poem'. There is much further speculation, involving 'wallet', 'axis' and even *versus*, the Latin 'turn in the furrow'. But even Carson plumps – not in the end, because all the meanings are abundant with association – for 'the mouth of the Farset' or 'the approach to the sandbank or ford'. Calvin Klein's 'Obsession', a poem in Carson's collection *The Irish for No*, ends with the thought that 'maybe it's the name you buy, and not the thing itself'.

If the name is indeterminate, so too is the land. It is not accidental that Michael Longley, a poet who has dedicated his working life and his art to his native city, quoted St Paul's Epistle to the Hebrews when looking for the title of his first book: 'For here we have no continuing city'. This pious place, whose citizens still take religion, as distinct from sectarian politics, seriously; which still, despite new Tory laws allowing Sunday pub opening, mainly rests on the seventh day and goes to church or chapel dressed in Sunday best, the men in suits, the women in hats, where a forest of spires conduct God's lightning into the preachers and through their hands into the foreheads of the faithful; this pious place is not built on rock but on sand, mud, sleech or slobland.

In *Thomas Russell and Belfast*, Brendan Clifford quotes S. Ramsey:

> have we ever asked ourselves how it came to pass that on a site so unpromising –
> on what may be described as a mud bank or a morass – one of the chief cities of
> the United Kingdom has risen? Why, if there were to be a town in this part of the
> world at all, is it not found where the sea waves beat against the solid rock, as at
> Carrickfergus or Bangor, or like a second Glasgow ten miles up our river, at
> Lisburn? A string of loaded carts makes our houses quiver as with an earthquake
> – a heavy sea floods our streets – to obtain a sufficient fall for our drainage taxes
> the utmost engineering skill – and if we wish to build anything much heavier than
> a cottage we must spend the labour and time and money in securing an artificial
> foundation below the treacherous upper soil.

The questions were put just over a century ago to the Rosemary Street Presbyterian Church Young Men's Guild, and were published as *The Early History of Belfast*.

Many Belfast houses are still strangers to the right angle and the square. The city has its own leaning tower, the Albert Clock, whose eccentricity grows more alarming every year. Even the prettiest parts of the city, such as the houses of the Crescent between University Road and Botanic Avenue, display this vernacular feature of subsidence. They were thrown up by a speculative builder in the last century as fashionable houses just outside the city boundary: the old toll cottage, now replaced by an ugly postmodern brick frivolity, was round the corner in Shaftesbury Square. In his design the builder had a vague notion about Bath, mixed up with Regent Street. He only managed two sides of a horseshoe (the third was filled in later with a terrace of ordinary brick houses) and he was not as rigorously consistent as he might have been, yet the square that is the Crescent is an adornment.

It was threatened for several years that another of Belfast's grandiose roads would be cut through the Crescent, to join the Ormeau Road and Sandy Row. When this idea was first a gleam in a civil servant's eye, Northern Ireland had no system for listing buildings of architectural merit. It was only after the introduction of direct rule from Westminster in 1972, in the early years of the Troubles, that the system was introduced, one of several examples, from homosexual law reform to the Sunday opening of pubs, of how the end of the Unionist government's care for 'their own country' allowed Northern Ireland to catch up with Britain. The Unionists were always very good at roads, however, and Belfast must have one of the most over-elaborate road networks anywhere, so that drivers complain if they have to wait for a few minutes at its busiest junctions in the rush hour, and city councillors find themselves trying to devise schemes whereby residents can be assured of being able to park their cars directly outside their homes or offices without having to walk more than a few yards down the street. All this in a place that most of the time feels strangely empty to the traveller from southeast England.

The road through the Crescent threatened to demolish, in the same way as Ramsey's string of carts, the street's half-crumbling and half-restored terraces, for the houses already trembled every time the Dublin train went by in the cutting behind them. After lobbying aided by David Cooke, Belfast's first and so far only non-Unionist Lord Mayor, and after several changes of mind by the various sections within the Department of the Environment, the road scheme was abandoned. When renovations took place in the wake of the decision, it began to be suspected that some houses in the terraces had been holding up the others. The builder had had a habit of not worrying where his walls ended, whether they actually made it to the corner or up to the ceiling. When the road was dug up for cable-laying the sandiness of the soil was obvious: one expected to find seashells. To live at the top of such a building is to be conscious of faded elegance and the transitory nature of human endeavour: the respectable residents who once took afternoon tea on the green have given way to students in flats and workers in offices. Certainty in Belfast involves the life to come: the mundane things like living from day to day in peace, or in a solid house, are more difficult.

The city has risen after its fashion, almost *sui generis*. When redbrick replaced the half-timbered buildings in the late eighteenth century, local builders exploited the clay under their feet. Great brickyards sprang up in the town. Many buildings were constructed from bricks made from clay dug up and fired on site. The walls rose out of the earth they stood on. Needless to say, these rough bricks have proved more attractive as they have weathered more over the years than modern smooth bricks. There are no brickfields in Belfast any longer, and the new imported bricks develop a tidemark of salt as soon as a building is put up, as if the house has just been dragged out of the sea.

As for the flooding Ramsey mentions, that is no longer such a problem, but it took three-quarters of a century for it to be dealt with. Frank Ormsby has written a poem, 'Floods', which commemorates the sense of strangeness and unease the 'subversive' waters brought, and implicitly uses this ready-made metaphor the city offers to touch on other worries and incivilities: 'Blame fall on the builders, foolish men.' Into the sixties, the floods could reach, for example, Great Victoria Street, where they would threaten the cinema organ of the Ritz, which was stored underground ready to rise, illuminated and booming, before the big film. If the environmentalists are accurate in their predictions about global warming, our children will have to deal with the problem all over again. The city centre might have to retreat to Balmoral, and Belfast might become a fringe of suburbs around a sunken Venice.

Ireland's first settlements of Mesolithic people have been carbon-dated to 7,000 BC. If, as Henry L. Snyder contends, they came from Scotland, they would have landed first on the northeast coast on either side of Belfast. The links between eastern Ulster and southwest Scotland have always been important: their landscapes and dialects can seem interchangeable still. In the seventeenth century settlers would cross back to Scotland to attend church services, and in the middle of the nineteenth century a young man sailed across from Scotland merely to shake the hand of his hero, the Presbyterian divine Henry Cooke.

A new theory suggests that Ireland's earliest people crossed over land-bridges further south, but let us say they settled around Belfast. The Neolithic people, who brought farming, probably arrived in about 5,000 BC from Brittany. They were, says Snyder, small and dark-skinned. Their stone axes, pottery and burial places have been found. They worked copper and gold, and they exported bronze vessels and jewellery.

The trouble comes when we talk about the Celts, for everyone has a stake in who exactly they were. It is fitting that there are football teams named after them. One complication is that the Celts wrote their own history, for their own purposes, with their own conventions and assumptions. Nora Chadwick, in *The Celts*, says that Ireland is the only independent Celtic country in a continent which was once dominated, in its northern half at least, by Celts. Robert Jerome Smith is prepared to assert that 'Ireland can only be defined in terms of what it was when free – in terms of beginnings, of the past.' This sounds absolutist and idealistic: presumably Belfast could never be defined, since it was and has remained the creation of the invader. Is that why it remains fascinating?

Everyone is anxious to justify themselves or what they see as their tribe by appealing to beginnings, and there is a lot of scope to do so. According to the theory, the Celts were dominant in Europe by the start of the third millennium

BC, or succeeded the Neolithic people in about 1,200 BC, or can be traced back to the beginning of the Iron Age in Europe, about 1,000 BC. They were originally Bohemians who spread west through France, Spain and Britain to Ireland, south to Italy and east to Turkey, where they were known as the Galatians, and received a letter from St Paul. They had chariots, iron swords and an art which was geometrical. By 500 BC the La Tène culture emerged, with an art less restrained, full of curves and spirals, luxuriant plants and animals. It takes its name from the Swiss site where votive metal objects decorated in this fashion were found. It is to this style that the modern Celtic revivalist artists have often looked.

The father of history, Herodotus (490–425 BC), mentions the Celts twice, as living around the source of the Danube, and as being the most westerly nation of Europe, apart from the Cynesians, living beyond the Pillars of Hercules. Herodotus is also known as the father of lies, partly because he was also given to recording hearsay and what people believed to be true.

As Jonathan Bardon points out, fierce academic argument rages over the precise order of Celtic settlement. But according to one version the Celts' arrival in Ireland was in four stages. The first, the 'P-Celts', left traces only in northern Britain, where they became known as the Picts. The second, the Builg or Erainn, who also came via Britain, gave their name to Ireland. The third, the Larginian group of tribes, came from Gaul and settled in Leinster and Connacht. The fourth, the 'Q-Celts', came directly from the European continent. Irish, Scots and Manx belong to the group of dialects shared by this fourth wave, while Welsh, Cornish and Breton belong to that of the first wave: where one group would use the sound p, as in *pedwar*, meaning 'four', the other would use a q sound, as in *cethair*. The La Tène culture probably came to Ireland with one of the later waves, though by the time from which written records survive, the end of the heroic age in the late fourth century AD, the Celtic groups had merged and spoke a common language.

There are more confident and amusing approaches to the origins of the Irish. Eoin Neeson, for example, concentrates on the Milesians. Blending hints from Herodotus, the *Leabhar Gabhala* (Book of Invasions) and coincidences like the apparent Phoenician sun symbol at Newgrange, he plumps for a proud, civilized and spiritual origin for the Irish, far superior to that of the English. According to him, the nearly 'indigenous' Firbolgs/Fomorians, savages 'very much like the Picts who flourished until much later in the neighbouring island', were conquered by the mystical and visionary Tuatha de Danaan. Eventually these Picts were civilized by the Roman legions and by warlike Irish settlers. The moral seems clear: when the British were painting themselves blue, the Irish were a cultured and religious people from the cradle of civilization, art and democracy.

On the other hand, Nora Chadwick suggests that the Milesians, the sons of Mil, may have been an invention to placate Christian sensibilities: the Tuatha Dé Danaan (as she spells it), 'the tribes of the goddess Danu', led by their poet Amargin, were regarded as gods by the Celts, who had the euhemeristic habit of deifying former kings and peoples. The Milesians, it is proposed, were invented as conquerors of these gods, who were relegated from gods to fairies. As *aes side*, supernatural beings or fairies, they lived in *sídhe*, or burial mounds. The Celts were, however, as powerful as Neeson could wish. They raided the British coast and controlled northern and western Britain and Wales. The Romans called them the *Scotti*, and their domination of the north provided its name, Scotland. Their attacks encouraged the Romans to leave Britain, and when Vortigern took over from the Romans, he had to call in Saxon mercenaries to combat the Celts. This led in turn to the Anglo-Saxonizing of England.

In many respects there have always been differences between Ulster – and in particular the counties of Antrim and Down – and other parts of Ireland. These differences existed among the Celts. The O'Neills, for example, are often referred to as the kings or earls of Ulster, and it was frequently implied, on the accession of Captain Terence O'Neill as Prime Minister of Northern Ireland, that his ancestry gave him a regal as well as a political entitlement to rule Northern Ireland. The Uí Néills, descended from Niall of the Nine Hostages, ruled west of the Bann. They controlled the ancient religious site of Emain Macha and sponsored Christianity. The new religion spread from the south, but the cult of St Patrick flourished around Armagh, which became the centre of the Irish Church. The kingdom of Dalriada, which covered Antrim, Down and western Scotland, was rather slower to adopt Christianity.

Missionaries sailed out from Derry, but it was not until saints Columbanus and Gall set out from the great abbey at Bangor founded by Comgall in AD 555 that the greater Belfast area can be said to have begun 'civilizing' western Europe. Ian Adamson felt able to entitle a book *Bangor, Light of the World*: he points out that young men came from all over Europe and Asia to study philosophy and mathematics in Greek at Bangor, and that its liturgy, in the *Bangor Antiphonary*, had a fundamental influence on Christian worship. Authorities have compared the significance of Columbanus, who was born in AD 543, to that of Charlemagne; Pope Pius XI attributed the 'rebirth of Christian virtue and civilization' in Gaul, Germany and Italy to him. Adamson notes the rivalry between St Columb, himself an Uí Néill, and Bangor, and records battles fought between the Uí Néill and Dalriada.

In another book, *The Cruthin*, Adamson neatly turns the Neeson approach on its head, and makes a potentially irenic contribution to the culture of Northern Ireland. For him, the Cruthin were in Ireland long before the Gaels. They were the last of the Picts, who lived in both Ireland and Britain and were driven out by the sword by Johnny-come-latelys: 'traditional, historical and linguistic considerations all support the conclusion that the Gaelic settlement of Ireland was a LATE event in Irish history' (*sic*). He deplores the dominance of 'Gaelic' history and language, which has become synonymous with 'Irish' (and frequently extends to 'nationalist' as well), when in fact the real picture is much more complicated.

13

In the *Táin Bo Cuailgne*, (The Cattle Raid of Cooley), which was probably written down in the seventh century AD, Gaelic storytellers tell of a war between the Ulaid and the Connachta which supposedly happened in the first century AD. Adamson argues that the Ulaid (from which comes the word 'Ulster') were an aristocratic warrior caste who came from Britain to Antrim and Down, where most of the people were Cruthin. The hero of the *Táin* is nicknamed Cúchulainn. His real name is Sétanta, which Adamson says is cognate with a British tribe living in Lancashire. Adamson is arguing that when the Scots Protestants, Picts or Cruthin, came back to reconquer the northeast corner of Ireland, they were merely coming home, and behaving no worse to the Gaels than the Gaels had behaved to them. He also finds comfort in the role of the Belgic tribes who established Dalriada, and formed a confederacy with the Cruthin.

This theory would be more attractive if it had not been so enthusiastically taken up since its publication in 1974 by the cultural department of the Ulster Defence Association and the inhabitants of the House of Orange, that ugly modern white building on the Dublin Road that is 'World Headquarters' of the Orange Order. Adamson provides a justification for the presence in Ulster of Protestants descended from Scots. It is touching to see the eagerness with which some Protestants (who, since the national revival at least, have tended to feel that the Catholics have more 'culture') grab at this rare example of literature and history being on their side for a change. In the past the puritan dislike of art and artifice, combined with a feeling that very often the devil does have all the best tunes, had encouraged a turning-away from the arts in Belfast, and a prickly uncertainty about cultural identity. If you believe, as some protestant sects do, that novels are mere lies, it is hard to avoid feeling inferior about the arts when they are the topic of conversation, or indeed turn out, after all, to have their uses.

It would be fair to read Adamson rather than concentrate on his promoters, but he is involved in myth-making rather than conventional history. If his myth of origins involves exaggeration, speculation and special pleading, his motives and aims are honourable. While many nationalist 'Gaelic' scholars of the generation before the present one took an essentially racial view of Irishness and the rights and wrongs of Irish history, Adamson emphatically does not. The various 'peoples' represent linguistic groupings rather than genetically distinct nations. The Celts were composed of different physical types, and their languages were imposed on or adopted by a variety of other tribes. The Gaels and Britons, in medieval times, thought of themselves as separate, despite having similar social, legal and literary forms, and did not know they had a common Celtic origin. In contrast, the Anglo-Saxons, for example, were less 'bombastic', as Adamson puts it, about their origins, but never lost sight of their links with the Old Saxons of Germany.

The cover of the 1986 edition of *The Cruthin* uses an illustration by Jim Fitzpatrick: Cúchulainn stands before a runic stone with a blood-stained axe over his shoulder, his right hand on the scabbard of an elaborate sword. His hair looks like flames. He appears to be wearing blue eyeshadow, and his leather boots are attached to his chain-mail jerkin by what can only be described as a forerunner of the suspender. It is in Fitzpatrick's familiar style, a case of twilight sword and sorcery, or a psychedelic-Celtic version of the posters of Alphonse Mucha.

Taking advantage of the current upsurge of interest in cartoon strips, or so-called graphic novels, which were formerly a French peculiarity, Island Publications of Newtownabbey has started a series of publications with *Cúchulainn, Champion of Ulster*. The text is by Michael Hall and the artwork, with all the conventions of the comic strip but alas without the draughtsmanship of Fitzpatrick, is by Gary Hamilton. Books 2 to 4 of the series *Ancient Tales of Ulster* promise to deal with *The Táin, The Death of Cúchulainn* and *Deirdre of the Sorrows*. The appearance of such a publication, aimed at a popular audience, suggests an impulse to retrieve the tales from scholars and school editions. Hall is at pains to emphasize that Cúchulainn was not a Gael (describing him as small and dark, whereas Gaelic heroes have normally been depicted as tall and blond) and that he was not one of the Ulaid either.

Perhaps the cartoon strip is an appropriate way of treating these stories. Thomas Kinsella's translation of the *Táin* is a work of admirable scholarship, but at times, it has to be admitted, it seems very remote. For example, in Cúchulainn's 'warp-spasm', as he mounts his sickle chariot in preparation for battle, he changes shape in an horrific way: his calf muscles switch to the front of his shins, one eye sinks into his head, the other rolls out along his cheek, his lips draw back so that his liver can be seen flapping about, and so on. Kinsella's prose is marvellous, but the passage, like many in the tale, is overdone and draws attention to the storyteller rather than the story. The concept of the secret weapon, the *gae bolga*, a sort of many-headed spear which must be thrown by the toes from under water, is difficult to grasp. Kinsella calls the *Táin* the 'oldest vernacular epic in Western literature': it is vivid, immediate, earthy and amusing, but in many ways is only comprehensible as literal transcriptions of oral poetry, complete with the humorous exaggerations that are more effective in a performance than in a literary work.

The stories of Achilles or the Cyclops suggest a comparable taste for the fantastical (and, incidentally, bloodstained heroes of psychopathic enthusiasm), but the *Iliad* and the *Odyssey* seem to have been organized under a literary consciousness at an early point. It may be that those brought up on the classics rather than Gaelic are more familiar with Greek monstrosities than Irish ones, but it does seem that the syncretic service of rendering the scattered oral fragments around the figure of Cúchulainn into a great, unified epic has not been performed. In the same vein, when it came to rendering it into English, Kinsella found that there were numerous adaptations and bowdlerizations of parts of the story, but no straightforward, organized translation of what had survived. Adaptation to cartoon form seems as honourable a ploy as any, especially since the more fantastical flights of the *Táin* are no more impossible than the exploits of superheroes like Batman and Superman.

The Ulster Cycle, of which the *Táin* is part, is pre-Christian and deals with the conflict of the Ulaid and the Uí Néill. It predates the Uí Néills' taking of Emain Macha, and the latest theory is that it refers to events earlier than 100 BC. By the time the *Táin* took literary form, the Celtic language had changed. It had once had more resemblances to the Romance languages than other Indo-European language groups: it had similarities to Gaulish and Latin before the fourth century. The name 'Vercingetorix', for example, uses an ending comparable to the Latin *rex*, meaning 'king'. But by the seventh century AD the Gaelic language had changed, often in an aesthetic direction. It became softer and subtler, many final syllables and medial vowels were lost, while medial consonants were simplified or lightened. *Eech* meant 'horse', *equus* in Latin. It was a language poor in verbs but rich in nouns and adjectives, as Gantz says, static but vital.

It is tempting to interpret, to infer a culture given to ornamentation and ceremony, description, naming and praise rather than action: Neeson quotes Herodotus in mentioning vainglory and ostentation. More interesting and significant is the point of similarity rather than difference. The old stories, myths, legends and histories were, amongst other things, attempts to discriminate and identify. The lists of 'peoples' or tribes around the Mediterranean, Asia and Europe whom Herodotus tags have an air of unreality. The naming and labelling could have been a way of marking differences that were otherwise by no means apparent. Sean O'Faolain, in *The Irish*, says that the inhabitants of the island are a mixture of peoples, from a succession of incoming waves – Celts, Normans, Norsemen, Spaniards, Scots, English, French – whose qualities have contributed to the richness and diversity of Irish life. They have made a mixture that is not homogeneous but lumpy. It is the unexpected unevennesses of Irishness that contribute to its vitality, its never-failing interest, and perhaps also its lack of equilibrium. If these things began to be true three thousand years ago, they have continued to be true, perhaps especially in Belfast, to the present.

The *Annals of the Four Masters*, also known as *The Annals of the Kingdom of Ireland*, dates Belfast's debut in history as AD 666:

> *The battle of Fearsat, between the Ulidians and the Cruithini, where Cathasach, son of Laircine, was slain. The Fearsat here alluded to was evidently at Bel-Feirste, now Belfast, on the river Lagan, in the county of Antrim.*

The *Annals* were compiled in the 1630s by a number of monks in Donegal. Under the year 680 they have the following entry:

> *. . . Cathasach and Ultan, princes of the Cruithinians of Dalaradia, leagued with the Britains to invade Ireland, and united their forces at Rathmore, in Magh Line . . . .*

Benn comments: 'Such it may be said, are examples of the public transactions which continued for centuries among the chiefs of Dalaradia or Dalriada. Wars among themselves and their kindred in Scotland or the Isles were the pastimes of their lives.'

The Vikings began their depredations after the golden age of Irish Christianity had already passed. Though scholars question his existence, Turgesius is supposed to have landed in 831 and taken Armagh. The Northmen's ships used Belfast Lough for shelter, and they must have raided what they could find in the area. Like belfries and watchtowers, the round towers so characteristic of Ireland – there are eighty whole or in ruins still remaining – were a method of defence against the Vikings. The round towers were from seventy to 120 feet high, with a door seven or eight feet off the ground. The monks could climb into the tower by a ladder which could be pulled after them. It seems a very rudimentary form of defence, and suggests that the Northmen could not be bothered with sieges or demolition work. There are the remains of a round tower at Drumbo, due south of Edenderry, though little is known about the monastery to which it was attached. The remains of a church were still visible in 1744. The Vikings might have been able to navigate the Lagan in their longships up to a point near Drumbo, then going overland after the monastery's treasure. But they might have been too nervous about leaving their boats for long to set about extracting the monks and their treasures.

The usual view of the Vikings is as bogeymen: the monk shivering in his cell thanks God for the storm, because rough seas mean there will be no raid tonight. But, as we might expect, Johannes Brondsted, in *The Vikings*, is more sympathetic. Contrary to popular belief, the Vikings were not always as fierce as Kirk Douglas. They began by raiding, but went on to colonize, and their impact on England was most profound through the Danes and their descendants, the Normans. They also affected Ireland, encouraging the growth of the first Irish towns in the south of the island – Dublin, Wexford, Cork, Limerick and Waterford. The north, less troubled by them, was also free of towns for longer, and had to wait for the Normans to found Carrickfergus. In the struggle against the Vikings, Brian Boru became the first effective king over all the Irish. He finally defeated the Vikings at Clontarf on Good Friday 1014 (though he died in the battle), but the Vikings, or Ostmen, stayed on. They gave Ireland her first currency, and encouraged the formation of a fleet, the exploitation of fishing and foreign trade. The Church was reorganized into parishes and followed the authority of Rome.

At around the time when Turgesius is said to have first arrived, there was a king of Ulaid called Madagan, who ruled from AD 838 to 855. It is from him or from a later Ulidian King Madagan (933–48) that Cave Hill got its first recorded name, Ben Madagan. The later Madagan's grandson, Eochaid Mac Ardgal, was killed at the battle of Crew Hill in 1003, and it has been suggested that he gave his name to McArt's Fort on the same hill.

The skyline of Cave Hill gives Belfast its most spectacular and recognizable feature. From many parts of the city, if you lean your head to one side, you can see along the scarp edge the profile of a man's face, remarkably reminiscent of Napoleon Bonaparte's: hence the nickname for McArt's Fort, Napoleon's Nose. But was it only after the French Revolution that someone realized there was the face of a huge sleeper looming over Belfast? Whose face was it before 1789? Or was it a piece of United Irishman propaganda that placed the genius of revolution slumbering over radical Belfast, ready to be awoken?

McArt's Fort is the top of a promontory that juts out from Cave Hill, more than 1,000 feet above sea level. Below two thirds of its edge is a sheer drop of 500 feet to the sloping grounds of Belfast Castle, with its hazelwoods. Looking out, the effects of height and the proximity of the city are enhanced. Belfast Lough seems so close that you almost feel you could throw a stone into it. On a clear day you can see the graceful peaks of the Mourne Mountains far to the south, but the whole of Belfast is laid out before you and does not seem far away at all.

The flat top of the fort is 150 feet from north to south and 180 feet from east to west. It is cut off on the landward, western side by a ditch ten feet deep and twenty-five feet wide. If Eochaid Mac Ardgal ever fought in his fort, it must have been a desperate battle, for there is nowhere to go but down. Besides, it is exposed and has no water supply. Perhaps the Vikings were as impatient here as at Drumbo. Like other apparently ancient monuments around Belfast, such as Dundonald Moat, McArt's Fort may have been adapted and rebuilt by the Anglo-Normans.

Fulmars can be seen flying around the promontory: they fly with stiff, outstretched wings, and are sometimes called woodenwings. On the higher slopes of the grounds of Belfast Castle are tormentil, a small yellow flower, and patches of white bedstraw. Further down there is milkwort, a small blue flower, and woundwort, and in the damper ground yellow irises. The harebell, or Scottish bluebell, grows in profusion on the dry ground, uncommonly close to the city. There is also the fragrant meadowsweet. Some 200 yards behind McArt's Fort, on the flat summit of Cave Hill, there is a low, round cairn.

Like the site of Emain Macha near Armagh, Cave Hill has been threatened with mining. A campaign to save it has recently been set up in the face of confusion over a Northern Ireland Office promise that the entire area would be safe: when the prospecting licence was granted, it was not clear exactly how far the area of protection would extend.

The caves which gave Cave Hill its modern name are a mystery. They are man-made, cut from the rock like others around Belfast at Knockagh Hill, Ballymartin and Donegore. They may have been occupied in the early Christian era, but could have been excavated earlier. Underneath them, potsherds were found in rubbish. The lower cave is accessible from the Sheep's Path, which is now in disrepair and interrupted by a landslip. The others are at varying heights, from seventy-four to 133 feet above the path, in the face of the almost perpendicular cliff. There are the remains of two narrow and broken paths but, strange as it sounds in an island not noted for high mountains, many people have lost their lives trying to reach the caves, and rescuers are frequently called out to save would-be explorers.

The grounds of Belfast Castle are favoured by courting couples. (Do these places concentrate the magnetism of the fertility goddess, or has it merely been that lovers in puritanical Belfast have had to get away from their parents?) But McArt's Fort is a favourite jumping-off point for suicides. At one time a whole love affair could have been conducted in the environs, from the meeting at the Floral Hall in Bellevue to the surreptitious dates, to the healthy afternoon walk to see the view, to the wedding reception in the Castle, or to a more gloomy end, when it all went wrong. The site of Wolfe Tone's oath to fight for Ireland's freedom is also the most romantic place to kill yourself. It is fitting that the hill's presiding god should be the most histrionic, megalomaniac figure from the birth of violent revolutionism, Napoleon Bonaparte, because when you look down on things they seem simpler.

Life, like landscape, is not so straightforward. The city is bifurcated by the River Lagan and Belfast Lough. As Robin Bryans said in *Ulster: a Journey Through the Six Counties*, approaching Northern Ireland the best way, by boat to Belfast, the difference between the two shores is striking. County Antrim's 'forbidding escarpment', protean as the daylight changes, 'vaguely menacing' in silhouette at night, faces a gently undulating landscape of blues and greens dotted with beech and oak and dappled with cloud shadow. It is epic drama facing pastoral. And between them, where the bows of the boat are pointing, are the frantic jumble of the city under its smoke and the huge machinery of the shipyard at the mouth of the river, the point where Belfast makes its marriage with the sea.

On the extreme edge of the city opposite McArt's Fort, from the front-room windows of the houses along the Lower Braniel Road where the Castlereagh Hills begin to rise, there is a panorama just as breathtaking. But since it is from gentle County Down, the viewpoint seems a more protective one. On the right, near Dundonald, the white classical parliament building of Stormont stands in its grand setting at the top of a mile-long hill, shining out its wholly compromised idea of a Protestant parliament for a Protestant people. You can see all the areas of Belfast: from Gilnahirk and Tullycarnet, the Short Strand and Ballynafeigh, to Carnmoney Hill, apart from the rest; you can see the gap up to Glengormley, where terriers are tamed, to Wolf Hill, where the last wolf was killed, and Divis with the head of the waters, one stream flowing north and west to the Bann and Lough Neagh, the other east to Belfast Lough. Then the Black Mountain. In between, out of the haze of the city centre, the shipyard's cranes rise, you see the great cylindrical oil containers, the reclaimed land thrusting into the lough, the green dome of the City Hall and the few tall buildings here and there, the white arch of the King's Hall, Balmoral. Within the city boundary the land rises from soft mud at sea level to black basalt at 1,500 feet. Looking across you have the compulsion to identify and name each place you recognize, to comprehend it, to understand the delights and hurts it had the power to inflict.

CHAPTER TWO

JOHN DE COURCY

Sometimes tired, as it were, of the true and the serious, Nature draws aside and goes away, and in these remote parts indulges herself in secret and distant freaks.

In this way Giraldus Cambrensis, Gerald of Wales, introduces his *The History and Topography of Ireland*. Giraldus was born in about 1146 in Pembrokeshire, the grandson of Nest, mistress of Henry I. He was a member of the influential Geraldine family who, as the FitzGeralds, were the main protagonists in the Norman invasion of Ireland.

Giraldus was educated at Paris, which he revisited later in life, he made four visits to Ireland, went to Rome several times, and set out on a crusade, though he was absolved from his vow before he reached Palestine. Although he was several times offered bishoprics, he always refused them. He was determined to become Bishop of St David's and to assert its independence from Canterbury – if necessary, suggests Lewis Thorpe, by martyrdom in emulation of Thomas à Beckett. He never got his wish. Although Giraldus was a member of Henry II's entourage in 1184, accompanied Prince John on his visit to Ireland in 1185 and was a powerful and valued courtier, Henry no doubt did not wish to create another martyr by appointing a Welshman to the see of St David's. Giraldus wrote seventeen books, and was a practised propagandist, whether for his own very strict, and even puritanical, views on church discipline, for a separate Welsh Church, or for the adventure in Ireland.

His purpose in *The History* is to whet Norman appetites for the conquest of Ireland with tales of its temperate and healthy climate, its fertile but unexploited farming land, its abundant falcons, fat stags, plentiful wild boar, and natural wonders. He is careful to flatter the King and to suggest how the Irish Church might be reformed. As a result the book is a mixture of delightful tall tales of curiosities and miracles, shameless sycophancy, and racist abuse of the barbarous, lazy, vicious and untrustworthy Irish. Ireland, he says, is an exotic country with natural resources ready and waiting to be exploited by a more efficient, energetic and religious group like the Anglo-Normans, as long as they are not taken in by the sweet talk of the natives. He even describes the weaponry they might encounter: the Irish fight 'naked', without any armour, ride without saddles, bridles or bits, and their most effective missile is the stone. Giraldus is also impressed by the great axes he says the Irish adopted from the Ostmen: the Irish walk about holding them like staffs, ready to use them at the slightest provocation. It sounds a bit like the Wild West, with the battleaxe in place of the six-gun.

The previous wave of Northmen, the Vikings, had been absorbed into Ireland, but since the death of Brian Boru in 1014 the Church had become weak and corrupt, and the authority of the High Kingship had declined. Turlough O'Connor, the last powerful native ruler, had died in 1156 and did not have a successor. Pope Adrian IV, the first and only English Pope, gave Henry II his blessing in 1159 to invade Ireland, but Henry waited for nine years, until he was invited by Dermot, King of Leinster, to mount an expedition against his enemies. By 1171 Henry himself had taken over the campaign. Waterford and Wexford were taken, and Hugo de Lacy was made the first English viceroy. De Lacy was given Meath to curb the power of Strongbow, leader of an earlier Norman wave which had established itself in Leinster.

In *The Conquest of Ireland* Giraldus reports the remark of Maurice FitzGerald at the siege of Dublin in 1171: 'to the Irish we are English, and to the English, Irishmen'. T.E. McNeill, in *Anglo-Norman Ulster*, comments that this was quite a claim, considering that the Anglo-Normans had arrived only just over two years before. Yet apparently it was not strange to Giraldus or his audience. The descendants of the wandering Scandinavians seem to have had a chameleon-like ability to adopt whatever colouring they found themselves amongst, from Norway to Normandy. Brondsted sees them as pillagers in more senses than one, who took more than they gave to Europe.

James Lydon claims that, after the coming of Christianity in the fifth century, the Norman invasion was the most important event in Irish history. The invader with the biggest reputation, 'the man around whom the most fantastic legends were spun', was John de Courcy. The future 'Prince of Ulster' and 'King of Erainn', came from minor gentry in Somerset. Giraldus says he was blond, tall and lanky, immensely strong, bold and brave, and an impetuous warrior who behaved more like an ordinary soldier than a leader. He was also modest and although he was generous to the Church, he could be mean and unreliable. It sounds as if his meanness was most keenly felt by his soldiers. The sixteenth-century *Book of Howth* compares him to Lancelot and Hector: every stroke of his two-handed sword killed at least one man.

The Norman-French chanson 'The Song of Dermot and the Earl' claims that in 1172 Henry II told de Courcy that he could have Ulster if he could conquer it by force: other authorities suggest de Courcy acted without Henry's permission. In 1176 de Courcy arrived in Dublin with ten knights. He persuaded another twelve to join him and he set off to invade Ulster with 300 foot soliders, at least some of whom would have been Irish. They had to travel in winter for three days through enemy country, for the Normans controlled only parts of Meath and north County Dublin. They seem to have managed it without alerting the inhabitants. It was an age of miracles and heroic chivalry, for the English at least. According to Giraldus, a prophecy said that a white knight on a white horse, with birds on his shield, would invade Ulster; de Courcy fitted the bill. More significant, perhaps, when it came to battle, was the effect of the heavy cavalry. The Irish, when they saw the Norman knights covered in armour, with superior weapons and mounted on enormous horses, had a tendency to run away. It is unlikely that they all had heavy axes, and their short spears and darts would have been ineffective against knights in armour. The Normans also had archers who used the longbow.

Ulster was divided by warring groups. Those in the west were pressing upon the Ulaid, in counties Antrim and Down. With a mixture of military victories – helped no doubt by the sight of the heavy horses and the terror his reputation inspired – and the exploitation of local squabbles which divided the Irish, de Courcy established himself in Ulster.

At the second battle of Down, de Courcy was vastly outnumbered – Giraldus says there were 15,000 against him – but the Irish fled before a blow was struck. Many holy relics that they had brought with them to ensure victory were abandoned. The most important was the Book of Armagh, reputedly written by St Patrick himself. De Courcy restored it to the monastery of Armagh. It is now in Trinity College, Dublin.

Giraldus approved of de Courcy's reverence for the Church. Perhaps he really was devout, but he turned his devotion to political advantage, using local religious feelings to cement Norman authority. He claimed to have discovered the bodies of saints Patrick, Colmcille and Brigid in a vault in Down, and he had them translated to the cathedral. He changed the name of the cathedral to St Patrick's, and the name of the town to Downpatrick. He imported monks from England to alter the composition of the Irish Church and to rewrite its history. The Cistercians propagated the story that it was St Patrick who had converted Dublin and that therefore Armagh, Patrick's seat, had a superior claim to be the headquarters of the Irish Church. It remains so to this day, both for the Roman Catholic Church and the Church of Ireland. One side effect of his policy was that he secured a good press: both the Normans and the Irish Church had an interest in promoting his image.

Ironic light is thrown on the tangle of origin in Ireland by a recent claim of scholarship regarding the continuing cult of St Patrick that was so assiduously promoted by de Courcy. The tradition that Patrick banished all the venomous reptiles from Ireland is mentioned by Giraldus, who is always fascinated by unlikely yarns. It seems, however, that *Padraig*, the Irish form of Patrick, could have been confused by Norse speakers with *Padreker*, or 'toad-expeller', and taken to explain the absence of poisonous toads and snakes.

De Courcy challenged the primacy of Dublin and even issued his own coinage with the image of St Patrick where the King's head should have been. In 1180 he married Affreca, daughter of the King of Man, thereby gaining access to the Manx fleet. Through her he was related to the lords of Galloway and of Argyle. The latter also had a fleet, and the Galloways went on to control parts of mid-Antrim. Henry II appointed de Courcy Justiciar of Ireland in 1185.

At the time of de Courcy's victory at Down in 1177, Henry had made his son John Lord of Ireland, again with the Pope's blessing. Prince John visited Ireland in 1185 at the age of nineteen, but he only succeeded in offending the local chieftans and weakening Norman influence: he ridiculed Irish fashions and manners, for example, a failing to which Giraldus was also prone. De Courcy, on the other hand, seems to have been sensitive to local pieties.

John succeeded his father in 1189, and Ireland ceased to be a separate country, but it remained the personal fiefdom of the King, not an English dependency, an arrangement which obtained until Henry VIII. Historians given to seeking solutions in the past for the problems of the present regret that John did not happen to be crowned separately as King of Ireland. The idea of a dual monarchy was to be resurrected in the nineteenth century as an alternative to the Act of Union. John's second visit was more productive than his first: he established English forms of government and law, and divided the country the Normans controlled into twelve counties.

De Courcy and his like were adventurers. Their exploits were on their own behalf, and only secondarily for their monarch. It is easy to see that conquest would have been attractive for an ambitious young man from relatively humble origins: in Ulster the son of even an unimportant family could turn himself into a king. The Normans in Ireland were unruly and some opposed John's reorganization. De Courcy's control of Ulster was only ever partial, covering the areas of those tribes he had defeated in east Down and south Antrim, but John might have felt he was getting too big for his boots. He had failed to pay tribute on John's accession, and had spoken about the king's alleged murder of Arthur of Britanny. De Courcy was expelled by Hugh de Lacy, who was made Earl of Ulster in 1205. But the same trouble recurred with him, and King John had to come back in 1210, this time with de Courcy, once more in favour, and pursued de Lacy to Carrickfergus. De Courcy received a pension.

At this time, as Benn admits, Belfast was not the main centre. The big towns were either ecclesiastical like Downpatrick, where de Courcy had his capital, or military, like Dundrum or the great Norman castle of Carrickfergus, which remained an important military centre into the eighteenth century and is still a most impressive building. Belfast may have had a small castle guarding its ford, and a few small churches, but it was only one of several places of secondary importance. On the other hand, its position gave it an increasing geographical significance.

When de Lacy returned to Ulster in 1223 he was able, with the help of the

O'Neills from west of the Bann, to regain his earldom. He remained Earl of Ulster from 1227 until his death in 1243, though he had to contend with new rivals, Scots, to whom the King had granted lands north of Larne.

De Lacy extended the control De Courcy had established to include north County Antrim, but the Normans were never secure in Ulster, and never completed their conquest. Their organization was superficial: they took possession of the land and charged rents from those to whom they granted leases – farmers, burgesses and a few cottiers. They built mottes, such as that at Dundonald, at sites where they could see trouble a long way off, and to which tributes were brought. But they did not substantially alter the Irish way of life: their Irish farmers did not live in villages or use more advanced methods. On the other hand, McNeill finds that the Irish voluntarily adopted some Norman ways, despite the shared interest of the promoters of the Normans and the friends of the Irish cause in emphasizing their difference. The Irish started building castles and mottes in the Norman style. They intermarried, and at least some of the Normans understood Irish culture. De Courcy, for example, always kept at hand a book of the prophecies of Colmcille, written in Irish, which he frequently consulted.

The Norman earls were powerful but their local representatives were thinly spread. They depended on military strength, the co-operation of the locals, and the exploitation of local divisions. They could live as well as English earls, though they spent more time on war than administration: Ulster provided a healthy income for the English treasury, yet the tenants were not worked hard. To expand, the Normans tended to rely on taking more land and on a growing population (in this period numbers were rising throughout Europe). They could not attract many men from England willing to act as common soldiers on their behalf in return for the modest rewards of tenant farming.

McNeill traces the beginnings of 'nationalist' resistance to the Normans to the attempts of Brian O'Neill to revive the High Kingship and gain the support of other Irish kings against the Normans in Ulster. The earldom, which had lapsed after the death of de Lacy, was revived so that Walter de Burgh, Lord of Connacht, could take over from the Dublin government the task of containing Brian's Cenel Eoghain. Rather than do so by attacking into their territory, de Burgh let Aedh Buidhe O'Neill marry his second cousin. Treaties and alliances were signed. Walter's son Richard carried on the policy of encouraging friendly leaders of the O'Neill rather than attacking them. As Earl of Ulster and Lord of Connacht he was the most powerful man in Ireland, yet he had to deal with squabbles amongst the Normans themselves in which Irish leaders had become entangled. Westminster, Dublin and Edinburgh all had an interest in his activities.

The collapse of Norman influence in Ulster is usually attributed to two events. One is the attack by the Scots. Robert the Bruce, according to legend, spent a dark night of the soul in a cave on Rathlin Island watching a spider 'try, try and try again'. He defeated Edward II at Bannockburn in 1314. His brother, Edward Bruce, came to Ireland the next year to stop aid from Ireland reaching the English. He remained for two years and had the support of the Irish in Ulster, as well as the acceptance of many Anglo-Normans. Domnall O'Neill, son of Brian, sent a Remonstrance to the Pope seeking to widen the conflict into a national one against the English.

Edward Bruce was killed in 1318. He provides another might-have-been for the 'if only' school of history: if only the Scots, in alliance with the Irish and with the connivance of the hibernicized Normans, could have liberated Ireland from English rule. . . . All sorts of possibilities, all of them better than what actually happened, present themselves: a Celtic confederation; kings of Scotland and Ireland. . . .

The second apparent cause of Norman decline occurred in Belfast. Richard de Burgh's young heir, William, was assassinated near 'Le Ford' between Newtownards and Carrickfergus; another account says he was killed between the Castle of Belfast and Carrickfergus; another mentions the church at Shankill. His own barons, John de Logan and Robert and Richard de Maundeville, did the deed on 6 June 1333. The supposed cause was a family feud caused by de Burgh's insulting behaviour to his sister Gyle, Richard's wife. The crime appears to have happened spontaneously: noticing that the de Logans outnumbered the Earl's servants, Richard de Maundeville, 'while saying morning prayers with him . . . cleft his skull with a sword-stroke behind'.

The Normans probably took one of the ancient tracks first used in the Stone Age. The main road through Belfast from east to west, for example, would have run along the present Newtownards Road, crossing the river near the Queen's Bridge, then going along North Street and the Shankill Road. They might have passed three churches: those at Knock in the east and Shankill in the west were about a hundred feet above sea level; the Chapel of the Ford was the only church on the valley floor.

McNeill points out that the receipts from Ulster did not fall disastrously as a result of Edward Bruce's depredations, nor did the Irish push out the Normans in any decisive battle after Earl William's murder. Nevertheless the Clann Aedha Buidhe O'Neill, with help from Magennis and MacCartan, gradually re-established Irish control of the northern part of the weakening earldom. It was the Clandeboye O'Neills, who gave their name to the area around Belfast, who had to deal with the next, successful wave of invaders.

In 1366 the Statute of Kilkenny set up the Pale, the part of Ireland controlled by the English, but under Edward IV its size was reduced. In 1465 the laws against Irish culture were strengthened, and in 1480 all trade between the Pale and the rest of Ireland was prohibited. The English maintained their foothold in Ireland, but the forms of government, such as the Common Council, which had been established in Ireland at the end of the thirteenth century, were largely only forms.

Nevertheless, Brendan Clifford insists that such precedents are historically significant. Besides, the Pale may have enclosed half the population.

Many Anglo-Normans were assimilated into the melting-pot, or Irish stew, and became 'Old English' – in a sense, Irish in all but origin. An Act of Edward III suggests that this was felt early. It stipulated, rather hopefully one feels, 'that no difference of allegiance shall henceforth be made between the English born in Ireland and the English born in England, by calling them English hobbe, or Irish dogge; but that all be called by one name, the English lieges of our lord the king'. The Irish also made the distinction: at a later date, the term of abuse *bodach sassenach*, Rev. George Hill says, would only have been used of new arrivals from England, with their 'cold', 'supercilious' and 'coarse' manners.

On the other hand, the intolerant Giraldus, in at the beginning of the Norman adventure, gives plenty of evidence of a basic culture clash, and ominously foretells future troubles arising from it. He was openly contemptuous of the 'wild and inhospitable' Irish who, though physically handsome, were neither 'strong in war nor reliable in peace'. He deplored the way their treachery and expediency could 'contaminate' any foreigner who came into contact with them. But he did allow that the Irish were incomparably skilled in music, and suggested that the music of Wales and Scotland had been learned from the Irish. His brief technical remarks in his discussion of Irish music suggest that he understood something about it, so that his opinion on this subject is probably more reliable than his natural history (he could mistake an ouzel for a kingfisher, for example).

Giraldus deplored the state of the Irish Church, and its preponderance of monks and monasteries. He admired the monks' celibacy, their observance and their readiness to fast, but he deplored their drinking. Giraldus felt that contemplation was of strictly limited value, and indeed his whole character suggests that he would prefer action. He believed that there should be clergy to reprove the sinner and lay down the law. John J. O'Meara notes that many of Giraldus's criticisms had some validity, while the traditional Brehon law circumscribed the authority of the Church. This system was the atomistic common law passed down case by case by wandering law-givers, or Brehons, since pre-Christian times. Because these laws were simply that, without any organizing idea or basic principles, and often dealt with apparently mundane affairs such as defecating dogs, the safety of cattle, or the crime of causing your neighbour to blush, they can seem footling and unimportant. They are easy to have fun with, as does a recent book, *Irish Laws*, by Mary Dowling Daley. The Brehon law died out, or was stamped out, in the seventeenth century, and with it went the 'Gaelic order', including surprisingly modern-looking laws about divorce and married women's property.

Giraldus observed that the Irish Church had lots of confessors, but no martyrs. He records a conversation with Tatheus, Archbishop of Cashel, in which Giraldus said that no one had become a martyr defending the Church in Ireland. Tatheus replied that, while it was true that the Irish were barbarous, yet they had never attacked churchmen or saints. 'But now a people has come to the kingdom which knows how, and is accustomed, to make martyrs. From now on Ireland will have its martyrs, like other countries.'

Giraldus differed from Henry II's policy of combining military conquest with local alliances. He had no time for those who accommodated themselves to lax, lazy Irish ways: his manner was proud, restless and aggressive, and his Christianity was puritanical and severe. He found in Ireland that even the cocks were lazy; in every other country they would crow three times before dawn, but in Ireland the cocks crowed only once. If the Normans were too divided amongst themselves and too dependent on local support to sustain their conquest of Antrim and Down, their descendants succeeded where they had mostly failed. The attitudes that prevailed more resembled those of Giraldus than those of the adaptable de Courcys and de Burghs. Ireland was indeed to have its share of martyrs.

CHAPTER THREE

SIR ARTHUR CHICHESTER

The man who finally subdued Ulster and established Belfast as a bastion of the English presence advised his masters in London that in order to defeat the Irish it was necessary to occupy Ireland. But he did not mean that the English should adopt Irish ways.

Both Benn and Bardon list the many occasions, from 1476 to 1523, on which Belfast Castle was taken, demolished, sacked or 'broken' by O'Neills, O'Donnells and FitzGeralds. It is uncertain exactly when it was built or where: it was probably begun some time after John de Courcy's arrival, to guard the road from County Down to Carrickfergus, and was either at the bottom of the present High Street, or at Castle Junction, on the south bank of the Farset, 300 yards upstream from the Chapel of the Ford. It has been suggested that it was originally an earthen fort between the mouths of the Farset and the Blackstaff rivers. This spot was once known as Ballyrecoolegalgie, 'town of the fort of Calgach's Corner'.

In 1556 Philip Butler, Secretary to the Lord Deputy, Sussex, wrote of an expedition during which he had camped on low ground 'under Banne Vadagan', or Cave Hill. He claimed that the Great Cave was where the O'Neills of Clandeboye hid their treasure. At this time the area around Belfast was divided into Upper and Lower Clandeboye. The O'Neills had their base on the brow of the Castlereagh Hills, but they also claimed ownership of Belfast Castle. The Irish practised transhumance, moving their cattle from winter to summer pastures and living beside them in small farmsteads. Thick woods stretched from Strangford Lough (or Lough Cone) to the River Blackwater in County Tyrone, while Coill Ultach, the Ulster Wood, was untouched north of the Lagan.

Besides being full of wolves, the woods were one of a list of reasons why the English found it so difficult to push back into Ulster. There the Gaelic culture was strongest, behind a barrier of difficult country – forest and bog, in which the lightly armed Irish were at an advantage in the skirmishes of guerrilla warfare. Jonathan Bardon says that Queen Elizabeth expended more money and blood on the conquest of Ulster than she did in the defeat of Spain.

She sent Sir Thomas Smith in 1571, but his inadequate forces were unable to capture the shores of Belfast Lough. Two years later she sent Walter Devereux, the Earl of Essex, with many more men. She gave him the deeds to Clandeboye,

Belfast and other places. He might have achieved his object without bloodshed, for Sir Brian McPhelim O'Neill, the chief of Clandeboye, seeing Essex's powerful array at Carrickfergus, was apparently about to submit until a dispute arose over cattle. Bardon says that Essex stole Brian's cattle, but Sean O'Faolain claims that Brian, who arrived to do obeisance with ten thousand cows (which seems a lot), left the next morning having taken all his own cattle and all the English ones as well.

The armies fought at the ford of Belfast and the English prevailed. They camped there that night and in the dark could hear the Irish keening for their dead. When Sir Brian was at last persuaded to submit, Essex entertained him for three days at Belfast Castle, 'pleasantly and cheerfully'. Bardon explains what happened next as springing from the desire for revenge of a man whose dreams of an easy success had been delayed. The *Annals of Ulster* say:

> *As they were agreeably drinking and making merry, Brian, his brother, and his wife, were seized upon by the Earl; and all his people unsparingly put to the sword, men, women, youths, and maidens, in Brian's own presence. Brian was afterwards sent to Dublin, together with his wife and brother, where they were cut in quarters.*

Essex excused himself by claiming that this would terrify the Irish, but instead it roused them to anger, and he was forced to retreat on the best terms he could. O'Faolain records another atrocity on Rathlin Island, where Essex's men pointlessly slaughtered women, children, the sick and the old – Scots sent there for safety. Their kinsman, Sorley Boy MacDonnell, stood on the County Antrim shore and watched it happen as he heard their screams, according to the story. Rathlin Island is certainly visible from County Antrim, but you would need good eyesight to be able to make out figures on it.

Besides being responsible for Belfast's bloodiest early atrocity, Essex was also one of the first to see the potential for its future:

> *Belfaste is a place meet for a corporate town, armed with all commodities, as a principal haven, wood and good ground, standing also upon a border, and a place of great importance for service.*

He asked the Queen to pay for fortifications around the spring and for a storehouse; he and his followers would build their own houses. But few were enthusiastic for such pioneer settlements. After his defeat and withdrawal Essex persisted in trying to persuade the Queen to finance a colony: 'I resolve not to build but at one place; namelie, at Belfast. . . .' He argued that Belfast could guard the ford, supply Carrickfergus with timber and command the plains of Clandeboye, but Elizabeth was not interested. Essex died in 1576, possibly murdered.

Again, O'Faolain's account is rather different: he presents Essex as a reluctant campaigner, sick of the Irish rain, the Irish and his own discontented soldiers, who only wanted to get back to England. He also claims that Essex was poisoned by his wife in Dublin, who soon after married her lover, Leicester.

Despite setbacks, the war with Spain made it necessary to prevent England's next-door neighbour from forming an alliance with its enemies, and Elizabeth extended her control of Ireland. In 1595, Hugh O'Neill, Earl of Tyrone, began a rebellion that lasted nine years and made him one of the most celebrated heroes of Irish nationalism. O'Faolain entitles his biography *The Great O'Neill*, but he points out that Hugh was a reluctant patriot. His earldom had been granted at the recommendation of the butcher Essex, who regarded him as the only Irish leader he could trust. To begin with, at least, Hugh was more interested in a personal quarrel with Turlough Luineach than with keeping Ireland for the Irish.

In 1597 Shane McBrian O'Neill of Lower Clandeboye took Belfast Castle while the officer commanding Carrickfergus was 'making merry'. His men hanged and disembowelled all the Englishmen they could find. Sir John Chichester went north and recovered Belfast, slaughtering the defenders. But he made the mistake of antagonizing the MacDonnells, Island Scots who had become lords of the Antrim Glens, and who had stayed out of the war being waged by Hugh O'Neill. On an expedition from Carrickfergus, Sir John was ambushed by James MacSorley MacDonnell in Old Mill Glen near Ballycarry, and beheaded.

Hugh O'Neill suffered an irreversible defeat at Kinsale in County Cork in 1601, having marched the length of Ireland in winter to try to relieve a Spanish force pinned down there. Jonathan Bardon says that Kinsale meant the end of Gaelic Ulster. But Hugh did not surrender for two more years, and the Lord Deputy in 1601 said that the conflict in Ulster was 'as busy a war as any in the world'. During it the English under Lord Mountjoy created famine by stealing Irish livestock and burning Irish crops. The tactic was most effective. Three children were seen cooking and eating their dead mother on the Castlereagh Hills, and it was common to see corpses whose mouths were green from trying to find sustenance from nettles and docks. Hugh's own soldiers, as he surrendered, killed English horses and fought over the meat. It was only after he had signed the surrender that he was told Queen Elizabeth was dead.

Arthur, the brother of the murdered Sir John Chichester, had been appointed Governor of Carrickfergus in 1599 and had been one of Mountjoy's most ruthless officers. His letters to Whitehall show him as an enthusiastic soldier:

This garrison . . . hath done as good days' work in killing, burning, taking of cows, and destroying the rebels, as any one in Ireland, and I hope to continue it.

A few months later he reported to Mountjoy his progress on a campaign:

we have killed above 100 people of all sorts, besides such as were burnt, how many

I know not. We spare none of what quality or sex soever, and it hath bred much terror in the people, who heard not a drum, nor saw not a fire there of long time.

But he had time to think of other things. In between his slaughterings around Carrickfergus and his terrorizing of Dungannon, he wrote to London asking to be given Island Magee: 'It is a thing of small value.' He was also an advocate of Mountjoy's grim policy:

The traitors in many places receive blows, though we kill them not in multitudes, which cannot be, howsoever we beat them, they are so swift of foot. It is famine, not the sword, that must reduce this country to what is expected.

On 5 November 1603, eight months after Hugh O'Neill's surrender, he was granted 'the Castle of Bealfaste, or Belfast'.

Sir Arthur Chichester, the founder of Belfast, was born in May 1563 near Barnstaple in Devon. He matriculated at Oxford University at the age of nearly twenty, unusually late for Elizabethan times. Brendan Clifford calls him a 'highwayman', and he had to flee to Ireland after robbing one of the Queen's purveyors, or tax collectors. He was granted a pardon, and served on a ship against the Armada in 1588. Seven years later he sailed with Sir Francis Drake on his last expedition. Some reports have it that he was a captain in the Armada and commanded a ship with five hundred men for Drake, but it seems likely that he was in charge of marines. He fought at Cadiz, and was Sergeant Major General, third in command, at Amiens, where he was wounded. Henry IV, who converted to Catholicism to gain the French throne, knighted him.

Chichester was serving as a captain in the Low Countries when Sir Robert Cecil sent him back to Ireland with a command of 1,200 men. It is said that the Lord Deputy, a later Earl of Essex, was so impressed by the drilling of Chichester's men when they arrived at Drogheda that he made a mock charge at his pikemen at the head of the cavalry. Chichester took him seriously, and Essex had to retreat with a slight wound. But he did not take it personally, and on leaving Ireland Essex recommended that Chichester be made Sergeant Major General of the English army in Ireland. Chichester preferred to stay at Carrickfergus.

He understood the difficulty of fighting the Irish on their own terms:

We defend the heart, and care not greatly for the limbs; but those being taken away, the heart cannot long be in safety. This enemy can never be beaten, but by dwelling and lodging near him, and in his own country. Journeys are consumptions of men, more hurting ourselves than those we seek to offend. The kingdom is great, and Her Majesty's force of 14,000 men are scarcely seen in it.

His letters, which are in the *Calendar of State Papers*, have the eloquence of much

Elizabethan prose, horrific though their subject often is. He writes with exceeding humility to Cecil, and constantly apologizes for the length of his letters, but the style is matter-of-fact and he is less pompous than Essex.

His opinion of the Irish, comparable to that of Giraldus, was no doubt sharpened by the fact that the struggle in the Carrickfergus military area (which included Belfast) was most intense: 'They are the most perfidious generation that ever Christians lived with and there is little hope of a quiet government until they are absolutely confounded, especially within this command.'

One of the most interesting recent publications about this period is the facsimile reproduction of a book first published in 1581, *The Image of Irelande with a Discovery of Woodkarne* by John Derricke, edited by David B. Quinn. The most rewarding part is the twelve large woodcuts, which illustrate Irish customs and the nature of the fighting between the Irish and English. Verses seek to glorify the Lord Deputy of the time, Sir Henry Sidney, and justify his punitive actions by showing Irish atrocities and by satirizing their 'primitive' – certainly, to the Elizabethan English, strange – habits at table, for example. The book was originally printed by John Day, the most important printer of illustrated books of the time, and a staunch Protestant: it seems that the blatant racism of the book must have had some religious animus against Catholicism. The author at one point feels he has to justify his portrayal by explaining that the plate showing the most swinish behaviour depicts northern manners, not those within the Pale. The implicit assumption of the book and, it must be, of the English commanders, is that the Irish are criminals against their Queen, and deserve punishment.

Chichester no doubt reflected the common attitudes of his time. But it may be significant that the strategy he favoured involved a new, more thorough cultural oppression to go with a more relentless military oppression:

> We follow a painful, toilsome, hazardous and unprofitable war by which the Queen will never reap what is expected until the nation be wholly destroyed or so subjected as to take a new impression of laws and religion, being now the most treacherous infidels of the world and we have too mild spirits and good consciences to be their masters. He is a well governed and worthy gentleman whom their villainy does not deceive. Our honesty, bounty, clemency and justice make them not any way assured unto us, neither doth the actions of one of their own nation, though it be the murder of father, brother or friend, make them longer enemies than until some small gift or bienge [buying?] be given to the wronged party.

Chichester did not understand the Gaelic mode of settling a quarrel, and he sounds like one of those who feel that the only way to find a 'solution' is to make the Irish become like the English. (In the 1960s Terence O'Neill, Prime Minister of Northern Ireland, argued that prosperity would induce Catholics to behave like Protestants.) There was a gap like that between cowboys and Indians.

When they are down, it must be good laws, severe punishment, abolishing their ceremonies and customs in religion, and lordlike Irish government, keeping them without arms more than what shall be necessary for the defence of the honest, and some port-towns erected upon these northern harbours that must bridle them, and keep them in perpetual obedience.

When he became Lord Deputy of Ireland in 1605, Chichester issued a proclamation abolishing the Irish system of tenantry, by which farmers owed rent and allegiance first to their local chieftain, who in turn paid allegiance to the King or Queen. In future, tenants were 'to depend wholly and immediately upon his Majesty . . . and not upon any other inferior lord or lords. . . .' In fact the Irish chieftains did not so much own land as hold it in trust for their people. Chichester made a survey of landholdings around Belfast by consulting the Brehons. But the plan was not a complete success in Ulster, where there was resistance to the creation of freeholders paying fixed rents. The new system, of course, was designed to reduce the chieftains' political power.

James I encouraged the persecution of Catholics, but his Lord Deputy, surprisingly perhaps, was less enthusiastic:

I have dealt as tenderly as I might, knowing well that men's consciences must be won and persuaded by time, conference, and instructions, which the aged here will hardly admit, and therefore our hope must be in the education of the youth; and yet we must labour daily, otherwise all will turn to barbarous ignorance and contempt. I am not violent therein, albeit I wish reformation, and will study and endeavour of it all I may, which, I think, sorts better with his majesty's ends that to deal with violence and like a puritan in this kind.

Though he felt that Catholics could not be persecuted into becoming Protestants, he regretted the difference in religion and way of life: 'Ignorance, colour of religion, desire of liberty and detestation of civility makes them to hate us with a deadly hatred. . . .' On Chichester's advice the measures against Catholics were relaxed. He prompted the translation of the Book of Common Prayer into English, and distributed it throughout Ireland.

Following the start of the Plantation of Ulster, a means was devised of electing an Irish Parliament with a built-in Protestant majority. In 1613, the year Chichester was made Lord of Belfast, the town was incorporated: though it was no bigger than other towns like Bangor, Donaghadee or Comber, it became one of forty new boroughs, each of which sent two members to Parliament in Dublin. Despite the loyalty of such lords as Chichester, who sent their own men as MPs, the assembly immediately dissolved into squabbling. In February 1614 Chichester was summoned to England to explain what was going on, and when he returned to Ireland was told to resume the policy of Catholic persecution. He managed to have the measures modified a little, but in August the Parliament was dissolved and in November Chichester was relieved of his duties. He died in 1625 and was buried at Carrickfergus, where the Chichester family monument was erected. His only son had died, so the title went to his brother Edward who 'partook but little of the ability of his predecessor', according to Benn.

Brendan Clfford, never mealy-mouthed, claims that what distinguished the Chichesters' ownership of Belfast was their lack of civilized interest in it. His view of the incorporation is that it provided Sir Arthur with a pocket borough and two tame MPs. The Lord of Belfast was given 'over-riding powers' over the Corporation – initially twelve burgesses who elected a Sovereign, or mayor, selected from a list of three names supplied by the Lord. They held office for life and replacements were by appointment only. They elected the two MPs, but in effect these were the personal appointments of the Chichesters too. They could only make laws on the Lord's advice and with his consent. This situation obtained until 1832.

The town grew and improved through the energy of its humbler citizens, largely without the help of its owners, and occasionally despite them. For example, in the eighteenth century the Chichesters published threats to parents in the town who sent their children to the progressive school run by David Manson rather than to the school sponsored by them, and it has been suggested that they were not above fomenting sectarian strife in order to manipulate their tenants. In the nineteenth century they were reluctant to allow the Harbour Commissioners the use of land on the lough shore to enhance the port and shipbuilding facilities until the level of their compensation was raised. According to Estyn Evans, the granting of perpetuity leases in the 1820s and later in the century removed a significant obstacle to greater prosperity. Clifford says he is unable to find a Chichester who interested himself in politics until the nineteenth century. But Bardon points out that their Dublin house was used by the Irish Parliament until the building of College Green, and that the first Marquis was a politician, albeit an incompetent one. The Chichesters did interest themselves in the Plantation rather more effectively.

There are several versions of how the Plantation was set in motion. One involves the Flight of the Earls. Hugh O'Neill, the Earl of Tyrone, was in dispute with one of his dependants, O'Cahan, who appealed to Lord Deputy Chichester to adjudicate. As O'Cahan read out his petition, Hugh snatched the paper from his hands and tore it up. They then agreed to go to London to have their dispute settled by King James, but Hugh feared he would be arrested in England, and fled with Tyrconnell and others on 25 September 1607. Some commentators point out that after his defeat Hugh had been harried and pestered by Chichester's spies and *agents provocateurs*: the English were determined to remove his traditional authority, and it must have looked as if things could only get worse for him.

Hugh never returned. He lived out his days in Rome, on pensions from the dimension, his awareness of the Counter-Reformation and the implications of national struggles, has been largely diluted through the appropriation of his story by the insular patriots, atavistic and anti-intellectual, in the very tradition he sought to transform.

His departure made possible a large-scale plantation of Ulster by the adherents of an opposing European idea. In 1608, following the resolution of new unrest west of the Bann, Chichester began. His original plan allowed for the land previously owned by the earls to be granted directly by the Crown to native Irishmen 'of note or good desert', and for the surplus to be settled by English and Scots if they would build and garrison castles to defend themselves. In fact Ulster was not planted in this way. Grants were made at the Government's whim, and many Irish were displaced from the most productive land.

In a letter of 18 July 1608, Chichester wrote interestingly about the habits of the native people, and his suggestions for enhancing the security and economy of the new colony:

Whereas the most part of the inhabitants of this countrie doe not live together in Villadges and Townshippes after the manner of his majesty's civill subjects in other parts of this kingdome; but doe all the Sumer season passe from place to place, grazing their Creaghts or heards of cattle, having noe other houses or dwellings, but onelie sleight Cabbans, which they make uppon every remove, not placing them together in forme of a Towne, but scattering and single, heere, and there, whereby there doe arise dailie many particular mischiefs, and general inconveniences, to the Comonweale of this Kingdome, namely in theis poynts following:

First, divers rebells and other malefactors which stand upon their keeping, and are not ameanable to laive, are daily receaved and releeved in thoose Creaghts, which being transitory, and removing from place to place, his majesty's forces or ordinary officers pursuing the said rebells or malefactors cannot but by meere chance, light uppon them to app'hend them and bring them to Justice, which they might certenly doe, if the said enhabitants which releeve them, had certen dwellings and habitacons:

Secondly, the Constables of the severall Baronies in the said countrie cannot, p'serve the publique peace, follow hues, and cries or execute warrants directed unto them from his majesty's Justices of peace, as they might doe, if the said inhabitants were drawne into Townes and Villadges:

Thirdely, the said inhabitants living single and scattred, are not able to defend themselves against any rebells, woodkerne, or outlawes, soe as the said rebells, woodkerne, or outlawes, doe many tymes take meat, and drinke of the said inhabitants against their wills; and doe manie tymes robb and burne their howses; whereas if they did dwell and inhabit together in any certen place, they would be able not onely to resist their violence, but to arrest and app'hend the said malefactors that they might be brought to Justice:

Fourthlie; this loose and unsetled manner of living, is the cause that there are few or noe trades or handicrafts in use amongst them, soe as they want such things as are requisite and necessarie for a civill life: Whereas, if the said enhabitants were gathered together into Villadges and Townes, trades and handicrafts would of necessity be exercised amongst them, and the said inhabitants would not onely be reduced to a more civill manner of living, but alsoe the Comodities of this Country would bee improved, and the people growe to greater wealth and riches:

The final page is missing, but it is an argument for the building of towns, and the destruction of the pastoral way of life practised by the Gaels and Celts.

In 1610 Chichester told King James he 'would rather labour with his hands in the Plantation of Ulster than dance or play in Virginia'. A year later he was building a new castle in Belfast, of bricks fired on the site (it burned down in 1708). Sir Moses Hill had built a fort at Hillhall, and was erecting a large stone house at Stranmillis. Many of the settlers came in the train of gentlemen from Devon, Warwickshire and Yorkshire. The Lagan Valley for three centuries formed the English sandwich filling between the Scots to north and south, though Belfast itself, not in the area of the official Plantation, was quicker to change its character. Into the nineteenth century, according to E.R.R. Green, people in the Lagan Valley prided themselves on the purity of their English, and could easily identify their English ancestors. Sir Arthur was an enthusiastic colonist, and if his descendants, as Clifford says, cared more about the rents from their properties than improvements to the town, Bardon says that, initially at least, it was useful for the new town to have a powerful protector, and one who was intent on developing what he owned.

CHAPTER FOUR

CON O'NEILL
AND THE PLANTERS

The *Montgomery Manuscripts* compiled by William Montgomery of Rosemount in the eighteenth century and edited by George Hill in 1869, tell the often extraordinary story of one family which, in a peculiarly enterprising way, was instrumental in giving the Belfast area its Scottish tinge.

The story begins in the sixteenth century with an episode from the life of Hugh Montgomery, Laird of Braidstane, the details of which 'might afford matter for a facetious pleasing novel, if they were descanted on by one of the modern witty composers of such like diversions (as they call them), which I think is not an appellative name expressive enough of their nature, because they are instructives and recreatives also'.

Hugh Montgomery spent some time at the French Court and served in Holland as a Captain of Foot under the Prince of Orange, the great grandfather of William III of England. Following the death of his parents, he returned to Scotland. At the Court in Edinburgh he kissed the hand of King James VI. His family were involved in 'bickering' with the Maxwells and the Cunninghams. Montgomery tried to challenge both Patrick Maxwell and William Cunningham to duels, but the latter fled to the Hague. Montgomery pursued him and, as he thought, ran him through with his sword, 'yet it pleased God that the buckle (like a toorget) saved his life'.

Montgomery was thrown into prison, but former comrades with whom he had served in Holland were in the Hague, and he asked a kinsman, a sergeant, to help him escape. On instructions, the sergeant seduced the daughter of the marshall of the prison, and Hugh married them in his cell, in the Scottish fashion. At a drunken dinner, the sergeant persuaded the merrymakers that, to make the celebrations complete, the Prince of Orange had pardoned Hugh. The marshall, 'as a gouty man', was led to his bed, and Montgomery, his servant, the sergeant and his new bride made off to a waiting Scottish ship, which took them home to Leith. We can only speculate on whether Robert, the sergeant, and the marshall's daughter lived happily ever after. Astonishingly, this experience was to prove valuable in the acquisition of Belfast.

When Queen Elizabeth died in 1603, James VI of Scotland became James I of England. The Scots assumed that his wealth was limitless and the King was said to be 'overhastily liberal'. His Scottish courtiers saw a chance to enrich themselves. The Montgomerys kept the King informed about events in Ulster, with which they had trading links, and the area around Belfast, in counties Antrim and Down, was the nearest and most obvious place for such southern Scots to exploit.

A few months before the death of Elizabeth, Con O'Neill, the Chief of Upper Clandeboye and the Great Ards, got himself into trouble. Being 'in a grand debauch' at Castlereagh, he had sent his servants to fetch wine from Belfast. They returned, having been robbed of their wine and beaten by soldiers, although they outnumbered the soldiers two to one. The servants were very drunk. 'Con was vehemently moved to anger; reproached them bitterly; and, in rage, swore by his father, and by all his noble ancestors' souls, that none of them should ever serve him or his family . . . if they went not back forthwith and did not revenge the affront done to him and themselves by those few Boddagh Sasonagh soldiers (as he termed them).' The servants, still drunk, snatched up some weapons and 'engaged the same soldiers (from words to blows).' There was a scuffle, and one of the soldiers received a wound from which he died that night. The servants ran off to the safety of Castlereagh: some were 'sore wounded and others killed':

> Then in a week after this fray, an office of enquest was held on Con, and those of his said friends and followers, and also on the servants, and on all that were suspected to be procurers, advisers, or actors therein, and all whom the Provost Marshall could seize (were taken); by which office the said Con, with some of his friends, were found guilty of levying war against the Queen.

Chichester imprisoned Con in Carrickfergus, though he was able to walk about the town and entertain his friends during the day. He expected a pardon from the new king as soon as the disturbances raised by Sir Cahir O'Doherty in Donegal were settled. King James had after all openly supported the MacDonnells of Dunluce, and secretly supported Hugh O'Neill in his recent rebellion, sending supplies from Scotland. James pardoned the rebels and promised them they could keep their lands, but Chichester persuaded him to opt for Plantation rather than reconciliation.

Hugh Montgomery decided to repeat his tried and tested ploy for escaping from prison. He employed a kinsman who owned a barque and traded with grain to Carrickfergus to carry a message to Con. The trader, Thomas, was to pretend to kidnap Con and bring him to Braidstone, provided Con agreed to Hugh's terms.

> Thomas aforesaid (as the Laird had formerly advised) having made love to the Town Marshall's daughter, called Annas Dobbin (whom I have often seen and spoken with, for she lived in Newtown till Anno 1664), and had gained hers and parent's consents to be wedded together. This took umbrages of suspicion away,

and so by contrivance with his espoused, an opportunity, one night, was given to the said Thomas and his barque's crew to take on board the said Con, as it were by force, he making no noise for fear of being stabbed, as was reported next day through the town.

The Reverend Andrew Stewart, a Presbyterian minister at Donaghadee, gives further details. Annas acted as a go-between. She arranged for the boat 'to come from Bangor, which, being light, might even come under the castle, and receive Con out at a window at a certain hour'. She had brought him 'two big cheeses, the meat being neatly taken out, and filled with cords, well packed in, and the holes handsomely made up again . . . and left him to hank himself down from the window at such a time when, by moonshine, he might see the boat ready, and so begone as it was already contrived. All this is done accordingly, and Con brought over to the church of Bangor, where, in an old steeple, he is hid, and kept till such time as Hugh Montgomery might be advertised to send a relief for him.'

Con was greeted at Largs the next evening by a mounted and armed guard of honour, and he was entertained courteously at Braidstane. There he signed an agreement to give half his lands to Sir Hugh, on condition that Sir Hugh obtained a pardon for him, and the favour of the King, as well as a legal entitlement to the remaining half of his lands.

Con might have been foolish or merely unfortunate. Liam de Paor calls him 'a befuddled sot'. But Bardon reports a recent thesis by T.P.F. McCall which modifies the picture. Con was lucky to survive at all, for his drunken brawl was more like rebellion. He was also lucky to retain any land, for his claim to Upper Clandeboye was tenuous. Presumably the Montgomerys had an interest in glossing over these details. Despite the initial intentions of the King and English talk about fair play, it seems clear that the Gaelic chieftains in this period were harassed and harried by Chichester. But McCall points out that many lost their lands because, unfamiliar with English methods of collecting rent, they got hopelessly into debt. Bardon portrays the chieftain of a vanishing culture watching Belfast being built under the Castlereagh Hills on land which had been taken from him, and points out that Con is only remembered now in the name of the 'foetid stream' that runs through east Belfast, the Connswater.

Con was taken to kiss King James's hand and the agreement was made, with the proviso that Hugh Montgomery undertook not to allow 'any person of meer Irish extraction' to have a lease. But the eventual terms turned out to be even more humiliating for Con. Sir James Fullerton, 'a great favourite, who loved ready money, and to live in Court, more than in waste and wilderness in Ulster', had persuaded the King that Montgomery's deal with Con was too generous, and that 'such an Irishman' did not deserve to keep so much. Instead the 'overhastily liberal' King decided that the land be divided into three, between Con,

Montgomery and another Scottish courtier, Sir James Hamilton. A year later Con had signed away more lands and forests, and rapidly the environs of Belfast – in the most intensely and stubbornly Gaelic province of Ireland – ceased to be Gaelic. Belfast became, not Scottish or English but its own place, quite different from the rest of the island.

Hugh Montgomery lost no time bringing over settlers from Braidstane. His plantation began in the north of County Down, around Newtown, as New-townards then was, and 'Gray Abbey'. The names of those who came with him include Shaw, Nevin, Moore, Catherwood and Cunningham.

He occupied 'the stump of the castle', and brought 'divers artificers, as smiths, masons, carpenters', and others. The materials for making 'cottages and booths' – sods, wattle and thatch – were all locally available. Her ladyship started the manufacture of linen and wool. They were 'supplied with necessaries from Belfast (but six miles thence)' and two or three times a week 'in the fair summer season' they would receive supplies from Scotland. Donaghadee was 'but three hours from Portpatrick', and people could come over for the day from Stranraer to go to market, despite 'evil report of wolves and woodkerns'.

His lordship kept a blood (in Scotland called a sleuth) hound to trace out thieves and woodkerns (so were torys then termed) which was a great terror to them, and made them to forbear to haunt in his bounds.

They also built a 'place of God's honour' for, from the perspective of the early eighteenth century as reflected in the *Montgomery Manuscripts*, 'our forefathers were more pious than ourselves'.

They had all they needed, including a ready-made working class: 'there were Irish Gibeonites and Garrons enough in his woods to hew and draw timber for the sanctuary'. The reference to the Book of Joshua may sound an echo of the Dutch Reformed Church and its theory about the perpetual bondsmen destined to serve the congregation, but the comparison might have been with the American Indians rather than South Africa. Belfast was slow to get started, compared with some places across the Atlantic.

Later Montgomerys looked back on this pioneering period as a 'golden, peaceable age', for the family's fortunes were never certain in Ulster. But even during this calm beginning, between 1610 and 1618 there were 'divers debates, controversys and suits' between Sir Hugh and James Hamilton, as well as quarrels and disputes with other gentlemen.

Sir Hugh, who was made first Viscount Montgomery, was of medium height and ruddy face; he had a 'manly, sprightlie and chearful countenance'. He was 'sober and temperate in meat and drink, and chaste also'. His recreations were all physical: 'before he was nobilitated' he had hunted badgers and hares on foot; when he grew more grand he chased deer, fox and wolves on horseback. He liked tennis and wildfowling, 'but he delighted little in soft easy recreations (fit only, as he said, for ladies and boys)'. He built a harbour at Donaghadee and a school at Newtownards, and built or improved various churches. There is a vivid portrait of the old man:

> His Lordship was very obliging by his condescending humility and affability, his usual compilation was kind (often in his ultry grand climaterick years), calling inferior men, my heart, my heart, and naming them; his worst word in reproaching them was baggage, and his most angry expression was beastly baggage, and commonly followed by the lifting up the staff at the trespasser, or a committal to constable or stocks; this was his latter days intercomuning with his misdoing servants and yeoman tenants; but towards gentlemen or the nobility, his behaviour and discourse was no otherwise than as befitted them.

In 1635 Con's son Daniel O'Neill, a Protestant, petitioned for the return of his father's lands. Clifford says the suit was rejected because of a personal antipathy between O'Neill and Strafford, the Lord Deputy. This contradicts the *Montgomery Manuscripts*, which claim Strafford plotted with O'Neill and was only thwarted by Sir James Montgomery. Daniel O'Neill served the Royalist cause during the Civil War, and was a friend of both Charles I and Charles II. Rather than pursue his claims in Clandeboye, he settled for life in London where he owned a piece of Pall Mall. Clifford, for whom he is the favourite O'Neill, records that he was granted a monopoly on the manufacture of gunpowder and became Postmaster General.

Hugh Montgomery died in May 1636 aged about seventy-six. A year later Belfast received a boost when Carrickfergus lost its right to one third of the duties on trade into and out of Belfast Lough. But the golden age soon ended, and all order was swept away by the Scottish army. There were troubles ahead, but the first Viscount's 'body and nerves were agile and strong, beyond any of his sons or their children'.

On 24 October 1641 while King Charles I was at war in Scotland, the 'native Irish' rose in a rebellion. There was panic among the planters. The Scots and English expected to be slaughtered, and many, including Lord Edward Chichester, attempted to escape from Belfast by boat. (He died in Devon in 1648). Captain Lawson, who owned the ironworks at Old Forge, ran through the town trying to organize some defence. Bardon quotes his report of how he

> blamed them for offering to leave the town, and intreated for some arms, either by buying or lending, but could not prevail. At last I found in Mister le Squire's house seven muskets, eight halberts, ready in the street to be shipped to Carrickfergus, which arms I took, and bought a drum, and beating the same through the town, raised about twenty men, who came with me again up to the Iron Works, having

Mr Forbes, and some number with me, where I also gathered in all about 160 horse and foot.

He marched to Lisburn, where he was able to prevent Sir Conn Magennis taking the town by driving cattle against the gates. He delayed the rebels until he was relieved by larger forces. A month later, a bigger Irish army failed to take the town. An earthen rampart with a ditch was built to protect Belfast. The Protestants were in a state of terror:

rebels have intercepted many arms . . . and increase daylie in strenthe, and goes on in their former crewelties withe all sorts of persones, young and old; and except speidie assistance be sent from Scotland, be all outward appearance they will find but few of ther cuntrie men to welcom them, and verie evil landing heir; for we ar few and verie naked for want of armes to withstand them.
. . . The rebells burne and kill everie other night within a myl two or three unto us, neither can we help it; for what they doe is in the night, and if we send out a partie they have centinells on all the hills, and will not stand but reteir to the woods.

Great numbers of English and Scots fled from many parts of Ulster to seek safety in north Down, or in Scotland; there was a garrison of three or four hundred men at Belfast. There were atrocities all over County Down, though historians say that the popular idea of their scale was exaggerated. Help arrived in Belfast before it or Carrickfergus were taken. The Scots soldiers brought their own problems: their eagerness to disarm all the Papists in Ulster tended to exacerbate the situation. They were an 'unruly Scottish mobb, and common soldiers, who would make the pretence of searching for arms and ammunition an opportunity to quarrel and plunder'.

1641 is one of the most important dates haunting the psyche of Ulster Protestantism. The legend of the massacres inflicted by the Catholics on the Protestants (as the two sides were now coming to be seen) is used as a reminder of how precarious the planters' foothold has been, and how vigilant and unyielding they must be. Clearly the exact scale of the atrocities is a matter of controversy, and it may be prudent to opt for a conservative estimate. But Henry L. Snyder may be taking the wish to avoid sensationalism a bit far: 'Estimates of those killed vary: the number is generally reckoned to have been less than 25,000, but the effect was that of the large-scale massacre which was rumoured to have taken place'. Certainly the fear was real enough.

The long, confused struggle of the English Civil War and its aftermath haemorrhaged into Ulster. The element of religious difference became more and more important. James I had boosted emigration to Ireland when he introduced the episcopacy in Scotland. In August 1636 Presbyterian ministers had been summoned to church in Belfast for questioning about their loyalty to the Church of England. Five were deposed, and they set sail in September 1636 on the *Eagle's Wing* for America, though storms meant they had to turn back. The zealous Scots were more successful colonists than the English, and it seems they were more determined too. Episcopalians had fled in fright at the rebellion with their ministers and bishops, and left an inviting vacuum. As *A True Narrative of the Rise and Progress of the Presbyterian Church* puts it, 'the Lord began more openly to erect a new tabernacle for himself in Ireland, and especially in the northern parts of it, and spread more the curtains of his habitation'.

A Scots army under General Robert Munro arrived in Belfast in April 1642 to protect it from the rebels. But when the Civil War broke out Colonel Chichester and Monro found themselves on opposite sides. At first Monro stayed in Carrickfergus while Chichester, loyal to the King, held Belfast. Bardon says that it was only fear of the rebels that prevented open conflict breaking out. Then Chichester tried to stop the Scots administering the Covenant, and Monro seized Belfast. Though sent packing from Belfast, Chichester had his reward for issuing his proclamation against the Covenant when he was made first Earl of Donegall.

The Viceroy arranged a ceasefire but the Scots, newly pledged to drive out 'Popery, Prelacy and Heresy', were not interested in peace, and engaged Owen Roe O'Neill in battle at Benburb on 5 June 1646. Monro was ignominiously defeated and had to flee without his wig and coat. He was lucky to escape back to Belfast, having burnt what strongholds he could. He lost all his guns and half of his men, one of whom was the third Viscount Montgomery, who had succeeded his father at the age of about twenty in 1642. The youngest colonel in Monro's army, he was imprisoned at Cloghwooter Castle, on a lough in County Cavan, for two years.

James Seaton Reid's *A History of the Presbyterian Church* explains what happened after the battle:

> This caused a general consternation; great numbers fled into Scotland; and the counties of Down and Antrim would have been lost, in a great measure, if either by accident or by an adventurous policy, all Monroe's ammunition had not been blown up when the battle was lost; and if the nuncio, who received the news of the victory on June 13th at Limerick, had not despatched an express to O'Neill to congratulate his victory, and to desire him to march with his forces to support him in his opposition to the peace. The messengers overtook O'Neill at Tandragee as he was ready to fall into the Scots quarters . . .

Following Parliament's defeat of the Royalists and the fighting between the Scots and Parliament, Colonel Monk, the commander of a strong Parliamentary army, took Belfast in October 1648. But when he returned to England Belfast was reoccupied by Royalist and Scots forces. Amidst all this the feud between the Montgomerys and the Hamiltons was made up. Their mutual antipathy to Monk encouraged the Montgomerys and the Hamiltons to bury their differences: the third Viscount Montgomery and the first Earl of Clanbrassill, James Hamilton, became comrades.

The distinctive flavour of Belfast theological debate begins to be detectable amongst the Scots Presbyterians who came over with Monro. During the Royalist occupation of the town in 1649, they denounced Parliament's edict for religious toleration. They said that this scheme of the Sectaries in Parliament was 'an innovation overturning of unity in religion, and so directly repugnant to the word of God'. John Milton wrote a long and disgusted reply to the Belfast Presbytery, the members of which he called 'blockish presbyters of Clandeboye'. He was no less contemptuous of Belfast, which he had never seen, but which he did not like: 'a barbarous nook . . . whose obscurity till now never came to our hearing'.

Cromwell, after his massacre at Drogheda, sent Colonel Robert Venables into Ulster. He besieged Belfast for four days in the autumn of 1649 and it surrendered to the Commonwealth. Bardon points out that this was Belfast's only siege. The hasty nature of the earthwork that was thrown up to defend it is a reminder that Belfast, despite its sanguinary early entries into history and its strategic position, was not essentially a military town but a trading and manufacturing one.

For many people, Cromwell's treatment of Ireland has left the bitterest memories of all. 1641 and Drogheda: there is a tendency to cherish our particular atrocities as multi-purpose justifications for current behaviour. Snyder estimates that 30,000 Irish soldiers left the country after the final treaty. Following the Act of Settlement of 1652, only a fifth of the land was owned by Catholics; previously, three fifths had been Catholic-owned. Protestant Belfast largely escaped, as it had escaped in 1641. Those who suffered under Cromwell tended to be the poor (as always), the Gaelic landowners and the Old English, those descendants of the Normans who had often adopted Catholicism and Irish ways. The Presbyterian Scots who increasingly populated the town of Belfast were left alone, no doubt because, as fellow Protestants, they made up Protestant numbers in case of another 'native Irish' or 'Catholic' uprising. The Montgomerys got off lightly: 'Yet I confess the English are civil enemies.' Montgomery, the Royalist general, was exiled to Holland, though he was later allowed to stay at Melifont, outside Drogheda, and in Dublin:

> This unactive manner of living at Millifont and Howth, and the temptation of a bottle of wine (which in the city was often offered and accepted from the loyalists to remove heaviness of heart, to forget poverty and to remember misery no more) made his Lordship corpulent and unhealthy.

When Oliver's son Henry Cromwell was made Lord Deputy, he tried to reconcile the Protestant churches and had some success in Dublin and Leinster, but not in Ulster: 'These parties could not be twisted together more than a rope can be made of sand.' The Montgomerys thought there might be a change in their fortunes:

> *his Lordship now, hoped for more favour than from the Rump Republicans, Anabaptists, Independents, or such like locusts, which the bottomless basis of anarchy had vomited upon us.*

In the confusion before the Restoration, Montgomery was arrested in Dublin at the instigation of the Anabaptists, who were powerful in the Dublin Council. But his friends seized Dublin Castle and overthrew the Anabaptists. The Montgomerys retook one of their houses, Rosemount, in February 1659.

Richard Cromwell – nicknamed Tumbledown Dick or Queen Dick (for his 'womanish condescending') – was still, temporarily, Lord Protector following his father Oliver's death on 3 September 1658. The Montgomerys invited Charles II to take the crown first in Ireland but he waited until 1660, when an invitation came from England, and General Monk, to restore the monarchy. The Montgomerys were restored to their various titles and offices, and the Lords in the Dublin Parliament – 'Oliver's myrmidons' were still powerful in the Commons – passed a law intended to readjust the titles to land and the debts owing from the years of war.

The third Viscount Montgomery was made first Earl Mount-Alexander, the name taken from his residence near Comber. He died in 1663, 'the most regarded Scottish man in Ireland'. He had a red face and curly red hair, 'which denoted vigour of brain'. He was tolerant:

> *His Lordship had no hatred or love solely for country sake; English, Scotts and Irish were welcome to him, yet he liked and esteemed the English most (both his Ladys being such) and bore the greatest friendship to the most loyal.*

On the other hand, he 'was intirely addicted to worship God by the Common Prayer Book (in publick or in his family) when he could have it, and therefore was hated by the Scotts of all sorts'. Nor did he have much luck with his staff: his servants did 'clandestine and outward mischiefs' to him.

Most remarkably, he was a walking medical curiosity. William Harvey met him at the Court of Charles I, and made careful notes of what he found. Harvey was told that, when a child, Montgomery had fallen and fractured his left side, which led to an abscess:

> *Between the 18th and 19th years of his age, this young nobleman, having travelled through France and Italy, came to London, having at this time a very large open cavity in his side, through which the lungs, as it was believed, could both be seen and touched.*

Harvey met him and at first, like doubting Thomas, could not believe the story because he looked healthy:

> he immediately showed me everything, and laid open his left side for my inspection, by removing a plate which he wore there by way of defence against accidental blows and other injuries. I found a large open space in the chest, into which I could readily introduce three of my fingers and my thumb . . .

Harvey, having quelled his amazement and ascertained that Montgomery was genuine, and safe, brought him to the King. The two of them examined the young man again, and decided that what was thought to be the lungs was in fact the heart, and that it had no sensation when Harvey touched it with his finger. The King remarked, 'Sir, I wish I could perceive the thoughts of some of my nobilities hearts as I have seen your heart.'

The Montgomerys' troubles did not cease with Charles II's restoration. The first Montgomery of Ards chose the motto *honneur sans repose*, which 'hath been a prophesy, or rather a caveat for us in all future adventures'. The remnants of the Mount-Alexander estates were sold to the members of another band of settlers, the Huguenot families of De la Cherois and Crommelin, in 1764. The stone chair in which the chiefs of Clandeboye had been inaugurated at Castlereagh is now in the Ulster Museum; some stones from the castle were used in a wall, but no other trace of it remains.

CHAPTER FIVE

KING BILLY

Belfast's favourite historical event, celebrated annually in one of the world's biggest street festivals and depicted on the gable walls of the city in its own peculiar art form, did not take place in Belfast. It is Belfast's favourite event because it marks the triumph of one group in Ireland over another, so it could well be Belfast's most hated event too. The triumph was over Catholicism and yet, as every barstool wit will tell you, the Protestant side had the blessing of the Pope. Nor was the battle of the Boyne a decisive, glorious deliverance of the Protestants who were rapidly transforming the north: arguably the real struggle for the ownership of Ireland only got under way after that battle was fought. There is also doubt in some quarters about King Billy's white horse.

On his restoration in 1660, King Charles II promised that he would give back all the land which had been taken from the Irish and Old English under the Cromwellian settlement. He also promised, however, that the new colonists would be allowed to keep what they had acquired. The Lord Deputy, the Duke of Ormond, remarked that a bigger Ireland was needed. Some of the King's favourites were rewarded, but the process of colonization was not reversed, and in Ulster particularly the new arrivals were very strong. Towards the end of Charles's reign Ireland prospered and drew in many more: Peter Berresford Ellis claims that in 1672 alone 80,000 Presbyterian Scots arrived, but others find this figure far too high.

All over Europe Catholicism was contending with Protestantism – or at least religious differences were entangled with national and political ones – and James II's accession in February 1685 seemed to mean that England would take the side of the Catholic powers. Louis XIV, the Sun King, had made France the superpower of Europe, and Charles II, in some respects a sincere admirer (his idea for the Royal Hospital in Chelsea was in imitation of Louis's *Invalides*), had secretly contracted the Treaty of Dover with him. This reversed England's previous posture and joined France in opposition to Holland.

In 1686 Louis revoked the Edict of Nantes, and 100,000 French Protestants – Huguenots – fled to Holland, Switzerland, the Palatinate and England. A significant number settled in the Lagan Valley. Everything Louis did, from his daily habits to his choice of architects, was designed to enhance his own power, and there were pragmatic political reasons for his persecution of Protestants and his wars against Protestant states, but Pope Innocent XI thought his treatment of the Huguenots was foolish, and when Louis sent an army against Rome he made an enemy of the Pope.

It became increasingly clear that James's sympathies lay with Catholicism, and when he replaced Clarendon with Richard Talbot, Duke of Tyrconnell, as Viceroy in January 1687, the Protestant settlers, who had been twitchy since the excesses of 1641, felt more and more insecure. On his appointment Clarendon had announced that James would not change the land settlement. Tyrconnell's appointment helped keep alive Catholic hopes that James would overturn it.

In the summer of 1688 a London court refused to convict seven Anglican bishops of seditious libel for their criticism of the King. A group of noblemen (the modern equivalent, perhaps, of the 'men in suits' who, according to the political columnists, have a quiet word with the leaders of the Conservative and Unionist Party when it is time for them to go) invited the Prince of Orange to depose James.

William had proved himself an able, warlike prince. Since 1672 he had been winning back Dutch provinces from Louis. He was married to James II's eldest daughter, Mary, who had confidently expected to become Queen of England on her father's death. But late in life James's wife had unexpectedly given birth to a son. The prospect of a Catholic succession might have spurred the men in suits, perhaps it spurred on William. He landed at Torbay on 5 November 1688. Louis might have saved James by attacking the Dutch provinces and forcing William to turn back, but he sent his armies to Germany instead. James's second daughter, Anne, joined William at Nottingham. James was captured but escaped at the second attempt to France in December. In February the Glorious Revolution was announced when, at William's insistence, he was made joint monarch with Mary rather than merely regent. The Declaration of Rights limited the sovereign's power and established the supremacy of Parliament. The revolution was a bloodless coup in England, but it was less glorious in Ireland.

Prior to James's flight, Tyrconnell had begun changing the administration of Belfast. A newly enlarged council of burgesses had been set up that removed control of the town's administration from the Chichesters. Because there were no Catholics in Belfast who met the property qualifications, Tyrconnell's men had to be imported. Of the thirty-five burgesses, nineteen were now Catholic, and the rest were Anglican or Presbyterian. A few months previously the corporation had refused a request by the Bishop of Clogher, Tyrconnell's secretary, to provide a place of worship in the town for the Catholic officers who had been newly appointed to the army garrisoned there.

The Presbyterians were particularly pleased at William's elevation and sent a minister to warn him of the dangers to Protestants in Ulster. Soon after, on 3 December 1688, warnings to the Protestant settlers were conveyed by curious means. Anonymous letters addressed to prominent people were dropped in the streets of towns around Belfast. In Comber, Lord Mount-Alexander was warned that a massacre of Protestants was planned to begin the next Sunday. A warning reached Derry in time for thirteen apprentices to close the gates of the city against the Earl of Antrim's Redshanks.

The second Earl of Mount-Alexander, caught between Protestantism and loyalism (like the Anglicans in Derry), had 'retired to County Down' when it had become clear that James II was going to act against the Protestants. But now he and a group of local noblemen tried to organize a defence: he was elected General Commander of 'yᵉ Protestants of Ulster' to prevent a repetition of the massacres of 1641. William sent a message to Mount-Alexander to assure the 'Protestant nobility and gentry in the North of Ireland'

> *how sensibly we are affected with the hazards you are exposed to by the illegal power the papists have, of late, usurped in this kingdom, and that we are resolved to employ the most speedy and effectual means in our power for rescuing you from the oppression and terrors you lie under . . . And because we are persuaded, that there are, even of the Romish communion, many who are desirous to live peaceably, and do not approve of the violent and arbitrary proceedings of some who pretend to be in authority; and we, thinking it just to make distinctions of persons, according to their behaviour and deserts, do hereby authorize you to promise in our name, to all such as shall demean themselves hereafter peaceably and inoffensively, our protection and excemption from those pains and forfeitures, which those only shall incur who are the maintainers and assertors of the said illegal authority, assumed and continued contrary to law; or who shall act anything contrary to the Protestant interest, or the disturbance of the public peace in the kingdom.*

He wanted to avoid a sectarian bloodbath.

The Anglicans and Presbyterians, threatened alike, acted in concert. Attempts to take Belfast and Carrickfergus were vain, though only a 'mobb' of unruly and unarmed soldiers had been left in the latter while the crack troops marched south. Mount-Alexander was defeated at the 'Break of Dromore', and the Jacobite forces marched through Antrim, Hillsborough and Lisburn, capturing abandoned cash and cannon. The Protestant settlers were thoroughly frightened. The Jacobite forces had withdrawn from Belfast, and the locals proclaimed for William and Mary, but only two days later General Hamilton and his victorious Jacobite army reoccupied the town. 'The best part of yᵉ British escaped to Scotland, England, or the Isle of Man': with them went the Earl of Mount-Alexander, who stayed in England until 1691, when much of the excitement was over. He had to wait another seven years for preferment from William and Mary. The Sovereign, or mayor of Belfast, Thomas Pottinger, tried to ensure that looting in the deserted town was kept to a minimum. James promised a pardon to those who had been resident in Belfast for more than a year and who returned within forty days, but few accepted.

In March 1689 James landed at Kinsale and on Palm Sunday, twelve days later, he entered Dublin. He convened a parliament, at which his behaviour began to suggest that he was not the champion the Irish were looking for. They voted for 'liberty of conscience', a removal of restrictions on Catholics. James, however, would not agree to the separation of Ireland from England in a separate monarchy. He could only be induced to allow that the English Parliament should not have the power to legislate for Ireland, and went so far only because he feared that refusal would make it difficult to retain the support he needed. Most reluctantly, he had to allow the assembly to invalidate the Acts of Settlement. James was fighting for the Stuart succession, not the rights of Irish Catholics.

He and his Irish supporters did not like each other. After his defeat, James was dismissive of Irish abilities at soldiering and leadership, and he even went so far as to advocate, like the most arrogant of Protestant invaders, that Irish children should be educated in English ways so that they might be 'weaned away from their natural hatred toward the English'. Education should 'by degrees wear out the Irish language, which would be for the advantage of the inhabitants'. Friction arose between the Irish and the French soldiers in the army, and the French harassed Protestants in Dublin, with the result that James lost any lingering loyalty he might have hoped for from them. In the summer of 1689 Protestants were imprisoned in Dublin.

There was some delay in gathering a Williamite army, but at last the Duke of Schomberg arrived in Belfast Lough in August 1689, two weeks after the siege of Derry was finally raised. According to which account we are reading, he landed at Groomsport, Bangor or Ballyholme Bay. When the Jacobites saw his ships they fled. The local settlers were 'so comforted that the shore was soon covered with horses, cows and sheep for the benefit of the army; a quarter of mutton sold for 6d'. There was general rejoicing: 'The shore was all crowded with Protestants, – men, women, and children, – old and young falling on their knees with tears in their eyes thanking God and the English for their deliverance.'

The Jacobites had two regiments at Carrickfergus under Cormac O'Neill and MacCarthy Mor, and a force of horse and dragoons in the Belfast area, but they offered no resistance despite Schomberg's fears: 'If they have one dram of courage or wit they will attack us this night since they will never expect the like opportunity.' Fearing that Belfast was to be burned, Schomberg took the town, and went on to besiege Carrickfergus. It was fiercely defended for a few days, and when it surrendered Schomberg had to try to restrain the colonists from committing outrages upon the Catholic defenders.

By September 20,000 troops had landed. Their tents stretched from Mill Street in lines up Malone and the Falls. The army included experienced and well-trained Dutch troops, Danes, Huguenots and locally raised regiments, including a group from Enniskillen, who arrived with a large number of cattle. The Williamite army had smart uniforms, so the ragged irregulars from Fermanagh looked all the more outlandish. They were fierce fighters who would 'give little quarter to the Irish': at one point they told William that they were no good at taking orders and preferred to fight in their own way. William was to lead them in a charge at the Boyne. They were nicknamed 'the Duke of Schomberg's Tartars'.

Schomberg secured Ulster and restored Belfast to the Protestant burgesses and justices. Protestants returned, while many Catholics fled from the province. Schomberg marched south in September but the two armies did not engage. He encamped near Dundalk. James's army was poorly equipped and his French advisers were telling him to avoid a confrontation. The seventy-five-year-old Schomberg was increasingly criticized for excessive caution. But some of his Huguenots were deserting, while an epidemic had broken out in his army. In the Great Hospital of Belfast, formed to receive the sick, almost four thousand men died between November and May. The sickness spread to the town itself:

> it was impossible to come into any house but some were sick or dead, especially at Belfast where the hospital was. I have sometime stood upon the street there and seen ten or a dozen corps (of the townspeople) go by in little more than half an hour.

The Grand Alliance was battling to turn the tide of the fortunes of Catholic France on the continent, but William's blow was to be struck in Ireland. In June 1690 William sailed into Belfast Lough determined, it is suggested, to ginger up Schomberg's somnolent campaign. He came with six men-of-war commanded by the celebrated Sir Cloudesley Shovell, and a great number of other vessels. A contemporary was delighted and relieved:

> The Lough between this and Carrickfergus seems like a wood, there being no less than seven hundred sail of ships in it, mostly laden with provisions and ammunition, so that now we fear no more Dundalk wants, the plenty and order of all things here is most wonderful, and scarcely credible to those who witness it.

William landed at Carrickfergus with men, horses, artillery and a galaxy of glittering commanders from Europe's noble houses. Schomberg met him at Whitehouse: the chair William sat in was preserved for posterity. When he rode in Schomberg's carriage into Belfast there was, we are told by Cathal O'Byrne but not by others, an earthquake. He was greeted at the North Gate by the Corporation and by George Walker, who had been Governor of Derry during the siege. The people

> at first could do nothing but stare, never having seen a king before in that part of the world, but after a while some of them began to huzzah; the rest all took it up

*and followed the coach towards His Majesty's lodgings, and happy were they that
could get a sight of him.*

He was already a hero in Belfast, but in some ways he was unprepossessing. He
suffered severely from asthma and, at the age of thirty-nine, he had a racked,
pale, lined face. He was physically weak and followed an abstemious regime,
avoiding excesses of food and drink. He had a poor command of English (one
wonders whether, in private, Mary spoke to him in Dutch) and as a result gave
the impression of being cold and blunt. Nevertheless, he was obliged to give a
speech to the citizenry, which he did. It was quite bland, except that he called
for a fast to be observed. He slept in the Castle:

> *At night the streets were filled with bonfires and fireworks, which were no sooner
> lighted than the alarm signal was given by the discharge of guns, so planted that
> from one place to another throughout the whole country all places had notice of
> the King's arrival, and in three hours made bonfires so thick that the whole country
> seemed in a flame.*

On 15 June William attended a service at the Church of Ireland church in High
Street, where Dr Royse, his Chaplain, preached on Hebrews 11, 33: 'Who
through faith subdued kingdoms . . .'. Afterwards his officers bought dinner for
four shillings at Rourke's. As during World War Two, Belfast was abuzz with
excitement and prosperity from the large numbers of foreign troops spending
money there. Reinforcements continued to pour in. William had fifty pieces of
artillery, and a thousand horses were needed to pull them. The Long Bridge, ('one
of the stateliest Bridges in the Kingdom', being over half a mile long across the
mud and water) was damaged by the weight of the Williamite cannon. Seven of
its twenty-one arches collapsed a couple of years later. James had only a dozen
cannon: the English had neglected to develop artillery since the Civil War,
according to Ellis.

On 17 June William reviewed a regiment of horse in Belfast Park. He
anticipated the opinion of military leaders like Field Marshall Montgomery that
it was useful for a general to make himself known to his men. William's physician
advised him to leave Belfast, which was 'very unhealthful' in the hot summer
weather, but he did not go for another couple of days.

Legend has it that he was riding out to Lisburn when he was caught in a shower
of rain. He had a bad headache, and asked for shelter at a house. Ellis says the
house was 2 miles outside Lisburn, but claims it was called Malone Grove, which
seems unlikely, since the Malone area ends a long way before Lisburn. Cathal
O'Byrne gives two contradictory stories: one house was at the junction of the
Stranmillis and Malone roads, opposite the gates of Botanic Gardens, which
would seem to have been in the midst of the army tents, and the other, which

seems most likely, is the house he claims was originally called The Rookery. In any event the owner, John Eccles, managed to convince his fellow citizens that the Prince of Orange had stayed there. He changed its name to Orange Grove and preserved the beer mug William drank from and, until it disintegrated, the bed he slept in. Many years later the house was inherited by the distinguished botanist John Templeton, a friend of Thomas Russell and the McCrackens. Later its name was changed again, to Cranmore (meaning 'great tree'), because of sightseers. The grounds are now playing fields owned by the Royal Belfast Academical Institution, and science masters still take pupils there to botanize. The 'great tree' under which William tethered his horse must have gone.

Resuming his journey to Lisburn for a strategic conference with Schomberg, William is supposed to have met at Lambeg a Huguenot, René Bulmer. The Frenchman, delighted to meet the scourge of Le Roi Soleil, asked if he could embrace William. Seeing Bulmer's attractive spouse, William said, 'And thy wife also.'

On 22 June William and his army set off south to fight James. He had 35,000 men, only 13,315 of whom were English or Protestant Irish. That day an advance party was involved in a skirmish at the Moyry Pass, between the Cooley Mountains and Dundalk. This was mythic territory: it was here that Cúchulainn had defended Ulster from the armies of the south. Although a small force could have held up a much larger one here, James feared an outflanking manoeuvre, and abandoned Dundalk. His army fell back to Ardee, the place where Cúchulainn killed Ferdia in single combat.

The battle finally took place on 1 July on the Boyne River, between Drogheda and Slane, as Schomberg predicted. James had ignored his advisers, deciding that he must fight to defend Dublin rather than retreat any further in an attempt to avoid a confrontation. William was injured the day before the battle, and narrowly escaped being killed during it when musket balls hit his hat and the heel of his boot as he was leading the men of Enniskillen. The Duke of Schomberg was killed. Nevertheless it was a comparatively easy victory, thanks to William's generalship. He drew James's main force out of position with a feint attack across the river. Ellis estimates that about a thousand Jacobites and five hundred Williamites were killed.

William tried to prevent the pillage and slaughter that often comes in the wake of war, but the locally raised regiments were 'very dexterous at that sport'. James fled to Dublin complaining bitterly about Irish cowardice, and left Ireland without trying to rally his forces. The Boyne was the last battle fought between two kings. The cause of the Stuarts was defeated, but the Irish resistance to William continued. The French, and Tyrconnell, thought they should sue for peace when William entered Dublin, but the Irish, under Patrick Sarsfield, who was from an Old English Pale family, fought on with Tyrconnell's reluctant agreement. The Orangemen's marching song, 'The Sash My Father Wore', refers to 'Derry,

1. Captain Thomas Lee, 1594, by Marcus Gheeraedts the Younger. (*Tate Gallery*)
A swashbuckling commander under the Earl of Essex in the north of Ireland, Lee had
himself portrayed as half elegant Elizabethan, half barelegged Irish footsoldier, in the lee
of an oak, symbol of reliability. The image argues for his loyalty and promotes his
proposed treaty with the Earl of Tyrone. Lee was executed after Essex's 1601 rebellion.

2. *Above* Giant's Ring. (*B.N. Hartwell, Department of Archaeology, Queen's University*)

3a. *Opposite top* Dolmens in the Giant's Ring. (*Northern Ireland Tourist Board*)

3b. *Opposite below* Carrickfergus Castle. (*Northern Ireland Tourist Board*)

4b. *Below* Plate III from *The Image of Irelande* by John Derricke, 1581, republished in facsimile by Blackstaff Press, 1985.

4a. *Right* Sir Arthur Chichester. (*Ulster Museum*)

A   Now when into their fencedholdes, the knaues are entred in,
    To smite and knocke the cattell downe, the hangmen doe beginne.
    One plucketh off the Oxes cote, which he euen now did weare:
    Another lacking pannes, to boyle the flesh, his hide prepare.
C   These theeues attend vpon the fire, for seruing vp the feast:
B   And fryer smelfeast sneaking in, doth preace amongst the best.

3   who play'th in Romish toyes the Ape, by counterfetting Paull:
    For whichther doe award him then, the highest roome of all.
    who being set, because the cheere, is deemed little worth:
    Except the same be intermixt, and lac'de with Irish myrth.
D   Both Barde, and Harper, is preparde, which by their cunning art,
    Doe strike and cheare vp all the gestes, with comfort at the hart.

5. William III, by an unknown artist, 1690–1700. (*National Portrait Gallery*)

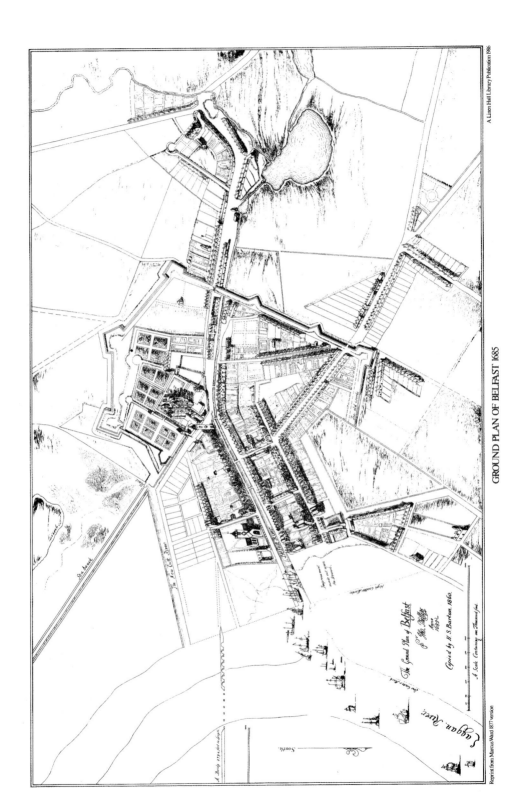

GROUND PLAN OF BELFAST 1685

A Linen Hall Library Publication 1986

Reprint from Marcus Ward 1877 version

The Ground Plan of Belfast
by Tho. Phillips
Anno 1685.

Copied by H. S. Buchan. 1860.

A Scale Containing one Thousand feet.

Laggan River.

6. *Left* Ground Plan of Belfast 1685 (with south at the top). (*Linen Hall Library*)

7a. *Above* High Street in 1786, from a copy of a contemporary engraving. (*Ulster Museum*)

7b. *Right William Drennan* by Robert Home. (*Ulster Museum*)

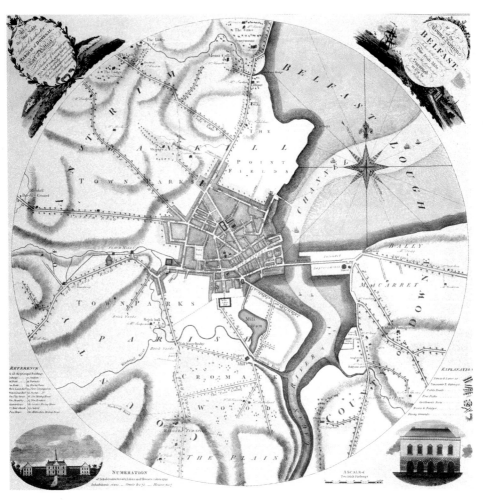

8. A Map of the Town and Environs of Belfast Surveyed in 1791 by James Williamson. (*Linen Hall Library*)

Aughrim, Enniskillen and the Boyne', and the decisive victory – and Ireland's bloodiest fight – was at Aughrim. A tough campaign followed the Boyne, and William, having been defeated at Limerick, handed over to Baron Ginkel, who won at Aughrim on 12 July 1691 only after the death of the French commander, St Ruth, threw the Jacobites into confusion when they were ahead.

Twelve thousand Irish soldiers went into exile after the Williamite campaign. As the 'Wild Geese', they assisted in the European wars of the eighteenth century, and their descendants supplied a French President, a Spanish Prime Minister, and an Austro-Hungarian Imperial Chancellor. The Treaty of Limerick vaguely promised 'not less toleration' of Catholics than before the accession of James II, and said Jacobites who laid down their arms would be allowed to keep their property. But these were empty promises, partly as a result of the limitation of powers to which William and Mary had agreed in the Declaration of Rights. The Parliaments of England, Scotland and Ireland all asserted their new independence, and the Irish Parliament refused to ratify the Treaty of Limerick.

Ellis says that a million and a half more acres were made available for colonization. Liam de Paor estimates that by 1703 Catholics held about fourteen per cent of the land. Both Catholics and Dissenters were persecuted. A quarter of a million Ulster Protestants emigrated to America as a result of early eighteenth-century Acts of Parliament which tried to punish those outside the Established Church. De Paor makes the interesting point that these laws were not an attempt to convert Catholics, for to do so would be to blur the distinction between the ruling class and others, but rather to make it impossible for non-Anglicans to hold offices of power, and to destroy the Catholic elite. By a series of laws which split up estates belonging to Catholics, and hampered Catholic education and entry into the professions, an entire class of landowners and rulers was destroyed by conversion, emigration or pauperization.

Ellis concentrates on the reactions of Presbyterians to their persecution. He quotes the Anglican Bishop of Armagh, Hugh Boulter:

> The worst of this is that it stands to unite Protestant and Papist and whenever that happens, goodbye to the English interest in Ireland forever.

Ellis argues that the failure to provide true 'religious liberty' after the Boyne led to the republicanism of 1798 and the United Irishmen. For him it was the defeat of the Presbyterian and Catholic republicans of 1798, rather than the Williamite campaign, which led to 'modern-day Irish sectarianism'.

This may be a simplification. The hysteria that surrounds King Billy and the Boyne is not new: it arose at the time from sectarian causes. *Kings In Conflict* makes obvious the widespread use of hysterical propaganda on both sides in Ireland and across northern Europe. Protestants – Anglicans and Dissenters – fully expected to be slaughtered by Catholics before Schomberg and William arrived, as they thought, to save them. They were so sincere that many dashed over to Stranraer for safety, leaving their homes and businesses behind. The Presbyterians expected to be treated like Protestants, not Catholics, after William's victory: they had, after all, dispossessed the Catholics, and were acutely aware of their vulnerability to those who wanted their land back. They have never ceased to be acutely aware. It is arguable that the exclusion of Presbyterians from office and the measures against Presbyterian marriages and services in the eighteenth century drove them apart (though most obviously in Belfast, and not decisively) from the other Protestants with whom they shared the town and certain political interests. Bardon points out that religious disability was 'a very minor factor' in encouraging the emigration of Presbyterians, while Beckett argues their attachment to the Penal Laws and their own internal disputes stopped them campaigning effectively against the restrictions they suffered.

In Belfast, despite background neuroses about genocide from Catholic aggression, Presbyterians were in a relatively strong position. Profiles of social class by denomination in present-day Northern Ireland show that the Presbyterians remain the most prosperous: the Church of Ireland still reflects its history of embracing the small ruling class and the large working class. It was Presbyterians who largely created Belfast and its prosperity and, since the town was so much, and uniquely, the synthetic product of incomers, they had little inclination to feel guilty towards Catholics in general. George Macartney, the town Sovereign, remarked in 1707 that 'we have not amongst us within the town above seven Papists'. Later in the century the Presbyterians in Belfast assisted in a near-revolution.

CHAPTER SIX

WILLIAM DRENNAN

George Benn's great work first appeared in 1823 with the full title *A History of the Town of Belfast from the Earliest Times to the Close of the Eighteenth Century*. Fifty years later Marcus Ward & Co issued the second volume, *A History of the Town of Belfast from 1799 till 1810*.

The opening and closing remarks of Volume One suggest that the author would not have seen much imbalance in treating the city's first millennium in 770 pages while devoting 238 pages to its next decade. 'Belfast, as a town, has no ancient history,' he begins. In the last paragraph of the 1887 edition he says,

All here is of modern origin and modern fashion; we have spacious streets, stately buildings, huge mills, and edifices of every kind and for every purpose. The life of the eighteenth century, so recent, so quaint in our eyes when a glimpse of it can be recovered, has been pushed into the well of forgetfulness. There was a Maypole in the last century at the Stone Bridge in High Street, around which the youthful population of the small town disported in rustic fashion. This, with many another custom as well, has gone the way of all gay garlands.

As he implies in the concluding few pages, the three-inch-thick doorstopper of a tome he laboured for a lifetime to produce was in a sense merely a preliminary account of an unusual town whose glorious history was outpacing its first major historian. Sometimes Benn refers cosily to 'our town'.

The climax of Volume One is his account of the United Irishmen and the revolt of 1798. In this Benn shows a feeling shared by historians, revolutionaries and romantics ever since. For some – for many – Belfast's astonishing response to the French Revolution is one of very few palatable events in the city's political past.

The exclusively Protestant Volunteers, 'the armed property of the nation', had been originally formed to repel an expected French attack. The first regular company was formed in Belfast in 1778. From the start it was patriotic, but when the military challenge did not come it agitated for political concessions. At a Convention in Dungannon in February 1782, the Volunteers called for the Irish Parliament to have the sole right to legislate for Ireland. A new and weak Whig Government conceded what in theory almost amounted to independence, though in practice what became known as Grattan's Parliament was less free. The United Irish movement was formed in the wake of the French Revolution to build on this success and to create a fully democratic system of government. It was founded by Protestants, but it gained much strength from its support of Catholic claims to political rights: as the eighteenth century had progressed the Penal Laws were less rigidly enforced, but Catholics were barred from political power. Presbyterians were also discriminated against. Benn says,

> The romance of the United Irishmen is yet unwritten. Something has been done quite recently, but chiefly in Dublin and other parts of Ireland, but not in the North, where the people were more stern and prosaic; still revelations of a romantic kind here are possibly for ever buried in oblivion.

But he need not have worried. The heroes of those times lose none of their glamour over the years.

The late Stewart Parker devoted his penultimate stage play, *Northern Star*, to the United Irish movement, and felt it salutary to dispel the aura of sanctity around the figure of Henry Joy McCracken, who led the rebels at Antrim. Almost every politician who opposes Unionism finds it expedient to invoke the shades of the United Irishmen. In recent years John Robb's New Ireland Movement cited the 1790s in Belfast as proof that Protestants and Dissenters really can join in political endeavour with Catholics. Poets, historians and pamphleteers can find much ammunition in those events – apart from anything else, the protagonists were authors of vivid prose. In doing so, they seem able to promote a variety of political positions, or indeed to pursue personal concerns.

One historian sees it as his task to rescue one of the main conspirators from the guardians of his memory. In *Thomas Russell and Belfast* Brendan Clifford says 'a biography of Russell cannot be written from the political standpoint now occupied by the Linen Hall Library'. No doubt libraries, like other bodies, can have political standpoints, but the statement is full of ironies, for Russell was the second Librarian of the Linen Hall until his execution for high treason, and his portrait hangs in a place of honour in the Library's Irish section, overlooking the tables upon which many works on the United Irishmen have been researched and written. The sentiment is not apparently shared by Seamus Heaney in his and Michael Longley's pamphlet *An Upstairs Outlook*: 'The Linen Hall is one of those living proofs that the golden age of the city was not lived in vain; the moral and imaginative quickening that took place in the late eighteenth century always revives for me when I go up those stairs.' But Clifford is also engaged in a battle between north Cork (his and Russell's home) and Cork city (in the shape of professors of politics and English at Queen's University, Belfast) 'across the wilderness of the Protestant middle class'. History can be used in many different ways.

More interesting to the rest of us are his assertions in *Belfast in the French Revolution* that 'The French Revolution was a major event in the life of Belfast. One might almost say it was *the* major event in the life of Belfast', and 'Belfast *participated* in the French Revolution.' If the episode of the United Irishmen was crucial to the city, it continues to cast giant shadows on crucial events of the present. For among the most ardent and assiduous worshippers at the flame of the United Irishmen have been the IRA. But the IRA is not the only group that claims legitimacy for its claim to be the sole heir of republicanism. The factions who assemble annually at the grave in Bodenstown of Theobald Wolfe Tone, whether their adherence to constitutional politics is ambiguous or not, are celebrating the 'physical-force' tradition. One suspects that a certain amount of horse-trading between the various self-styled heirs and the Gardai, the police force in the south, must go on to avoid embarrassing clashes between the rival marches.

When they arrive at the graveside there are further snags to be dealt with. For Wolfe Tone committed suicide in prison while awaiting execution. This might be seen as a heroic act of republican courage, thwarting the English in their hour of triumph, but for the amateur of Catholic doctrinal niceties it provides amusement. Suicide is a mortal sin in the Roman Catholic Church, so how could this saint of Irish republicanism be roasting in the fires of Hell? He did not die immediately by his own hand – perhaps he died of natural causes after all. Maybe he was finished off by a warder. Does Tone's Protestant background make all this irrelevant? In any case, he himself was more interested in 'the common name of Irishman' than religious divisions.

Benn, and R.R. Madden's *The United Irishmen, Their Lives and Times* call Tone the 'founder' of the United Irishmen. But he was not, as A.T.Q. Stewart has shown. It is strange, and perhaps revealing, that the error was promulgated, for Tone himself records that he was unexpectedly invited to a meeting of what was to become the Society of United Irishmen in Belfast on 14 October 1791. His pamphlet of the month before, *An Argument on Behalf of the Catholics of Ireland*, had so impressed the First Belfast Company of Volunteers, the 'green', more radical company, that they invited him to dine with their 'secret committee' and become an honorary member of the corps.

Tone and Russell subsequently acted as go-betweens, linking Belfast with Dublin radicals such as Napper Tandy (who helped to found the Dublin branch of the United Irishmen that November) and the Catholic Committee. Tone, Russell and Henry Joy McCracken are the beefcake of the rebellion. Russell was an impressive figure, if Henry Joy McCracken's sister, Mary Ann, is to be believed:

> *A model of manly beauty, he was one of those favoured individuals whom one cannot pass in the street without being guilty of the rudeness of staring in the face while passing, and turning round to look at the receding figure. Though more than six feet high, his majestic stature was scarcely observed owing to the exquisite*

symmetry of his form. Martial in his gait and demeanour, his appearance was not altogether that of a soldier. His dark and steady eye, compressed lip, and somewhat haughty bearing, were occasionally strongly indicative of the camp; but in general, the classic contour of his finely formed head, the expression of almost infantine sweetness which characterized his smile, and the benevolence that beamed in his fine countenance, seemed to mark him out as one, who was destined to be the ornament, grace and blessing of private life. His voice was deep-toned and melodious . . .

And so on. Russell had had a classical education and had spent five years soldiering in India. He was a gentleman, a scholar and a man of action. Although he clearly caused female hearts to beat a little faster, he does not seem to have prefigured Lord Byron in any less reputable way.

Wolfe Tone, however, was something of a ladies' man. His journal, supposedly written for his sons, is quite open about his conquests before and after marriage. The official icon of Tone, taken from a portrait by his daughter-in-law, Catherine Sampson Tone, is odd though striking. He seems to have a stiff back, thrust-back shoulders, a huge pointed nose and a thin, weak mouth. It is like the head on a coin or medal, not a character study. He is painted in his military uniform, with lots of braid (he was an officer in the French service for the purpose of the invasion of Ireland), and he certainly appears to posterity as a colourful, passionate figure. His frank and enjoyable journal records his visits to Belfast in ebullient and often frolicsome terms. Arch like a schoolboy, he gives places and people secret names: Belfast becomes 'the City of Blefescu', Tone calls himself 'Mr Hutton', Russell is 'P.P.', meaning 'Parish Priest'; Thomas McCabe is 'the Irish Slave', after a sign he hung outside his silversmith's shop, which was probably in North Street.

Accounts of social events in Belfast at this time, especially the Volunteers' celebratory or commemorative dinners, frequently mention the liver-threatening number of toasts drunk. Clearly the enjoyment of strong liquor amongst saloon-bar politicians, Presbyterian and otherwise, was as hearty then as now. Tone was no exception: 'The Belfast men get warm with wine and patriotism – all stout – Gog valiant – also the Irish slave; also the Tanner, also Mr. Hutton.' Or again: 'Huzza, huzza! – generally drunk – Broke my glass thumping the table.' Benn reassuringly adds: 'Their patriotism did not restrain their libations; it was the custom of the time in assemblages of more staid character in Blefescu than those in which Mr. Tone led the riot.'

Wolfe Tone must have been fun. He might have been one of the 'great Gaels' G.K. Chesterton had in mind when he noted that 'all their wars are merry'. Such sentiments seem unfortunate now, when the barbarities of the contemporary IRA are perpetrated in Tone's name, whether or not he would recognize them as his heirs. He was in the end an incompetent revolutionary, whose scheme to invade Ireland with French help terrified a large number of his potential allies in Belfast.

Russell's story, though immortalized, if that is the word, in Florence M. Wilson's poem 'The Man From God-Knows-Where', was similarly ignominous. He was in jail at the time of the 1798 rising, but he was determined to make his mark, and finally got himself executed for his part in the futile fiasco of Robert Emmet's rising in 1803.

A.T.Q. Stewart argues that the responsibility for the founding of the United Irishmen does not belong with these Byronic figures but to someone quite different. The man who first proposed the arguably disastrous tactic of secrecy (which led to the 'secret committee' which invited Wolfe Tone) was by comparison something of a moderate, a Belfast-born doctor (Tone was a lawyer by profession, and a Dubliner) who managed to outlive the United Irishmen and died in 1820 at the age of sixty-six. The evolution of Dr William Drennan's ideas provides a clue to one of the mysteries surrounding the events of the 1790s, that is, how it was that the most radical, Jacobin town outside France itself came in the space of three or four years to accept docilely the 1801 Act of Union and to embrace the most abject loyalty to Crown and Empire. The passage quoted from Benn in which he wonders at the remoteness of the late eighteenth century from the perspective of the Victorian age implies that there were transformations in the Belfast mentality as thoroughgoing as the transformations in the Belfast streets and industry. Nevertheless, as Brendan Clifford points out, this change from 'nationalism' to 'unionism' is more apparent than real.

Luckily Drennan and his sister Martha (or 'Matty'), who married Samuel McTier, were prolific letter writers, and their correspondence has been drawn on by numerous historians. If they were around today, British Telecom would be richer, but history would be poorer. *The Drennan Letters 1776–1819* is D.A. Chart's selection and arrangement of over 1,400 letters mostly between Drennan, Matty and Sam. For a period of some years while Drennan was practising in Dublin, there is an almost day-to-day account of political life at all levels, both in the capital and in Belfast. Apart from the high quality of their energetic prose, and the intrinsic importance of the subjects described, the letters are of interest because the correspondents were personally involved in the great events of the time. Unlike Tone, Russell and McCracken, Drennan did not travel with United Irishism to its bloody conclusion, so his most intimate confidences on the matter are especially revealing.

William Drennan was born in Belfast on 3 May 1754, the son of Reverend Thomas Drennan, the minister of the First Presbyterian Church of Belfast, and his wife Anne Lennox. This church was rebuilt in 1783 and it still stands in Rosemary Street (formerly Rosemary Lane) amongst the grand Victorian and flashy postmodern buildings of Belfast's commercial centre. It is a small but attractive building designed by Roger Mulholland, who was himself a 'very bad attender' at the meetings of the First Volunteer Company. The classical façade is modest enough: C.E.B. Brett says severely that it was 'ruined by coarse reconstruction in 1833'. But he allows that the interior is still remarkable. It is elliptical in shape. There are box pews on the ground floor and the central group of pews could almost be the skeleton of a Viking or Anglo-Saxon ship burial. Wooden Corinthian columns support an unusually serpentine gallery. John Wesley preached there, and on 8 June 1789 recorded an impressive visit:

> It is the completest place of worship I have ever seen. It is of oval form; as I judge by my eye a hundred feet long, and seventy or eighty broad. It is very lofty, and has two rows of large windows, so that it is as light as our new chapel in London. And the rows of pillars, with every other part, are so finely proportioned, that it is beautiful in the highest degree. . . . Great was our glorying in the Lord, so that I gave notice contrary to my first design of my intending to preach there again in the morning; but soon after the sexton sent me word it must not be, for the crowds had damaged the House, and some of them had broke off and carried away the silver which was on the Bible in the pulpit; So I desired one of our Preachers to preach in our little House, and left Belfast early in the morning.

Today a blue plaque stands in front of the church explaining its history and carefully insisting that the enlightened ecumenical views it promoted in the eighteenth century are still held:

> The members of this congregation believe in the right of individuals to form their own opinions and fashion their own faith free from compulsion or coersion from any ecclesiastical or civil authority. This right was first demonstrated in 1719 when the Rev. Samuel Halliday refused to subscribe to the Westminster Confession of Faith thereby giving rise to the word 'non-subscribing'.
>
> We do not seek to exclude any persons because of their beliefs, nor do we seek to impose ours upon them. We welcome all who are seeking to work out and understand the purpose of life – with freedom of thought and without constraint of uniformity.
>
> Our church exists to witness to the breadth of true faith and to assist individuals in the quest for life.

The Rosemary Street church and Clifton House, the Belfast Charitable Society poorhouse delightfully designed in the Georgian style by the printer and paper manufacturer Robert Joy in the 1770s, remain two of Belfast's best buildings. If we knew nothing else about them, we could guess that the people for whom these buildings represented modern architecture revered proportion, rationality, grace and the ideal. The modern International style of architecture is also based on rationality. There are some examples in Belfast, not all of them contemptible, but that idea has suddenly become less fashionable in Belfast with the reappearance of red brick (this time with blue metal window frames). The reaction may be against a rationality that seems at times arrogantly scientific and inhuman by comparison with that of the Georgians.

We also have the Georgians' writings and the memory of their actions. The Drennan letters confirm that the grace of their buildings was not accidental, but was serious and hard-won: the crowd to which Wesley preached in Rosemary Street sounds as unruly as an audience of teddy boys at a Bill Haley film; the poverty and degradation that the poorhouse was intended to relieve was an urgent problem at the time. Mary McNeill quotes a letter to the *Belfast News-Letter* of 1785 asking:

> *if it is not inconsistent in the inhabitants to be daily giving proof of taste and increasing opulence in opening new streets, in public erections, etc. when they never once turn their eyes to shambles that for nastiness have not their equal in the meanest village in Ireland – tho' they have been noticed by travellers and by some of them recorded to our discredit?*

The image we normally have of the past is formed from the middle and upper classes' accounts of themselves. Especially when considering this period, it is easy to forget how small a circle the protagonists were drawn from and how, though Belfast might have deserved to be called 'the Athens of the North', such a description could have interested only a small proportion of the population. The first three Presbyterian churches huddled together in Rosemary Street as if for protection. Benn says, 'Belfast has always been reputed a PRESBYTERIAN TOWN. But there was probably no time in which Presbyterianism was more influential than in the days of the volunteers, and up till the year 1820 at the least. . . . The principal and most wealthy inhabitants of the town at that era were certainly Presbyterians.' Yet they were a suppressed sect, excluded from power. It is not difficult to imagine the first three Presbyterian congregations meeting on a Sunday and feeling like a big but threatened family in a town clung on to by Anglicans.

The Drennans and the McTiers were cultured, educated, religious and middle class, but they were also second-class citizens. They were not quite in the extreme situation of the Catholics, who suffered under draconian Penal Laws which, had they been adhered to strictly, would have ensured that *every* Catholic, rather than most, was a pauper. Professions were often closed to Catholics, so that they looked to trade and brewing to make money. At the start of the twentieth century, Catholics had found a niche in alcohol, which was shunned by Nonconformists: of 1,093 publicans in Belfast, 885 were Catholics. Medicine, which was pursued by William Drennan, was open to Catholics; the law was not. But there simply were not many Catholics in Belfast at the time. In 1791 the population of Belfast was 18,320. Nine years later it was about 20,000, of whom about 1,300 were Catholics. The opening of the first Roman Catholic chapel in Belfast in 1784 was celebrated by the First Company of Belfast Volunteers, but Wolfe Tone recorded that even the politically active inhabitants of the town were 'wonderfully ignorant of their Catholic brethren'. The discontent of the Belfast Presbyterians arose from the frustration of a dynamic group growing in prosperity but being artificially held back by laws it had had no hand in drafting. They had built up lucrative businesses, but the English were fond of protectionist laws to hamper Irish trade.

Presbyterians were the dynamo of the town, but were not allowed title to it. Henry Joy was only Deputy Town Clerk from 1759 to 1772, though it seems clear that he was by no means second in command: calling him 'Deputy' was a way of getting round the Test Act, which would have barred him, as a Presbyterian, from holding office as Town Clerk. So, against its apparent will, he served the town by establishing a Chamber of Commerce and initiating the long series of improvements to the harbour which was to have such an important effect on the development of Belfast. He also participated in the building of the White Linen Hall, which was probably completed in 1785, and was a crucial development in Belfast's progress as a provider of finished cloth.

The Drennans and the McTiers belonged to this rising class or group of businessmen and professionals who nevertheless had reason to feel dissatisfied with the dispensation of society. At one point Samuel and Martha McTier moved into a relatively modest cottage, Cabin Hill, and in her letters Martha makes a virtue of necessity, passing it off as a fashionable rustic retreat. Martha, so ready to do charitable acts for others, is offended in one letter that William has paid the postage on his previous letter in advance. But Sam gets a job as Belfast's first Ballast Master, the principal officer of the Ballast Office, which later became the Harbour Commissioners, one of the most important institutions in the town's progress. Martha reports that as a result they should have about £140 a year, and that they spent that sum for the past three years' housekeeping.

Another important factor in the Presbyterian attitude, and a reason for the difference of Belfast, was the Scottish connection. Ulster differed from the rest of Ireland in the extent and effectiveness with which it was 'planted' with incomers, but counties Antrim and Down were the only counties in Ireland in which Scots predominated. In Scotland, the Dissenters had had their own record of difficult relations with the English.

William Drennan was sent off at the age of fifteen to Glasgow University. He gained an MA in 1771 and in 1778 he took an MD at Edinburgh. This was an age of private armies and duelling. Drennan himself narrowly avoided a clash with one James Ogle in the early 1780s. The panache of the Volunteers, who were political idealists, and combined the threat of armed discipline with established patriotic credentials, must have made soldiering attractive. The propensity for Ulstermen to march about in self-organized armies has not disappeared over the years: these days they may be adolescents in berets and combat jackets, or a band of Paisleyites assembled on a hill and waving their firearm certificates for the benefit of the press. But given later events, there is a certain irony in the fact that the regular companies of Volunteers were a revival of an episode in 1745 when young men had joined the garrison at Carrickfergus to defend it against an expected attack from the Young Pretender.

On 6 April 1778 the twenty-four-year-old William Drennan wrote to his sister from Edinburgh.

> *Seven Irish lads here have entered into a resolution to be taught by a sergeant from the castle, and he gives us hopes that we shall fire powder at least with perfect regularity in a fortnight or three weeks.*

It is noticeable how often the correspondence talks about uniforms: Martha presumably knew how her brother's mind worked when she described the regimentals of the Belfast Volunteer companies, who were no doubt a pretty sight in blue and white, with blue gold-laced hats. Benn also thought of the military as colourful:

> *It is said that the military in any town infuses into it a life and gaiety not otherwise to be gained. If this be so with occasional visitants, what must Belfast have been during the many years in which regular regiments, volunteers, and yeomanry had possession of it. To be sure, the most of them were but carpet-knights, who had never seen service; still they had uniforms, swords, guns, and drums. These they kept constantly in service, and the ladies and gentlemen of the town paraded Donegall Place, then the only flagged street in the town, listening to the delicious strains.*

In 1783 Drennan began practice, mainly as an accoucheur, or obstetrician, in Newry. Drennan and his sister had wondered whether there would be enough work in Belfast for a third doctor: by now there were two new ones, and six more promised. In Newry Drennan's only rival – and the rivalry seems to have been keenly felt – was a Dr Templeton, though there were also six apothecaries and a surgeon. Drennan paints a rather comic picture of his life in Newry, about which he might have had ambivalent feelings:

> *In the morning of the same day I attended at Mr. Montgomery's public funeral, and walked before the rest in a very disagreeable procession, preceded only by a ragged beggar-looking fellow who kept constantly jingling a little bell in his hand as if to apprise the whole town that the deceased and the doctor were just a-coming. This is a constant ceremonial in funeral solemnities at this place, and not satisfied with this, there is always one of these bell-ringers that go through the town informing everyone by their papistical bell who has died, at what hour, and when he is to be interred. I observe that these fellows always pull off their hats most respect-fully on meeting me in the streets as if certain of my being a future friend*

of theirs and looking upon themselves as acting pretty much in the same vocation . . .

At this time Drennan hoped to make between two hundred and fifty and three hundred pounds a year. He also reported that he had been offered six guineas by the wife of a schoolteacher whom he had successfully attended but, conscious of his patient's reduced circumstances, had accepted only three.

While he was in Newry Drennan's writings first began to be noticed, though they were published anonymously. *Letters of Orellana, or An Irish Helot* appeared in the *Belfast News-Letter* in November and December 1784. He had to endure a response that will be familiar to authors brought up in Ulster households, for his sister reported in December 1784: 'We had a fish for dinner to-day on which my mother bestowed more epithets of praise than she ever afforded the "Helot", or anything that appeared in print.'

Drennan is probably best remembered as a poet, and one or two of his pieces usually appear in anthologies of Irish verse: these are the highly political verses 'Wake of William Orr' and 'Erin'. The latter is the poem which gave us the phrase 'the emerald isle':

> Arm of Erin, be strong! but be gentle as brave!
> And, uplifted to strike, be still ready to save!
> Let no feeling of vengeance presume to defile
> The cause of, or men of, the Emerald Isle.
>
> The cause it is good, and the men they are true,
> And the Green shall outlive both the Orange and Blue!

But he was modest about his literary achievements, and regarded himself as an amateur poet.

In many ways it is Martha McTier's personality that shines out most strongly from these letters. Hers is frequently the brighter wit, the sharper tongue and the clearer eye. She continues, even into middle age, to take a maternal interest in her brother, in his political activities no less than in his professional life. Touchingly, he often turns to her for advice or simply to worry aloud about his problems. There is a recurring concern about the damage William's politics might do to his prospects. In 1785 he receives a veiled invitation via James Corry to join the Whigs of Charles James Fox, under the guise of general observations about 'ways of gaining distinction'. As reported by Drennan, Corry's approach is Delphic, and Drennan admits, 'You will immediately call all this fudge.' Yet he goes on:

I owned my ambition and my wish for honourable and conscientious competence. . . . I think I have within me an impregnable heart in politics. I am of belief that it is necessary to be a party man, and that a man can be so consistent with the strictest honour. I believe that there may, but never will be long, a ministry which an honest patriot ought to support.

He was a dissenter by nature as well as by religion.

Martha's advice is to 'be proud of your present independence. . . . Remembrance of service *past* is a frail tie.' Her political comments are frequently more outspoken and emotional than her brother's, though she is also quicker to revise her opinions in the face of violence or, for example, when Napoleon begins to deviate from the principles of the revolution. Yet in 1786 she wrote: 'I would be invaded, were I an Irish Volunteer, before I would volunteer it either with money or person for George III.'

When he moved to Dublin, Drennan involved himself closely in politics. He was impressed by the constitutionalist Grattan, whom he saw in procession in May 1790. He admired 'that fine enthusiasm without which it is impossible to be a great man'. Napper Tandy had 'all the surliness of republicanism, grinning most ghastly smiles' at 'the many-headed monster' of the people. Drennan is not carried away: he admires the slogans and logos of the banners, but 'I look in vain for a *Bill for Amended Representation*.' And despite the invitation at Newry, he thinks little of the Whig Clubs, saying the one in Dublin 'literally does nothing more than eat and drink. They have no fellow-feeling with the people, nor the people with them.'

On 21 May 1791 Drennan outlines to Samuel McTier the idea which A.T.Q. Stewart has identified as the one central to the United Irishmen. It is arguable that the plan expressed in this letter had disastrous consequences, not only for the movement itself, but also for the whole course of Irish history.

I should much desire that a Society were instituted in this city having much of the secrecy and somewhat of the ceremonial of Freemasonry, so much secrecy as might communicate curiosity, uncertainty, expectation to the minds of surrounding men, so much impressive and affecting ceremony in its internal economy as without impeding real business might strike the soul through the senses. A benevolent conspiracy – a plot for the people – no Whig Club – no party title – the Brotherhood its name – the Rights of Men and the Greatest Happiness of the Greatest Number its end – its general end Real Independence to Ireland, and Republicanism its particular purpose – its business every means to accomplish these ends as speedily as the prejudices and bigotry of the land we live in would permit, as speedily as to give us some enjoyment and not to protract anything too long in this short span of life. The means are manifold, publication always coming from one of the Brotherhood, and no other designation. Declaration, a solemn and religious compact with each other to be signed by every member, and its chief and leading principles to be conveyed into a symbol worn by every of them round their body next the heart. Communication with leading men in France, in England and in America so as to cement the scattered and shifting sand of republicanism into a body (as well as those malignant conspiracies which courts and classes of men have formed) and when thus cemented to sink it like a caisson in the dark and troubled waters, a stable unseen power. Why should secrecy be necessary? For many reasons. It gives greater energy within, greater influence abroad. It conceals members whose professions, etc., would make concealment expedient until the real trial comes, etc., etc. I therefore think and insist on your not even mentioning it, nor do not imagine I shall neglect my profession or injure my character by keeping bad company. You are not, I believe, a republican, but not many years will elapse till this persuasion will prevail, for nothing else but the public happiness as an end, and the public will as the power and means of obtaining it, is good in politics and all else is job. Such schemes are not to be laughed at as romantic, for without enthusiasm nothing great was done, or will be done.

This plan is almost exactly that which he had outlined in a letter to Reverend William Bruce in August 1785: the secrecy, the word *Brotherhood*, the religious oath, the emblem worn next the heart, are all mentioned. He also emphasizes that, though it should be secret, he is not advocating a violent attempt against the state:

I still and (however you may smile at such romantic boyisms) ever think that such a constitutional conspiracy ought to take place as a means of perpetuating the best and noblest of political objects in the minds of the best and noblest men in the country.

The conspiracy was 'constitutional', and remained so until 1795 for most United Irishmen. It was designed to revive the spirit of the Volunteers, whom Drennan thought had been 'stifled by an extinguisher which Lord Charlemont [the aristocratic leader of the Volunteers] has gradually slipped over it'.

Drennan is fairly open about one of his motives for secrecy: throughout the letters he expresses his wish to make a good living from his profession. Another possible reason may lie in the emphasis he places on the trappings of ritual and ceremony: is the Presbyterian impressed with the outward forms of Catholicism, or is he attempting to appeal to Catholics with 'impressive and affecting ceremony'? Although he is only borrowing their forms and not their philosophies, it may be unwelcome for the admirer of the United Irishmen to find that the basis of their organization leaned so much on the trappings of Freemasonry, an idea which also occurred to the members of the Orange Order in Armagh in 1795. But these ideas were in the air. The secrets of the Bavarian Illuminati were revealed in 1784, the year of Drennan's original letter to Bruce. And in 1791 Wolfgang Amadeus Mozart had become a Mason in Vienna. Wolfgang

Hildesheimer puts this latter event into perspective: for Mozart the ideal of brotherhood (meaning at the time male brotherhood), though 'revolutionary' in its aims and ideas, was 'expressed only in vague proclamations'. If Freemasonry was more a matter of words than deeds, Drennan's Brotherhood was, in his letter, concerned with propaganda rather than pious sentiment. Yet there hangs about any secret society, whether a male 'gorging and boozing' club (in the case of Mozart) or a political association, an atmosphere that cannot fail to be unsavoury: conspiratorial, exclusivist, questionable, a little absurd.

In the summer of 1791 Drennan proposed a flag for the movement, with a 'beautiful motto from Rousseau' saying that every man must be a soldier for the defence of his liberty and that to die in the service of one's country is too fine a deed to be entrusted to mercenaries. These are strong words, though they are less a call to bloody insurrection than a reminder of the patriotic origins of the Volunteers from which the Brotherhood sprang. In November Drennan reports that they are to have a 'medal of admission' to keep out strangers, 'perhaps to be worn at the meeting'.

On 8 November 1791 Drennan, with Napper Tandy and four others, was on the committee for the second meeting of the Dublin Society of United Irishmen. It was on this occasion that he proposed, and had adopted, his 'solemn Declaration, or Test', in emulation of the civic oath of revolutionary France:

> 'I, A.B., in the presence of God, do pledge myself to my country, that I will use all my abilities and influence in the attainment of an impartial and adequate representation of the Irish nation in Parliament and as a means of absolute and immediate necessity in accomplishing this chief good of Ireland, I shall do whatever lies in my power to forward a brotherhood of affection, an identity of interests, a communion of rights, and an union of power among Irishmen of all religious persuasions without which every reform must be partial, not national, inadequate to the wants, delusive to the wishes and insufficient for the freedom and happiness of this country.'

Wolfe Tone and Thomas Russell, not on the committee because they did not attend the first meeting, voted against the Test. Drennan suspected that they 'wish everything to follow [the Belfast] Society by adoption', though later commentators have suggested their motives had more to do with simple jealousy. They were still objecting in December, and a certain distance in Drennan's relations with them can be detected.

> My chief fault to them is that they are too reserved to some who are entitled to confidence, and that they aim rather at making instruments than partners. They don't conceal this enough, and, therefore, I think, don't know men as well as they will do. They are both sincere and able and zealous. They sometimes speak as

being officially representative of the Belfast Society, and Tone said if this had not been the case he would not have taken the Test.

The *Northern Star*, a newspaper begun in Belfast to put forward a more radical view than that of the more liberal *News-Letter*, published alternative Tests on 3 February 1792.

Drennan imagined that the ritualistic Brotherhood and the Test would impress Catholics: he found them 'most zealous for the Test, which I think indicates their sincerity. I observe that the solemnity is the thing they like, perhaps from their religion.' In the Public Record Office's collection of facsimiles relating to the United Irishmen, the point is made that the Test did not attract Catholics, and may have repelled them. One of the great aims of the movement was 'union' between Irishmen: the insistence on it tends to suggest a reality of disunion.

Ironically, Tone was acting on behalf of Catholics rather than, as he claimed and as Drennan doubted, for the Belfast Society. Yet at the same time Tone was enamored of the radicalism he found in Belfast: as Thomas Addis Emmet said a few years later, 'every man turns his mind more or less on speculative politics' in Belfast.

Though his own beliefs seem to have been fairly relaxed, Drennan was always secure in thinking his own sect the best, and regarding Catholicism in particular as lamentable. He accepted the idea that all Irishmen should have equal rights, but ecumenism, one suspects, would have seemed to him an unappealing concept. Occasionally his references to Catholics and Catholicism sound patronizing to a modern ear, though they are a long way removed from bigotry: 'Trust like a Papist, for, if you doubt as a Dissenter, the same restless faculty that rejects the Athanasian Creed . . . will begin to nibble at the Incarnation, the Miraculous Conception, etc. . . . I like the *morality* of the Gospel so well that I have not the least occasion for the supplementary proof of miracle.' But he was tolerant:

> *We will not vilify the religion of any man, far less will we presume to make those vanities of faith, which are natural, and perhaps necessary, the instruments of civil persecution and political usurpation to make what may be deemed the pleasures of the Creator, the causes of torture to his creatures.*

In 1791 Drennan opposed motions and petitions by moderate Catholics that he felt were too accepting of the '*established* constitution'. He felt that the Catholics wanted 'two strings to their bow', while Pitt was trying 'to separate them from the *furious* part of the Presbyterians'. An extract from one of Drennan's letters to Samuel McTier was handed about in Dublin, and was claimed to show that Drennan had accused Catholics of duplicity. Drennan confided that, though he could not remember having accused any individual of duplicity, he felt that the Catholics as a body had 'acted a double part'. J.C. Beckett makes the point that, particularly after Pitt's restoration of the franchise to Catholics in 1793 in the hope of gaining their support, the struggle was between the Dublin Parliament, representing the Protestant ascendancy, and the radical reformers. Drennan had strong views on that section of society:

I don't understand the term ascendancy; *it is really an astrological term denoting the star which had* uncontrolled dominion *over our nativity; and is the language of a soothsayer rather than a politician. My toast should be –* The Sovereignty of the People – *not of any party; the* Ascendancy of Christianity – *not of any church.*

He was disturbed by outbreaks of fighting between Catholic Defenders and the military, and between Volunteers and the police:

I see an impending storm. I see an array of men against each other and I feel a somewhat of panic before a battle which I fear is going to begin. God save the right. In the meantime I go to a ball.

For all the affected nonchalance, Drennan did not relish the prospect of violence, as one might have expected a devotee of the French Revolution to do. But as yet the open rebellion was years away, and 1792 saw only repression. Drennan, deploring the 'great stock of bigotry in this country', expected that Catholics would be suppressed more effectively as a result of their resistance.

In November of that year he stated clearly to Martha the problems he found in dealing with the Catholics, and the nature of the relationship between them and the Dissenters.

The Catholic cause is selfish, compared to ours, and they will make use of every means for success. . . . They will send their sanguine men into our Society, and the heads of their sect will not enter it, but stand off, sullen and reserved. In this they are wise; but certainly our aim, as men of Ireland, is to keep them up to the compact, the league and covenant, which is ample justice to them, and then their exertions with the northerns for Reform in parliament. We ought, then, to watch them, though their sincere friends, greater, perhaps, than they are to themselves.

Drennan felt that they must avoid the appearance of 'revolution and republicanism': 'Our present pursuits ought to terminate in an equal and impartial representation of the people, and let posterity go on to republicanism if they choose.' The two parties in the movement had different aims, and Drennan felt that his side had to coax the other to continue pressing for political, rather than strictly sectarian, aims:

The Catholics may save themselves, but it is the Protestants must save the nation. . . . There is evidently a misunderstanding taken place between the parties here, and both, perhaps, are in fault, but it is certainly proper, all circumstances considered, that the Protestants should not be damped and quieted and restrained, but, acting at first for the Union, let them now act for that Reform, which was their object from the first.

At this stage his patience was wearing thin:

They suspect me as an incendiary, and I, many of them as cunning, uncandid, close, plotting and circumventing, between ourselves.

At the end of February 1793 the Gunpowder Law allowed the Government to seize cannon in Dublin and Belfast, and some leading United Irishmen were arrested. Drennan wrote to Sam that every man in Belfast and around it should have a firearm handy in case an army should be required at short notice. He felt that if the Volunteers had resisted the seizures and arrests, Catholics might have followed, but was not sure. He suspected that the whole exercise was merely a stunt by the authorities, a calculated risk designed to prove their effectiveness to Pitt. Government action against the radicals stepped up. Repressive laws were passed and further arrests were made. Napper Tandy proved lacking in courage in the face of this, and Butler and Bond in Newgate prison were 'behaving ill': the United Irishmen societies supported them financially, but were dismayed when it was found their bill for fruit was twelve pounds, and their bill for wine a hundred. Following the emancipation of the Catholic Relief Bill, forced on the Dublin Parliament by Westminster, Drennan found the Catholics had fallen into a 'torpor'. The soliders billed in Belfast behaved riotously, and the United Irishmen were held in 'general opprobrium'. Drennan found patients hard to come by.

Belfast is often presented as the most extreme repubican town, but Martha McTier was not so sure on her visit to Dublin in April 1793:

where the company know each other they go much further in both sides than in Belfast, and there are no other denominations than Loyalist or Republican.

By August William wrote, 'I am heartily sick of politics'; in September he complained that women and Catholics (why this mixture of people is not clear) regarded him as one of the 'incendiaries and Jacobins and atheists':

I do believe that Siberia is better suited to be a republic than Ireland, and I do believe that every day will bring on a coalition of the Protestant gentry and the Catholics of consequence directly opposite in its nature to the supposed alliance lately in train between the Presbyterians and the Catholics, an alliance to keep everything much as it is.

One of his abiding reservations about the Catholic side had been that it was too influenced by aristocrats. At heart Drennan was a democrat, who might have been expected to think that revolution could not succeed if the bulk of the people were indifferent or hostile to its aims. Yet he was also the architect of vanguardism in the movement, insisting that a small, secret group of plotters could do more than a mass movement. What he saw as the unsophisticated self-interest of the Catholic faction as led by 'aristocrats', made this ally difficult to work with, though it was potentially of overwhelming weight; it must have been tempting to think that the unwieldy structure he was attempting to build could be kept secure by the secret caisson, a small, efficient circle who would not be constantly hampered by spies, *agents provocateurs* and disagreements within the ranks.

By January 1794 things looked bleak; more men were arrested, including the proprietors of the *Northern Star*, and the United Irishmen were attacked from the pulpits. A further matter of regret was his break with Wolfe Tone, whose 'literary talents' he continued to admire: it was a personal falling-out, but Drennan also objected to Tone's double-dealing, his habit of attacking a person one day and behaving towards him in a friendly manner the next. Nor was the problem of relations between Catholics and Dissenters any easier. Attitudes to the French Revolution divided the alliance; the Presbyterians were frank enthusiasts whereas the Catholics secretly deplored it because the Catholic religion had been overturned:

Now the Catholics are still more religionists than politicians, and the Presbyterians more politicians than religionists. The one still cherish their creed as the first object, the creed of the other is in general liberty and equality but then they are far from that conviction which makes practice.

In May 1794 Drennan was arrested and accused of seditious libel arising from his pamphlet *An Address to the Volunteers of Ireland*. Other United Irishmen were being arrested and sentenced to hang, whilst some set off for America. Drennan found it difficult to engage counsel: Thomas Emmet declined to represent him, and another friend, Butler, was in 'embarrassed circumstances'. But it seems that Emmet had judged that his own political reputation might harm the case, and Drennan was grateful to him in the end for acting 'in the shade most zealously and friendly'. Drennan was not hopeful about his chances: he told his family to expect his conviction.

After a trial of nearly thirteen hours, Drennan was acquitted, though the foreman of the jury, Sir John Thrale, complained that 'the jury were obliged to give a verdict against their inclinations'. Drennan had been in doubt to the last minute because many of the jury were 'known aristocrats, the foreman in particular'. Will and Sam were chaired and huzzaed home by a crowd of a thousand people. Drennan admitted that the judges 'were all very decent and impartial in their charges'. Reporting these events, and the bills for high treason issued against Tone, Drennan promised his mother that there would be 'a quietus in my politics, at least so far as to dabble in these fugitive and now dangerous papers.'

That phrase 'now dangerous' may be significant. For us who read now how the Volunteers played at soldiers with firearms and pikes, it is difficult to accept that the conspirators could think their activities not 'dangerous': until the 1793 Gunpowder Law the Volunteers held their own cannon. It is certainly true that the 'show of strength' has been a tactic much favoured by Northern politicians in recent troubles: in some manifestations the loyalist leader can seem more like the Grand Old Duke of York than a politician. But though at one point in 1791 Drennan had been in favour of violent revolution, a few years later he was a gradualist.

Although he maintained to the end of his life his interest in politics, his philanthropy and his lively observations of daily political events, Drennan's acquittal was the high-tide mark of his career as a United Irishman. In January 1795 he supported a call to resist the French, which he hoped would bind the Catholics and the Presbyterians in the continuing struggle for reform. He remained as ever opposed to the 'aristocratic array' that the anti-government forces of the other three provinces would make without the democratic leavening of the north and, in particular, Belfast. In April 1796 he observed, 'Some people look at me, as they pass, as if they said, there is the author of evil.'

Neilson and Russell were arrested in Belfast in September 1796, Russell on the premises of the Linen Hall Library of which he was Librarian. Martha McTier instructed her brother to visit them when they were transferred to a Dublin jail: '"I was in prison, and ye came unto Me." You were there also, and do not let anything prevent your doing a humane and a friendly action.'

His course had started in youthful high spirits: the lad of twenty-four had learned to fire a gun with his Edinburgh college friends, wishing no doubt he could be back in Belfast to protect Ireland from the royalist and Catholic French. He wanted to use a disciplined and principled force, the Volunteers, an entirely legal, respectable and patriotic body, to call for fair and equal treatment for all the denominations of Ireland. He led the movement for change, or at the very least assisted it, into secrecy and encouraged the adoption of the trappings of Freemasonry – medals, ribbons and sacred oaths. At first he applauded the French Revolution, to the extent in 1792 of calling for the death of King Louis. But perhaps he realized that violence can lead not to justice, but to more violence. Later he came around to Martha's opinion of Napoleon, and told her that he and his wife had turned his portrait upside down.

It is remarkable how much Drennan was prepared to say in his letters about political and even paramilitary activities. Occasionally Martha McTier comments acidly on the possibility that their mail is being opened by the Belfast Postmaster, Mr Whinnery – she even includes messages to him in her letters to William. A few of their letters were delivered by friends, but the general openness of tone suggests that they did not regard themselves as indulging in criminal activities.

The situation rapidly deteriorated. The demands of Grattan's liberal opposition in the Dublin Parliament were too moderate for the reformers. The war with France brought economic depression, which in turn caused unrest in the countryside. In the north this took a sectarian shape. The Orange societies, loyalist and almost exclusively Anglican, began to form at about this time, and their members often joined the yeomanry. The United Irishmen became increasingly extreme, but even in Ulster they represented only a small group.

In February 1797 Belfast was once again alarmed at the prospect of French invasion, and not as sanguine about its response as it had been on previous occasions. At a meeting called by the city's Sovereign, or mayor, at the start of January, an attempt to form a yeomanry had ended in disorder when it was suggested that anyone who took the yeoman oath, swearing to uphold the laws, would be promising not to pursue reform. The town was also suffering from the presence of a soldiery that Martha McTier portrayed as a drunken, murderous rabble rather than a disciplined army. Drennan's relationship with the Society had changed too, to his surprise:

Is it not curious, my dear Matty, that I, who was one of the patriarchs of the present popular societies, should be at present civilly shoved out of their company, and I, who of my own accord wrote the Test upon which the new associations are still, in chief, founded, should in pursuance of the spirit of this same Test, be excluded and treated as a frigid neutralist, until I take it again in their form, and all this without the smallest change in my political principles or practice, except in not writing so as to throw myself, as other patriot suicides, into the gulf of a prison which, whatever it may do with them, would soon close upon me in dark oblivion.

In the new circumstances, extremists have taken over the movement, and act without restraint or honour. To take the oath in the form they require would be a capital offence.

Drennan had been taken to the edge of the abyss, seemingly before he recognized it as such, and had been allowed to walk away. At the age of forty, bespectacled and balding (he wore a small wig), a doctor–poet whose inclinations were for tolerance and justice, who valued material success but had made sacrifices for his principles, he did not after all wish to wash his hands in the blood of even the aristocratic oppressors of his country. He knew that he had risked his neck, but regarded himself as innocent, even from the point of view of the government.

From the perspective of the Drennan letters, 1798 is less of a climax than an aftermath. It is clear even from this family correspondence that the British authorities were aware of most of what was going on (although they did not suspect that Drennan was the author, not only of the Test, but also of the prospectus which laid out the plan for the original Brotherhood and which later, at Tone's suggestion, was called the 'Society of United Irishmen': this only became known in 1931). Drennan's trial was the result of information given by an informer. Dublin Castle had a large number of spies in its employ, but it could not discover the names of the leaders, thanks in part no doubt to Drennan's advocacy of secrecy from the beginning, and in any case informers were afraid to make themselves known in court because of the risk of assassination: although many in the movement were against it, there was a faction which advocated assassination, and a newspaper was printed in Dublin which gave names of those to be murdered. The authorities were forced to wait until March 1798, when Thomas Reynolds, a leading United Irishman, at last revealed who the secret leaders were. Sixteen were immediately arrested (including all the members of the supreme executive except Lord Edward Fitzgerald) before the rebellion took place. In the north, a Roman Catholic farmer from Saintfield, Nicholas Magin, himself a leading member, caused many of the Ulster leadership to be arrested before a shot was fired: he had been in the pay of Dublin Castle for eighteen months.

Drennan had advocated violent revolution in a letter to Dr Bruce in 1791, though it was seed that fell on stony ground:

> The prosperity of a Nation depends more on Liberty than on Peace. . . . Reform to be anything must be a Revolution. . . . I think that revolutions are not to be dreaded as such terrible extremes, and that it was the highest probability, it would be as peaceful here as in France, as in Poland, as in Ireland itself in the year '79, provided the great irresistible voice of the whole declared itself explicitly upon the subject. I believe a reform must lead rapidly to a separation, and a separation as certainly to a reform; both are means, and both are ends.

By February 1798 he had the example of the Terror by which to gauge the accuracy of his powers of prediction as regards France, and his disillusionment with things nearer to home is clear:

> There is a degeneracy from pure principle into vindictive passions . . . as to their [the United Irishmen's] persons and conduct in many particulars, I am not altogether as well settled in my opinion.

By March, seven of his friends were in prison and five had fled, for which he did not blame them: 'The people look on me here as a solitary ninepin, standing by chance, when the other 8 are bowled down.' A year later, after further government legislation and with the prospect of more arrests, Drennan was able to say, 'Thank God, if there be a ready-made plot, and a directory in the country, I am totally unacquainted with it.'

The skittling was followed by executions. Martha described the hanging of Henry Joy McCracken in October 1798:

McCracken was offered a pardon at the gallows if he would inform on R[obert] S[imms]; his old father at the foot of it desired him to do all he could to save his life with honour. 'Farewell then,' said the son, embracing him, and was immediately turned off.

He was hanged in Cornmarket, and according to Stewart Parker the rope was made in his father's rope factory. It is reported that the assistants in Burton's men's clothes shop are frightened to go into one of the rooms in the store because they believe it is on the spot where Henry Joy McCracken was hanged.

That must be how legends are launched. Heroism is always attractive even though its effects, immediate and long-term, may be disastrous. Everyone else had to deal with the consequences of the botched revolution. In February 1799 Drennan could only suggest his notion of the double crown, in a sense the reverse of the boldest aim of the United Irishmen. Commenting on a history of the rebellion – and it is notable how quickly the writers and portrait-painters moved in to immortalize the conspirators, even as they conspired – Drennan observed, 'The savagery of the lower Catholics was even greater than the rule of retaliation could account for.'

He never renounced his principles – in his later years, following his return from Dublin, he reprinted propaganda relating to the Volunteers in his *Belfast Monthly Magazine* – but he thought the United Irishmen 'foolish'. He thought the supporters of the Act of Union were 'rogues', but in 1802 he was advocating gradualism:

We must in this country be content to get the substance of Reform more slowly in the way of peace and without, instead of suddenly (perhaps without a proper preparation of manners to principles), in circumstances of great and terrible trial.

The same letter goes on to claim that he was always fonder of the 'professed principles' of the democrats than of their persons, 'though I saw in most of them aristocracy in a shabby coat, aristocratic self-sufficiency, aristocratic vengeance, aristocratic intolerance under a Maratism of manners and of language.'

The rupture between the old style and the new was made clear by Robert Emmet's rising in the summer of 1803. Drennan called it 'this mad business', but Martha was eloquent on the subject in her letter of 2 August:

My rose beds were trimmed and flower pots dressed, and (if possible) it should *have been without green, for even the vulgarest of flowers (the orange lily) does not now raise such disagreeable ideas. . . . Nothing good can, or ought to be, brought about by means too cruel for savages, and no steps a government could take will damn the cause nor stigmatise the very name of Irish liberty equally with the deeds that usher in to abhorrence the ruffians who pretend to assert it. Let me ever live in a country enchained by rule, rather than freed to anarchy by desperadoes.*

It is difficult to know where disappointment at political performance ends and basic feelings of difference and even prejudice begin. Standards today are different from those of two centuries ago, and if she could refer to 'that native vulgarity of face you observe in the Irish' or he could use the term 'bogtrotter', it does not mean they were bigots. Moreover, Drennan saw himself as furthering Catholic interests. Martha McTier's sympathies are hardly in doubt, as in her sketch for some amateur dramatics:

I will never represent a Union, though I would be of a group as Erin, but if I wore an orange lily, I would stick it in my b— I would be chained to Albion . . . my dress should be green . . . I would be crowned with shamrocks, necklace and bracelets of strung potatoes, and if I am allowed to slip my chain, will dance a reel with my sisters merrily.

Brendan Clifford claims that Drennan's speech to a town meeting in Belfast in 1817 shows that he, like the United Irishmen in Belfast as a whole, were not nationalist but sought social and political reform, and that they only advocated separation because of Britain's support for the 'corrupt Irish Parliament': Henry Joy reported him as saying that,

in the event of a full, free and frequent representation of the people in parliament for the whole empire he would be reconciled to the Union. He would, not unwillingly, merge his country in a fair and faithful representation of these realms – for what is country justly considered, but a free constitution, and give him that well guaranteed, he would consider himself more an Irishman on the banks of the Ohio or Mississippi, than he does now on the banks of the Lagan.

Republicanism and nationalism have been appropriated by the majority of Irish people. The Presbyterian moment ended, and the two strands of Catholic resistance carried on, the physical force tradition whose headquarters is now Belfast, and the nonviolent tradition of O'Connell and Parnell, to which the Derry-born leader of the SDLP, John Hume, could be seen as heir.

The glamour tends to attach to the physical-force men and women, those who laid down their own and others' lives for Ireland. Almost all the anti-establishment of modern Belfast, by no means confined to supporters of the IRA, would be proud in some way of those who were 'out' or 'up' in '98. The 'volunteers' who fire volleys over the graves in west Belfast wear their black berets and sunglasses with the panache we might expect the Volunteers, in their blue coats, white waistcoats and gold-decorated hats, to have shown. In November 1798, barely five weeks after the execution of Henry Joy McCracken, Drennan reported that he was to be included in a series of biographical sketches of the 'leaders and instigators of the Irish Rebellion of '98'. He corrected the paragraph on himself to refer to 'honest and honourable independence, the best blessing for myself, and my first and last prayer for my country'.

In 1800 he married Sarah Swanwick, whom he had known for many years; it sounds as if her Shropshire family had thought it prudent to wait and see whether their prospective son-in-law would be hanged. William and Sarah quickly had three children and, on inheriting some money from an aunt in 1807, Drennan retired to an honest, honourable and independent life in Belfast. He had enlightened views on most things. His pronouncements on medicine, for example, would sound eminently sensible in the mouth of a modern doctor, even though his sympathy in one letter for his mother's indisposition was tempered by his view that the problem was a 'Donegall Street cold', due to the state of her house. The last batch of letters concerns the defence of the fledgling Belfast Academical Institution, known in Belfast as 'Inst', against the attacks of Dr Cooke, clerical champion of Union and 'Old Light'.

William Drennan is not the most celebrated of the United Irishmen, so perhaps he should be allowed to paint his own portrait. He wrote the following to his sister in 1794, after reading Rousseau's *Confessions*:

I find some resemblance to myself in the portrait, in the reserve of countenance, the awkward timidity, the shortsightedness, the voice . . . really frank and open, apparently sullen and shut up, mild, knowing, sincere, easily temptible, sociable, yet solitary, without address, art, dissimulation, prudence, hating vulgarity, loving the vulgar, gentle in manners, yet a stern republican, flexible in every other thing, his spirit tuned to a flat key, yet much latent enthusiasm, fonder of the fair than he appears, and hurt in his pride for being taken for what he appears . . .

In *Northern Star* Stewart Parker rewrote the final days of Henry Joy McCracken, before his arrest on Cave Hill, as an uproarious pastiche of styles from the great Irish dramatists. The playwright's own term for his subject was 'comedy of terrors'. The play asked what were the real consequences of 'heroic' action, and revealed how drama runs the risk of trivializing and distorting it. When McCracken makes his speech about Belfast, the character may be expressing the tortured ambivalence of the author towards his native city:

Why would one place break your heart, more than another? A place the like of that? Brain-damaged and dangerous, continuously violating itself. . . . As maddening and tiresome as any other pain-obsessed cripple. And yet what would this poor fool not give to be able to walk freely again from Stranmillis down to Ann Street. . . . We never made a nation. Our brainchild. Stillborn. Our own fault. We botched the birth. So what if the English do bequeath us to one another some day? What then? When there's nobody else to blame except ourselves?

Parker himself was crippled by cancer, which deprived him of a leg in his teens and ultimately killed him at the age of forty-seven. He was an exile from Belfast, where the theatres had failed to encourage him until he had achieved success in Dublin and London. In the speech above, McCracken speaks as a sort of exile, barred from the city he loves by the clash between his own idealism and its recalcitrance, or by his rash utopianism and its inconvenient and unwelcome realities. But the episode of the United Irishmen is the moment in the life of Belfast that holds out the hope – for liberal Protestants and ecumenists in particular – of its potential for progressive thought and action, tantalizingly squandered ever since in a way that can 'break your heart'.

Thanks to two strokes of luck Drennan was able to walk freely again through his native city, 'a town which has probably the same feeling for me as I have for it, which I esteem but do not love'. It is unlikely that future dramatists will feel a need to deconstruct the myth of William Drennan. The delivery of babies and schools is less sensational than battles with pikes and guns. A partial monument would be the classical façade of Inst, the school which he helped to found and strove to protect. Despite the unwelcome intrusion of the Technical College on the right-hand half of its front lawn, it still adorns the city centre.

In February 1805 Drennan discussed with his sister his ideas for educating his son, Tom:

People say that boys teach each other to be manly, but I think it is absurd to let good boys be educated under bad ones, which is always the case, and it is time enough for Tom to be manly ten years hence. I am quite against public schools for children. . . . I am not at all afraid of his getting any formality from old ladies, or of his being rendered timid; better even so, than boldness beyond strength, and that mimicry of manliness which is unnatural in a child.

The young man learning to use firearms in Edinburgh, handsome, manly Henry Joy McCracken, are shadows at the back of the fond father; he had disentangled himself from those who committed the cardinal sin of revolutionaries, failure, which only led to more bloodshed and disaster, to the third and fourth generation: better timidity than boldness beyond strength.

CHAPTER SEVEN

HENRY COOKE

A statue of the conqueror of liberalism stands in the city centre, dramatizing in bronze and granite the bitterness of the conflict between two strands of Belfast thought. In front of the Belfast Academical Institution helped into being by William Drennan is a likeness of its greatest enemy, Henry Cooke. He was an autocratic democrat, a fundamentalist maverick, a vituperative pastor, a political man of God, a quasi-prelatic minister – a bundle of contradictions, but hardly unfamiliar in Belfast today. The conditions under which Ian Paisley and his like operate can be traced back to the times of Henry Cooke: the disastrous nexus of religion and politics, the identification of Presbyterianism with Unionism, the Crown and conservatism, the broad front of 'Protestants' as against Catholics. If he was not their only begetter he was one of the most influential Presbyterians at a time when Belfast was growing exponentially and changing beyond recognition. Cooke was a charismatic leader who helped lead Presbyterianism, and Belfast, away from the vistas opened by the United Irishmen and their culture.

The great man's son-in-law, J.L. Porter, was responsible for a delightfully partisan biography in 1871 in which he claims that Cooke's father was descended from Puritans who came from Devon to County Down 'in the train of the Hills and Conways' in the early seventeenth century. Yet there are a number of uncertainties about the origin of the champion of orthodoxy. His family name, for example, was Macook, and the future Pope of Presbyterianism was to change this twice: when he was ordained in 1808 he called himself Cook; some time later he embellished himself with a final *e*.

John Macook farmed nine acres at Grillagh, between Maghera and Coleraine. R. Finlay Holmes, in *Henry Cooke*, says Macook came from 'the anonymous peasantry of Ulster'. Porter, in his biography, calls him Cooke, but emphasizes that his hero had a humble beginning, though John's second wife, Jane Howie, was of an 'old and respectable Scotch family' which came over with the Plantation. She brought to John Macook the income from her father's farm, and bore him two girls and two boys, of whom Henry was the youngest. Porter says he was born on 11 May 1788, but Holmes is not so certain: it is possible that he was born in 1783.

Later Henry Cooke was to claim illustrious ancestors; one was Howie of

Loughgoin, a hero of the Scottish Reformation; another had been present at the Siege of Derry, and Cooke described him thus:

At the first outbreak of the Rebellion all his family were murdered except one little child. Driven from a distant part of the county Down, with thousands of starving Protestants, he carried his child in his arms to Derry, and was, happily, one of those admitted into the city for its defence. When he mounted guard at night, he had no nurse or caretaker for his little one, so he carried it with him to the walls, and laid it between the embrasures where the cannon frowned defiance on James and slavery. Providence protected the boy in the midst of famine and death; and when, in after-years, he was asked how he fared for shelter, 'Well enough,' was the reply; 'I had the shelter of my father's gun.' Yes, God – the God of battles – protected the motherless and homeless boy; and he who now addresses you is that boy's descendant.

The *Londonderry Standard* was amused, in its obituary notice of 1868:

Every Greek is inclined to think that he had an ancestor at Marathon or Thermopylae, and we need not criticise too severely the pretensions of any County Derry man who has conceived the idea that one of his forefathers withstood the siege.

Cooke probably derived such notions from his mother, who was the dominant influence on him: 'Proud of the struggles of her forefathers in defence of faith and freedom, she never forgot fact or legend connected with their history in Scotland and Ulster.' He was her favourite. They were both clever and loved words and stories: 'Ballads, songs, legends, tales of border warfare, of Celtic fanaticism, of popish cruelty, were drunk in with keenest relish.'

Henry Cooke was educated in three hedge schools. The first was in a thatched cabin under the violent tutelage of Joseph Pollock, or Poak. The children sat on 'black oak sticks from the neighbouring bog' and a peat fire burned in the centre under a hole in the roof. The young Henry was an 'emaciated, delicate-looking boy, with sharp features, jet-black hair and piercing grey eyes'. He was Poak's star pupil, but he was also liable to distract his classmates with stories. Already he was honing his principal weapon, his voice, and becoming accustomed to being in charge: 'whether at home or abroad, in playground or in class, his leadership was asserted'. Poak instructed the sects in their respective catechisms.

The school of another teacher, Frank Glass, was removed five times, and ended up in a building with unglazed windows and stones for seats. In all, Cooke was taught by one Catholic priest, one former priest, and a Presbyterian probationer. He received a classical education, probably not dissimilar from the type celebrated in Brian Friel's play *Translations* or by William Carleton. No doubt there is some exaggeration of the quality of such schools but Cooke derived a background in Greek and Latin that turned out to be very useful. Although he had fun in later life imitating Glass's 'quaint' renderings of the *Odes* of Horace, it was the vituperative rhetoric of Demosthenes and Cicero that appealed to him most.

Porter provides another suggestive image. Young Henry was an expert on stilts, and would often cause consternation by walking past the windows of upper storeys. Glass's school was a long way away from Grillagh, across a bog and the Moyola River. Henry and his mother had decided that he could cross the river on stilts. On his first day she accompanied him to the Moyola, which he crossed without difficulty. He hid his stilts in the grass and walked on. Looking back, he saw his mother's tall figure pointing towards Cairntogher, where a farmhouse was burning, 'the house of a loyal man fired by the rebels'. This was in 1798, when Henry was probably ten. On another occasion, in a snowstorm, he fell into the swollen river and narrowly escaped being swept away.

Parts of Porter's biography are based on the reminiscences of an old man who was always given to flowery language and emphatic flourishes, so it is difficult to know how accurate it is. But Cooke's family would not have been alone among rural Protestants in their feelings about the rebellion fomented by the associates of William Drennan. It has been in the interests of republicans, nationalists and some Presbyterians to minimize the sectarian violence that accompanied the 1798 uprising. Cooke never felt so constrained. However far such things were from the intentions of its leaders, the perceived conduct of the rebellion, particularly in country areas, strongly reinforced Protestant insecurities. During that summer Cooke was in a state of terror, sleeping in barns or cornfields and watching homesteads round about go up in flames. This was the ten-year-old's experience of revolution. On the other hand he was not blind to social injustice. He earned the gratitude of various groups of workers in Belfast later in life for his interventions in industrial disputes.

The attitudes of Cooke and his biographer are not simple. Porter is transparently proud of the Volunteer episode, and scathing about the incompetence, corruption and injustice of the government of Ireland that the United Irishmen were seeking to remedy. On the other hand he repeatedly uses the French connection as evidence of the United Irishmen's nefarious purposes, and plays down the Presbyterian involvement: 'the prime movers' were Episcopalians, he claims, while the 'great mass' were Roman Catholics, though he does allow 'a few were Presbyterians'. One, the minister who baptized Cooke, had to flee to America.

Mrs Macook imparted her Scottish Calvinism in a way that even her son admitted could be 'cold and formal'. She used the Shorter Catechism, the Confession of Faith, and, like a good fundamentalist, 'the Bible was her final and sole standard of appeal. "She taught me that man is naturally corrupt; that Divine grace alone can quicken and renew; that the Spirit of God . . . is the only source of right principles and pure practical morality. . . . She charged me . . . to judge for myself."'

Thus equipped, Henry walked to Glasgow, like a lad o'pairts, to continue his education and train for the ministry. He was probably fourteen years old. At the time it was usual for Presbyterians to finish their education in Scotland. Groups of youngsters would gather in Ulster and make their way to the ferries: Cooke walked the sixty miles to Donaghadee. Such young men as he were a familiar sight on the road from Port Patrick to Glasgow, and along the route could call on local hospitality.

Most students qualified for an MA in four years, but Cooke does not seem to have been a happy undergraduate. Porter claims it was illness brought on by the move from country to city that prevented him from taking his degree, but then tells how much time Henry spent on walking tours around the Clyde. He also blames the dull lectures, but Cooke admitted that the fault was largely his own. Elocution was the only subject he studied thoroughly, and 'his provincial accent was almost entirely corrected'. According to John Hewitt, the Scottish universities at this time frowned on Scots and, presumably, Scots-Irish dialects.

Cooke managed to complete two divinity sessions and pass the Ballymena Presbytery's examinations for a licence to preach the gospel. Soon afterwards, in November 1808, he was ordained. But his first post, at Duneane (then Denain), near Randalstown, was inauspicious. He resigned within two years because, Porter claims, his 'fervent zeal' was not appreciated by the apathetic minister and congregation, who mistook his zealotry for 'Methodism'. Besides, he was expected to subsist on twenty-five pounds a year. He became a tutor for a few months in the family of a Farmer Brown near Kells. One Sunday, during the usual long communion service in Connor, Cooke was called in when the minister became ill. The flock was 'astonished and delighted' by his eloquence. It is the sort of story that is normally told about operatic tenors.

In January 1811 Cooke became minister of Donegore, near Templepatrick. Porter calls this the 'holy ground' of Ulster Presbyterianism, planted by the first Scots. It had more than five hundred families, and Porter presents it at first as an exciting step up the ladder, being full of intelligent and affluent people. When he feels the need to explain Cooke's reasons for leaving, he says it was infested with Arian heretics, and that the orthodox Cooke was completely isolated. The previous minister was not orthodox, yet when the congregation looked for a successor, they rejected the liberal Henry Montgomery in favour of Cooke. The two were contemporaries, and rivals throughout their lives. They had been at Glasgow together and they were to divide Presbyterianism between them.

At this time the Presbyterian Church was split in several ways. The austere Calvinism of the traditionalists, expressed in the Westminster Confession of Faith, was the official belief of the Synod. But an important number of Synod members felt that subscription to the Westminster Confession should not be compulsory on ordination: these were the followers of New Light, latitudinarians who often were liberal and even radical in their politics. Crucial divisive issues were the doctrine of the Trinity, and the belief in salvation by grace alone, which Old Light thought essential. As early as 1726 the Non-subscribing Presbytery of Antrim had separated from the Synod, though many holding similar views remained. At the other extreme, many conservatives had joined the secession movement which, like the Reformed Presbyterians or Covenanters, had come over from Scotland in the eighteenth century. Enthusiasts had also been wooed by Methodism (by 1800, nine years after Wesley's death, there were 20,000 Methodists in Ireland), and by the evangelical movement.

Many of the Volunteers and United Irishmen were followers of New Light which, like Ulster radicalism itself, was strongest in Belfast; the rural areas were more conservative. Holmes allows that New Light became less attractive when the idealism of 1798 was dashed, but he also argues that the changes of the industrial and agricultural revolutions demanded new spiritual forms which the cool rationalism of the eighteenth century could not supply.

Henry Cooke sounded like an evangelical but he did not, apparently, yet think like one. He quickly gained a reputation as an emotive speaker in country towns around the north, but his first sermon in Belfast in 1814, which was published, showed no trace of evangelical ideas.

Confronted with a congregation split between Old and New Light, he set about improving his education and studying the doctrines of his church. His congregation allowed him to spend two successive winters studying in Glasgow. In 1817–18 he studied medicine in Dublin, then the centre of the evangelical movement in Ireland. Perhaps his evangelical tendencies were encouraged. Soon after his return from Dublin he resigned from Donegore and 'answered a call' to Killyleagh. Since it was God who had called him, his flock could hardly complain that it had been abandoned. His successor in Donegore found that Cooke had not kept the register of births and marriages up to date.

Cooke's interventions in Synod became more and more significant and as he preached around the country he became the best-known speaker in Ulster. It was an era of orators: Daniel O'Connell was to make the state tremble by enchanting tens of thousands of people with the sound of his voice. From the start of his rise Cooke began to get involved in issues central to the development of Belfast. The way in which he conducted himself had important consequences too.

From his earliest sermons he blurred the distinction between the religious and the political, a tendency which has not diminished amongst political preachers. In Donegore he characterized 'National Infidelity' as female, and implicitly identified the temporal and eternal powers:

> she proclaims rebellion against heaven's King; she thinks it possible to dethrone the Omnipotent. It was only a few years ago religion fell in France before the infidel

phalanx, led by a Volney and a Voltaire. In our own country a Hobbes, a Hume, and a Paine, with a host of others, organized a crusade against the Cross.

Despite the adherence of some ministers of the church, God had preserved Britain:

white-robed peace has continued to scatter olives over our country. Justice lifts aloft her impartial balance. Plenty sheds abundance around. Commerce spreads abroad her wing, and is fanned by the breeze of prosperity. Toleration bids every man worship God as conscience dictates; while the smile of freedom brightens every British home. Let us then turn with grateful hearts to that God who has so signally blessed us.

It may be easier to forgive the floral elaborations of such a passage than the blatant misrepresentations. As Holmes comments, the Test Act and the Corporation Act were in force under 'impartial' Britain until 1828, and few Catholics would have recognized the rhapsodic picture of a country where conscience was free. It is also amusing to hear Cooke condemn the overthrow of Catholicism in France: he was not often so solicitous in later years.

Cooke earned his living and his influence by the force of his voice. Even his lifelong enemies acknowledged his power. He would write out his sermons and then memorize them. Perhaps this allowed him to address the audience without the appearance of consulting notes, as the autocue does for Mrs Thatcher. His manuscripts were much revised, and sometimes he would rewrite sermons completely. Many speeches, particularly those on controversial issues at Synod, were published in pamphlet form, and sold in thousands. Some must have been given extempore: several exist in differing versions, as if reconstructed by journalists, or revised by the speaker for publication.

Cooke courted Ellen Mann for seven years. A letter to her written in 1813 displays the 'spirit of deep piety' that would not be out of place in the pulpit. On this occasion Cooke was writing to his girlfriend about the death of her younger brother:

It is, I believe, generally supposed that the Bible condemns grief for the death of friends. It does not. Neither do I condemn it; nay, I approve of it. The Bible shows us Rachel weeping for her children, and refusing to be comforted, etc. . . . But, my dear Ellen, do not think that all sorrowing is to be approved. Far from it. We may sin in our grief. How? Whenever we murmur against God. Let every one carefully avoid that danger.

And so on. Evidently Ellen appreciated being spoken to like a church full of people, for they married and lived happily. On his incessant speaking tours and, later, lobbying trips to London, he would write to her tenderly and regularly.

But it is the public, lapidescent man who is of most interest. His war against the Belfast Academical Institution has been fixed in stone, and he was as unrelenting in the struggle as in anything. In 1814 William Drennan declared at the school's opening ceremony that it would provide a setting in which 'pupils of all religious denominations should communicate . . . in the common business of education, by which means a new turn might be given to the national character and habits'. Accordingly the different churches were invited to appoint their own professors of divinity.

This was not universally welcomed. The Presbyterians wanted to have a place to educate their clergy nearer to home than Glasgow, especially since a university education had become compulsory for ordinands in 1804. It was likely that they would form the bulk of the students. Reverend William Bruce, the head of Belfast Academy, wanted to do the job himself. He enlisted the help of Lord Castlereagh, a Presbyterian, who had been Irish Chief Secretary when the Act of Union was passed in 1800. Drennan would not have been surprised to find the aristocrat Castlereagh determined to stamp out the 'democratic party in the synod' and the democrats seeking to educate its future members.

Castlereagh sought to buy the loyalty of Presbyterian ministers through a greatly increased *regium donum*, the government grant paid to clergymen. However, rather than pay a lump sum to the Synod, as before, the money was paid to individual ministers who, to qualify, had to swear an oath of loyalty to the Crown. As for the Institution, it had begun to receive a government grant of £1,500 a year in 1815. This was later withdrawn. One pretext was an incident during a St Patrick's Eve dinner when, it was claimed, disloyal toasts were drunk by staff and founders. Apparently the Belfast liking for toasts had survived Wolfe Tone.

Castlereagh made his attitude clear to Peel, the Irish Chief Secretary, in November 1816. He argued that 'the Protestant body is the sheet anchor and Bulwark of the British connection in this Country', and that the Presbyterians made up half the Protestants. This showed 'the incalculable importance of not suffering Dr Drennan and his associates to have the power of granting or withholding certificates of qualification for the ministry in that church'. Threats were made to both Synod and college, but they resisted, and in 1817 the first Presbyterian Professor of Divinity was appointed. Cooke approved, encouraged no doubt by the fact that the new professor was an evangelical.

In 1821 the Institution, keen to placate its enemies, appointed William Bruce junior, son of the Head of Belfast Academy, as Professor of Hebrew and Greek. Unfortunately Bruce junior, though conservative in politics, was liberal in theology, while the defeated candidate was an orthodox seceder. At the annual Synod in 1822 Cooke launched a fierce attack on 'Arian ministers and professors in Belfast'.

Arianism was a challenge to the doctrine of the Trinity. In the fourth century Arius held that God was a single entity and that Jesus, being God's son, could not be coterminous with God, but was God's unique agent. These New Light views were shared by many of the ablest members of Synod, and were part of a more rational, tolerant philosphy which believed, as Porter put it, in 'freedom of thought and Christian forbearance'. Porter's, and Cooke's objection to this seemingly unobjectionable idea was that 'it was negative rather than dogmatic'. In other words, it was opposed to the emotional, aggressive and ultimately irrational evangelicalism Cooke increasingly adopted and which has characterized so many of the churches, halls and meeting houses that have infested Belfast ever since.

The Synod investigated the Institution and accepted in 1823 that Arian views were not being taught. Some professors promised not to teach Arianism. This was not good enough for Cooke, who objected that the Arians were preaching their views on Sundays. But there was general goodwill towards Inst and little enthusiasm for Cooke's campaign or for his enthusiasm. 'I seem this day to stand alone,' he said in Synod, but claimed that most lay Presbyterians were on his side.

Nevertheless, he had to work hard to cause a breach. He went on tour with his philippics against the Academical Institution, but he made little progress until 1824, when he was Moderator. He persuaded Synod to put forward its own candidates for chairs at Inst: the college, needing support for the payment of its grant, accepted. A pamphlet by Dr William Bruce senior was censured for Socinianism – expressing the idea that Christ was not divine. But Cooke suffered a setback when a committee failed to insist on subscription to the Westminster Confession of Faith: it offered presbyteries the alternative of 'such examination as they consider best adapted' to the purpose of ascertaining the soundness of candidates' faith. Many orthodox Old Light members were opposed to an inquisition.

In 1825 Cooke made two visits to London to give evidence, as Moderator, to parliamentary committees on Irish affairs. The publication in the Belfast newspapers of parts of his evidence, on emancipation, Inst and Arianism, brought an outcry. He took pains to explain the subtleties of his position: he had said that while he personally favoured limited concessions to Catholics (reserving the highest offices of state for Protestants), most ordinary Presbyterians were entirely against emancipation.

> I glory in the accusation [of being 'illiberal']. I was born the subject of a Protestant Government, the original liberty of which my Presbyterian forefathers chiefly contributed to establish and maintain. . . . . Yet I wish to extend its every blessing to all within the pale of its power, so far as I could be persuaded that the extension was consistent with the integrity and permanence of its structure.

In a letter to his wife, Cooke said they must agree to differ about emancipation: she was opposed. The Synod had voted in favour of Catholic emancipation in

1813, and his claim that most Presbyterians opposed it was potentially embarrassing. In the same way, he had repeated his accusations against the Belfast Academical Institution and against Arians, whom he explicitly linked to the United Irishmen: again his remarks diverged from recent Synod decisions, and they were attacked even by orthodox members of staff at the college, who accused him variously of lying, intemperate speech, mischief-making and trying to stir up 'popular prejudice'. He also gave evidence on sectariansim. He was opposed to Orange marches, but felt that Protestants were suffering from Roman Catholic aggression, as fomented by bodies like the Catholic Association.

The Synod of 1825 was expected to give a verdict on Cooke's conduct as Moderator and on the controversies he had aroused. It took place in Coleraine and the meeting house was crowded. At one point the gallery seemed about to collapse. Cooke's opponents claimed that many present were politically partisan, Orangemen drafted in to support Cooke. He seemed to be of the same opinion, for when he defended his evidence to Parliament he literally played to the gallery:

> I have been loaded with obloquy. I have been charged with publicly degrading the high office to which you elected me. I have been threatened with the censure of the Synod. Yet I stand before you, fearless, for I am conscious of rendering back my office clean and unsullied; and I know I can rely on the impartiality, the wisdom, and the justice of my fathers and brethren. I now stand in my native county; I stand in the Church in which I first preached the gospel; I stand in the midst of those reverend presbyters who first received me into the ministry; I stand in the presence of that august Synod which lately honoured me with the highest office in its gift; and here I this day fearlessly and scornfully repudiate the foul imputation cast upon me by the seven thousand Catholics of Dublin. I appeal to you, fathers and brethren, with whose censure I have been threatened, whether that evidence was 'false and unfounded'. I appeal to all around me – aye, even to those galleries, crowded with the free men of my native county, to whom I was told I dare not look lest a burst of indignation would overwhelm me – to you, to all I confidently appeal for a unanimous and cordial verdict of acquittal.

In response, says his biographer, came 'A burst of enthusiastic applause'. Holmes records that Cooke was immediately ruled out of order for appealing to the gallery, but he carried the day. A series of measures sought to restrict the independence of the Belfast Academical Institution, requiring, in effect, only orthodox candidates approved by a Synod committee to be considered for posts.

Cooke later wrote a letter to Sir Robert Peel, the Home Secretary, in which he said that the connection between the Church and Inst could either be dissolved, or continued with Inst under the control of the Ulster Synod. He asked what Peel wanted, and offered his services in future negotiations, which, 'so far as I have any influence would be managed according to your wishes.' Peel, though he was anxious to ensure the loyalty of Presbyterians and saw the Belfast liberals as a threat, in reply confined himself to general expressions of goodwill. If it had been made public at the time, th letter could have been personally disastrous. Holmes is scrupulously fair in pointing out that Cooke was trying to enlist government support.

On his first visit to London, Cooke had written to his wife that 'the Earl of Roden and Colonel Forde are at Cheltenham, so the poor parson of Killyleagh is here without any of his natural protectors'. Even the fair-minded Holmes baulks a little. Cooke's taste for hobnobbing, as Moderator, with the aristocrats of the ascendancy would have surprised many Presbyterians. Not a few of them retained Drennan's views on the aristocracy. Cooke never represented the views of all Presbyterians, nor even of all significant groups of Presbyterians, but Peel must nevertheless have been delighted to receive Cooke's offer to act as the Government's cat's paw against the Presbyterian wets.

Cooke was unable to build on his success, for Inst was determined to preserve its independence and non-sectarian character. It refused to accept the new restrictions on the grounds that the Moderator already had a vote in choosing professors, and Synod had its own Professor of Divinity. The education commission reported, despite Cooke's evidence, that Inst was not turning out theological students steeped in Arianism. The Belfast newspapers decided to stop printing letters about the controversy to give their readers a rest.

Cooke's star had already waned by the time of the 1826 Synod, which endorsed a compromise. His arch rival, Henry Montgomery, proposed that ministers should in future be prevented from taking chairs at Inst, thus removing one of Cooke's major objections. Cooke complained that he had been 'deserted' by his friends, and Holmes points out that 1826 marked a revulsion, even among the orthodox, against the *odium theologicum* Cooke provoked. Porter claims that the orthodox wanted peace at any price and that outside Synod Cooke was 'the most popular man in Ulster'. The *Northern Whig*, which rarely lost an opportunity to attack the modern Athanasius, crowed: 'It is impossible that the bigot can long continue to lord it over God's heritage.'

Following this reverse Cooke fell ill and went to Dublin for treatment. In the familiar evangelical way, his worldly fortunes were linked to the state of his soul. In the centre of Irish evangelicalism again, Cooke met the Swiss pastor Cesar Malan, himself a battler against Socinianism in Geneva. Cooke's letters home suggest he went through a spiritual renewal: he said the Lord had 'saved my soul from doubt, darkness, fear, and the power of sin. I am my Saviour's now. I shall be with Him through eternity . . . . if you really believe that Jesus is the Christ, then you are "born of God".'

He convalesced in the stately homes of Lord Mountcashel and the Earl of Roden. Besides being aristocrats, both were evangelicals. Cooke might have been in heaven already: 'Lord and Lady Mount-Cashell are in the highest degree kind and amiable. . . . Tell Rowan how I enjoy this society. We have ease without familiarity; we have elegance without forgetting our Saviour.' This renewed his fervour for an assault on the north: 'Oh! how I long for the honour of bringing souls to the Lord. I never rightly or fully knew the Lord before. I had heard of Him with the hearing of the ear, but now mine eye seeth Him. . . .'

The ecstatic letters suggest the experience of rebirth, the absolutist and deeply emotional change that so many preachers in Belfast today – in shopping precincts and meeting halls – insist on as the only authentic means of knowing God and controlling one's life. It allows for little subtlety or latitude, and no doubt that one might be in possession of all the truth. It may be surprising but it is not unusual that a lifelong believer such as this ex-Moderator should feel in need of conversion. No one sees the Indian rope trick without being told it is going to happen.

Holmes notes the tension between this personal assurance of salvation and the Presbyterian belief in predestination and divine sovereignty, and that such apparent contradictions never troubled Cooke. Although he was inflexible when it came to the triple godhead, he often said that minor doctrinal differences did not disturb him – particularly when he was seeking to emphasize the shared interests of his Church and the Church of Ireland. He was a member of the committee which, in the wake of the 1859 Revival, decided that the traditional Presbyterian beliefs were compatible with the sort of ecstatic possession and 'personal assurance' that became epidemic in Ulster.

The Arians began to declare themselves more openly. Henry Montgomery and the Clerk of Synod, William Porter, both acknowledged their views in their evidence to the Education Commissioners. The Clerk claimed Arianism was growing among the 'thinking few' in Synod, and was reported in the English Unitarian magazine, the *Christian Moderator* (of which his son was 'acknowledged editor', Cooke said), as saying that 'in Presbyterian Ireland orthodoxy and intellect do not flourish simultaneously'. William Bruce's 'heretical' pamphlet *Study of the Bible and the Doctrines of Christianity* was reissued in 1826.

A rage for separation seems to be associated with the evangelical experience. Phobic revulsion from what is thought impure – often most extreme when it focuses on what is closest – is an abiding factor in Ulster theology. Ed Moloney and Andy Pollak, in their book *Paisley*, identify this urge in the Free Presbyterian Church.

Cooke went to the Synod of 1827 determined on a showdown. The Synod took place in Strabane where, it was said, 'No surrender' and 'Down with the Arians' were interchangeable slogans. William Porter, the Clerk of Synod, was an advocate of Catholic emancipation and the only Arian minister west of the Bann: he was the target of the first attack, a motion calling for his dismissal. Cooke's biographer relishes the dramatic atmosphere of these occasions, and describes the excitement of listening to great orators as they do verbal battle in the midst of their passionately involved peers. The hall was crowded and the struggle lasted from Thursday to Saturday. Cooke called for what he had gone to Strabane to achieve, a split in the Synod and separation from the Arians.

Many of the orthodox were reluctant to follow Cooke's lead and had no wish to penalize their Clerk. An amendment was carried which merely expressed regret that he had called himself an Arian. Cooke then insisted that there should be a compulsory declaration of belief in the Trinity. This would have had the effect of exposing and isolating the Arians. To Henry Montgomery's amusement, the orthodox members then got bogged down in trying to define what they meant by 'Trinity'. In the end, they adopted the formula Cooke proposed, the definition in the Westminster Shorter Catechism.

Having decided what they ought to believe, they debated Cooke's motion on the compulsory declaration. Henry Montgomery spoke for an hour, and Cooke's son-in-law admits that he 'electrified the assembly'. He argued that such 'man-made creeds' were an interference in the right of private judgement and would lead to persecution of fellow ministers. The speech was later published and sold 30,000 copies.

Cooke concluded the debate. The extracts from his speech chosen by his biographer elide rather strangely, given the setting, the political and the religious. To Montgomery's charge that the declaration would be an infringement of liberty, Cooke replied, 'Opposed to liberty! it is a calumny. We are the determined friends of the British Constitution. We were so in days past, when some of those who now oppose us set up the standard of rebellion.' It is not recorded whether 'Down with the Arians!' or 'No surrender!' greeted these remarks. To Montgomery's appeal for tolerance and peace in the Church, Cooke replied: 'Peace! peace! without purity of faith, which is its fundamental principle . . . There can be no peace apart from purity and truth.'

The motion was carried and a crack in the Synod appeared, but many still refused to go to the extremes Cooke wanted. He resigned from a committee on the Home Mission, for example, when Arians were not barred from becoming members. Even the leading Scots evangelical, Thomas Chalmers, deplored 'the strife and vainglory' which had given orthodoxy 'so revolting an aspect': although he personally admired Cooke, Chalmers felt the Arians should not be forced out of the Synod. Further strife was caused by the New Reformation societies evangelicals were setting up for the purpose of converting Catholics. In April 1828 liberals tried to disrupt a meeting to form a Belfast branch.

Cooke published his aims in the forthcoming Synod of 1828 and called like-minded members to a meeting to plan their tactics. When the Synod began the excitement and expectation were just as intense in the Cookstown meeting house as they had been in Strabane. On Thursday those who had not been present at the Synod of 1827 were required to announce whether they accepted the doctrine of the Trinity. Of 117 ministers and elders, ninety-seven answered 'believe'.

The 'great debate' began the next day. Cooke did not allow the moderate orthodox proposal to go through unchallenged, and proposed that each candidate for the ministry must undergo an examination by a committee of Synod into his 'personal religion', his knowledge of Scripture, and 'especially' his views on a series of doctrines which divided the Arians from the orthodox. Once again Henry Montgomery gave a powerful speech, this one lasting two hours, in which he argued that matters on which there was a difference of opinion could not be regarded as fundamental, that it was wrong to change the rules under which ministers had already been admitted, and that the rights of congregations to choose their own ministers would be compromised by having to submit to the committee. Once again Montgomery was defeated, and a committee of 'emphatically orthodox' men was appointed.

Pamphlets were published, attacks appeared in the Belfast papers and public meetings were called. At one meeting in Belfast Montgomery attacked the 'system of inquisitorial espionage on the affairs of their brethren' which his opponents had set up, and accused Cooke, who was present, of sabbath-breaking: when George IV had visited Ireland in 1821, Cooke had rushed 'on the sabbath to bow the knee to an earthly monarch'. Cooke replied by accusing Montgomery of sabbath-breaking. Even Montgomery's supporters found the debate unedifying. After Cooke's withdrawal, a Remonstrance was adopted which rebuked the Synod for subverting principles such as 'sufficiency of scripture in matters of faith and duty' and 'the right of private judgement'.

In the wider world tension was rising over political developments. The Catholic Relief Bill had been defeated in the House of Lords in May 1828, Daniel O'Connell had won the parliamentary election for Clare but, as a Catholic, was unable to take his seat, and in September of that year thousands of members of the Catholic Association staged a 'peaceful invasion' of Ulster under the leadership of Radical Jack Lawless, which threatened to provoke civil war. The Orange Order had been dissolved in 1825 under the Unlawful Societies Act, and was beginning to be replaced by the Brunswick Clubs: many evangelicals became members but Cooke, unlike modern Unionist churchmen, never joined the Orange Order or its substitutes.

The 1829 Synod was largely taken up with the old problem of the Belfast Academical Institution. When restoring the £1,500 grant, the Irish Chief Secretary had offered the Presbyterian Synod a veto on the appointment of chairs, but the college had rejected this, and the Synod had agreed that the existing arrangement was acceptable. Even Cooke had to bow to the general support for the college. However, the college had rejected the Synod's candidate for the chair of Moral Philosophy in favour of Reverend John Ferrie, a former chaplain at Glasgow University. This was the first appointment in which the new committee was involved. Cooke accused Ferrie of being an Arian 'or something worse'.

Montgomery made the last of his great speeches in the Synod, in which he accused Cooke of inconsistency: when it had suited him, Cooke had praised Glasgow University, but now he found it expedient to deny its orthodoxy. Further, he had had ample opportunity to express any doubts about Ferrie before his election, but had said nothing. It was a personal attack, on Cooke's style as well as on his integrity. Montgomery had noticed that Cooke had been smiling as he was impugning Inst's representatives:

> I have heard of the vampire which fans its victim while it is sucking its blood, and such was the character of that smile. After the smile we had a laugh, but it was a laugh that foreran the dagger. I have, in common with other members of this house, been guilty of having been at the theatre; and I recollect having once witnessed Kemble's personation of Zanga in the tragedy of 'The Revenge', and of having been struck with the expression of his countenance when, in the triumph of his feelings, he sets his feet on his fallen enemy. Such was the triumphant look with which Mr. Cooke seemed to regard the Institution when he fancied it had fallen and he was trampling it under his feet. But then we are told that this arises from a love of truth, and a regard for the interests of the Redeemer. This would be tolerable if men's conduct did not betray their motives.

Montgomery ended by warning that the Remonstrants, weary of the struggle, would withdraw from the Synod if their Remonstrance was ignored. Cooke's biographer differs slightly from Holmes's wording: 'If we cannot live together in peace, in the name of God, let us part in peace.' His speech lasted two and a half hours.

Holmes describes Cooke's speech in reply as a superbly self-confident and psychologically acute performance, which instinctively played on the psychology of his audience. Cooke alternated humour and passion, defusing the spell Montgomery had created and making his own serious points more effective thereby:

> I have got a new lesson in natural history. Mr. Montgomery, from the fertility of his own imagination – from the dark chambers of his own dark heart, has drawn such a graphic picture of the vampire, and, by the waving and quivering of his outstretched arms, has given such a thrilling representation of the monster at its work of death, that I could not suppress the thought, the horrid conviction, as I gazed on that consummate actor, and was fanned by the motion of his hands – we have the living vampire before us. . . . But I pass from these personalities.

Cooke was quite an actor himself though:

> I now stand before you, sir – before the bar of this house – charged with the foul crime of perjury. Oh! may it never be the fate, sir – may it never be the fate of a

single individual in this vast assembly to lie for one moment under the stigma of so base, so terrible a charge! You will pardon, sir, the exhibition of feeling which I cannot suppress. You will sympathise with a man who stands charged with the crime of deliberate perjury. You will bear with him as he assails the foul impeachment – as he dashes to atoms the vile accusation – as he smites and shivers the atrocious calumny with the talisman of truth.

'Tears,' says Porter, 'burst from almost every eye.'

Commentators have noticed that, even at his most vehement, Ian Paisley seems to be enjoying himself enormously. Whatever one thinks of his opinions and actions, the demagogue can charm, or at least fascinate, a wide range of people: one can be attracted in some basic way by those who love words and can use them entertainingly, or extravagantly, by those who have a simple, apparently clear message emphatically put, and who are having fun performing for us. The ministers and elders in Cooke's day were connoisseurs of oratory, and they had plenty to relish. J.L. Porter frequently notes how even those who were being attacked would stand up and applaud speeches against them. The extract quoted above, composed to the classical rules of rhetoric, has a musical force, even though its content is nugatory.

Cooke ignored the question of Ferrie's real beliefs and answered Montgomery's accusations of inconsistency by an appeal for approval of his own integrity. Much of Cooke's speech must have been spoken off the cuff: he had only the lunch adjournment between Montgomery's speech and his own in which to prepare himself.

For all the éclat which greeted Cooke's speech (some listeners took off their shoes and banged them together) the debate ended when Montgomery accepted that 'It is too bad to give licence to two individuals to assail each other.' The evidence Cooke was able to muster for Ferrie's heterodoxy was unconvincing. As the committee knew, Ferrie had subscribed to the Westminster Confession of Faith, and had offered to do so again. And few shared Cooke's antipathy to Inst. A debate on the Remonstrance was postponed until a special meeting in August. The Remonstrants did not attend, but merely presented the Remonstrance itself and, once it was rejected, seceded from the Synod.

The departure was not peaceful. Demeaning squabbles over church property and the allocation of the *regium donum* began, and went on year after year, sometimes breaking into riots. One occurred in Ballycarry when Cooke attempted to join an orthodox party in occupying the meeting house of William Glendy. Glendy called the Synod a 'synagogue of Satan' and said it had 'the duplicity of Jesuits, the malignity of demons and the ferocity of bloodhounds'. Cooke rolled up in the new phaeton which had recently been presented to him, but was prevented from entering. He tried to hold an open-air meeting but stones were thrown and he fled to the nearest pub. He was burned in effigy outside and when he tried to escape, burning straw was tossed under the feet of his horses. Cooke's policy of encouraging even the tiniest minority in an overwhelmingly Remonstrant body to regard itself as the 'original and endowed congregation' did little to calm tempers.

In January 1830 the Bangor Presbytery refused to allow the Greyabbey congregation to withdraw from Synod. Cooke called in someone whose name was redolent of the pioneering days of Scottish settlement, the landlord William Montgomery of Rosemount. As magistrate, William Montgomery took possession of the meeting house, and arrested a Remonstrant minister who tried to break in. But then Henry Montgomery intervened and, as the magistrate admitted, 'completely opened my eyes to the deceits that have been practised on me'. He allowed the Remonstrants to have the meeting house, and charges of riot were dismissed.

In November 1829 Cooke answered the call to a newly built church in May Street, in the centre of Belfast. Designed by W. Smith in the Palladian style, it remains one of the city's finest buildings. It shares Rosemary Street's classical taste, but is grander and less homely, reflecting the growing fortunes of the town and the eminence of the first incumbent. C.E.B. Brett maintains that when the Presbyterians followed fashion later in the nineteenth century and started building in the Gothic style, the results were mediocre: the followers of Knox and Calvin took no delight in decoration.

When Cooke conducted the opening ceremony for the May Street church, and although admission was by ticket, many of 'the leading nobility and gentry of Down and Antrim', including the Marquis of Donegall, were unable to get near the door. (The Marquis was an admirer of Cooke: later, when the divine was ill, Donegall visited him every day. No doubt the admiration was mutual.) This was the appropriate setting for the triumphant Cooke, and soon his Sunday sermons were attracting audiences from miles outside Belfast. For eighteen years, we are told, he conducted three services every Sunday: often each sermon or lecture lasted more than an hour.

The Remonstrant Synod first met in May 1830 and declared its intention 'to lay the foundation stones of a temple dedicated to religous liberty . . . under whose ample dome every individual who chooses to enter, will be allowed to worship, in his own way, the one God and Father of all'. Some of Henry Montgomery's other activities, though, seem more opportunistic. Following the collapse of Wellington's Tory government, Montgomery celebrated the new Whig administration at a Reform meeting in Belfast at which he called for a system of ballot voting to reduce the power of landlords. The Belfast Reform Society arose from this. The day after O'Connell was arrested, Montgomery led a deputation of Remonstrants to the Lord Lieutenant, to whom he pledged their 'adherence' to the Union. This disgusted the repealers who supported O'Connell, but persuaded the Lord Lieutenant to recognize the Remonstrants' right to *regium donum.* At the same time the Belfast Academical Institution was protected from orthodox interference in its annual grant.

Cooke was soon embroiled in another war over education. In September 1831 the Irish Chief Secretary announced a new system for the 'combined literary and religious education' of 'the peasantry'. These National Schools sought to provide an integrated education system. Cooke attacked the proposal even before the details were published, saying that Protestants and Catholics would find it impossible to co-operate in schooling (an observation which integrationists are still trying to disprove). A special meeting of Synod was held in January 1832 to debate the new system, but only a third of the ministers eligible turned up. It decided that the Bible should be taught 'without comment' during normal school hours, which was unacceptable to the Catholic Church.

The growing self-confidence of O'Connell and his followers, and the reformist attitudes of the Whigs, caused alarm amongst more conservative Protestants. The Earl of Roden, Cooke's evangelical ally, told one of a large number of excited public meetings in 1831 that 'there never was a period in which the protestant institutions of this country were placed in such imminent peril'. Holmes suggests that the Tory landlords were grateful for the spectre of concessions to popery in their campaign against a government opposed to tithes and contemplating disestablishment. Cooke's own language at this time was inflammatory. His opinion of the education plan was that, 'If you were to encourage murder, it would be nothing to this.'

We may be reminded of the Democratic Unionist Peter Robinson speaking to a rally outside Belfast City Hall at the start of the campaign against the Anglo-Irish Agreement. Mrs Thatcher, he alleged, was 'murdering democracy'. No doubt Cooke, Robinson, Paisley and others like them would deplore physical violence. Yet such words are violent and, in an environment of violence, risk inflaming the passions of those who share their outrage. Whatever his intention, whatever careful distinctions he drew in his condemnations of the belief but not the believers, Cooke's legacy is a style of debate that exaggerates and dramatizes, that sharpens division, that stokes the passions and denies the possibility of accommodation.

When cholera came to Belfast, Cooke announced that it was divine judgement. From March to November 1832 there were 2,381 reported cases, and 417 people died, but it is unlikely that they were all Arians and O'Connellites. On the other hand, Cooke served on the Belfast Board of Health and made visits to the sick during which his medical training was no doubt valuable.

In the election of that year, the first after the Reform Act, Cooke openly supported the Tories Lord Arthur Chichester and Emerson Tennent, who were returned as MPs for Belfast. The reform candidates were accused during the campaign of Unitarianism and of being opposed to the reading of the Bible in school. Nearly all the 350 Catholics eligible voted for the reformers; all their

Protestant support came from New Light Presbyterians. Cooke made himself clear: 'Whilst I reject alike the name of Whig or Tory, I decidedly avow myself a Conservative. But of what am I conservative? . . . I am conservative of the rights of property. I am conservative of abstract and general Protestantism, whatever may be the form of the church in which it is contained.' In other words, he was not a diehard reactionary, but espoused the progressive, or reformist conservative policies of Peel.

At the mass meeting in Hillsborough in 1834 in which he laid out these beliefs, he made clear his wish to cement an alliance with the Established Church. His metaphors were military, and the enemy of the allies was obvious: the Anglicans and the Presbyterians were two columns in 'our noble Protestant army'. He called on the Protestant aristocracy and their tenantry to act together against the urgent threat to Protestantism.

In his campaign against the education proposals, Cooke had the support of 'great numbers of obscure persons of strong political feeling' who packed meetings and intimidated his opponents. Another report spoke of 'a disorderly party of mean-looking persons' which applauded everything he said and insulted those who disagreed with him. Cooke was criticized for his partisanship, and found at the 1834 Synod that many members did not share his antipathy towards the Education Board.

Another unsavoury alliance was with the solicitor John Bates, with whom Cooke transformed the Belfast Society into the partisan Belfast Conservative Society. Historians like Jonathan Bardon have accused Bates of sharp practices and even gerrymandering to ensure that Conservative supporters registered while known Liberals were disqualified on technicalities or by downright trickery. Nevertheless, Bardon says that the Conservative councillors of Belfast at this period were as energetic as all but the most radical group of Liberals in Britain in seeking improvements to their town. Cooke delivered a sermon excoriating electoral corruption, but he did not seem to feel this applied to John Bates.

Just before the Hillsborough demonstration, in October 1834, Cooke had offered to resign from May Street after complaints about his conduct. He was often absent, he had shown no interest in dealing with the large debt the congregation had incurred, and he had failed to have elders elected. He was allowed to remain, however, and in the next year made a trip to London to raise funds for the May Street debt. While there he spoke at Exeter Hall. The meeting was advertised as an exposure of the intolerance of the Catholic Church in Ireland. What he had to reveal was, Holmes says, 'less than sensational', but this did not stop him using violent language:

> I tell you that to have peace so long as the doctrine of war is hugged to the bosom of the Church of Rome is utterly impossible. We will have peace with the men, but with the principle I do proclaim an unchanging war.

This meeting came at a time when there was an upsurge of racist abuse of the Irish in Britain, provoked by the Whigs' alliance with the O'Connellites. Cooke's behaviour was ill-timed for the purpose of establishing 'peace with the men', but he increasingly believed that 'zeal against popery' was a sign of health in Protestantism, and it became 'one of the chief aims of his life'.

The influence of the Arians on Presbyterianism as a whole diminished, while the orthodox consolidated: the General and Secession synods combined in 1840 to form the General Assembly. In 1845, when Peel's government agreed to create what we would recognize as a modern university in Belfast, it was decided not to build on the Inst site. (Cooke's proposal for a grand campus sweeping down to the Lagan was also rejected.) The government wanted a non-sectarian college, but the Roman Catholic Primate pointed out that putting the university in Belfast would tend to make it sectarian. In 1853 the Presbyterians set up their own institution, the Assembly's College, of which Cooke was president for the last fifteen years of his life.

The National Schools system foundered over the question of Bible study. In 1839, following government attempts to meet Presbyterian objections, the scheme was being attacked by both Cooke and by Archbishop McHale. One saw it as attempting 'to conciliate Roman Catholics' while the other thought it was anti-Catholic. The Church of Ireland set up its Church Education Society in the same year, and by 1841 the government had allowed some schools to teach exclusively in the Presbyterian manner, thus reversing the original purpose of the scheme.

Two of Cooke's greatest victories – so they were billed – were yet to come. One was over Voluntaryism, the movement which held that churches were corrupted by state support and by tithes, that they should be independent of government and rely for their maintenance on the voluntary contributions of their members. William Drennan would have been a Voluntaryist, but so were people from a wide variety of political and theological opinions. Cooke was vehemently opposed, and he insisted on replying to the guest speaker, Dr John Ritchie of Edinburgh, at a public meeting in Belfast in March 1836. The meeting lasted for two nights, and on the first night Cooke, who had come from his sickbed, spoke for five hours, starting at half-past ten. Porter claims that the crowd only went home when Cooke released them from his spell, with dawn light filtering through the windows.

Ritchie's speech had been political, and Cooke was able to respond in similar vein. He attacked the conduct of the Voluntaryists, and was able to defuse their argument that the American churches thrived without state support, by attacking the slavery system. (Cooke was an active abolitionist, and once said that England's greatness lay not in her army or navy, but in William Wilberforce and the outlawing of slavery in the British Empire.) He also indulged in a little anti-American chauvinism.

On the second night, Porter tells us, Ritchie's reply was three hours long, and

Cooke spoke for a further hour. He argued, amongst many other things, that the abuses of an established church did not affect the principle that the state should support religion. He did not answer the idea that logic would dictate that Ireland's established church should be Roman. The meeting did not break up until six o'clock the next morning, when Cooke was carried home in triumph by his supporters, who believed he had inflicted a crushing defeat on Ritchie.

Porter claims that Voluntaryism was at an end because of the debate, but in fact Ritchie continued his campaign. At a Conservative banquet nineteen months later Cooke still thought it worth attacking Voluntaryism, along with O'Connell, the ostensible reason for the meeting. He claimed that if anything were to 'pervert the Presbyterianism of Ulster, the union of the three kingdoms is not worth a twelvemonth's purchase'. Other Presbyterians – in England and Scotland – had degenerated into 'Radicalism', but Ulster adhered to 'the genuine Establishment principles of the Mother Church'. Voluntaryism would lead to 'national Atheism', which would lead to 'a Cromwell, a Robespierre, or a Napoleon'.

Even Porter feels he has to excuse Cooke's unPresbyterian proclivities: the differences which divided the Protestant churches were only 'minor points'. But Porter has to admit that 'there can be no doubt he sometimes spake and acted in a way which gave offence to many of his Presbyterian brethren'.

After being overlooked for the presidency of the new Queen's College in 1845, Cooke was made agent for the *regium donum*. One of his last acts before his death in 1868 was to write to the Lord Lieutenant to ask that the post of agent for *regium donum* should pass on to J.L. Porter, his son-in-law and biographer. This proved unnecessary, as the post was soon to be abolished. The Church of Ireland was disestablished a year after Cooke's death.

The other 'triumph' came in January 1841, when Daniel O'Connell answered an invitation to visit Belfast. There is an element in this of the sectarian boundary-drawing perennial in Northern Ireland: the Orange marchers insist on parading through precisely those areas where they are unwelcome, because they are thereby asserting their ownership of territory. Emancipation and O'Connell's campaign for repeal of the Act of Union were making the Catholics less quiescent, and the proportion of Catholics in Belfast was growing: in the twenty years from 1830 to 1850, the town's population doubled in size to 100,000, and the proportion of Catholics was rising towards one third. There was nervousness about O'Connell's visit, particularly as his remarks about religion were not calculated to placate Protestants: 'The Catholic Church is the national church,' he was reported as saying.

Cooke challenged O'Connell to a public debate but the 'Liberator' gave a flippant response, referring to him as 'bully Cooke, the cock of the north', and later as a 'boxing buffoon of a divine'. Orangemen had organized in the expectation of trouble, but O'Connell abandoned his plans for a triumphal entrance and arrived quietly. A couple of days later he tried to address a crowd from the balcony of the Royal Hotel, but he was shouted down. In the evening rioting began outside the New Music Hall in Upper Arthur Street, where he was attending a charitable soirée. Mobs ran through the town stoning the homes of repealers and laid siege to the *Vindicator*'s offices. If O'Connell hoped to reawaken Belfast's Presbyterian radicalism, he was disappointed, for his initial Reform dinner did not attract Presbyterian support: even he could not help joking that he would be for Repeal in the morning. O'Connell left Belfast quietly, escorted by police to the ferry at Donaghadee.

O'Connell had saved the town the trouble of more rioting, but in the contest of swagger the loyalists felt they had won. The Conservatives were jubilant, and Cooke was their guest of honour at a meeting the next night. A 'munificent sum' of £2,000 was raised for the 'saviour of the country', or rather as provision for his wife and children, since his life had been threatened. A contemporary pamphlet celebrating the repulse of O'Connell contrasted this well-heeled gathering with the repealers and their 'ragged pauperism'. The common insulting epithet for O'Connell was 'the Big Beggarman'.

Cooke's speech refuted O'Connell's contention that Protestants had nothing to fear from Catholics gaining power: he cited 1641, 1688–9 and 1798. At the same time, he called for Catholics and their property to be respected, 'however we may oppose, nay, abhor, some of their doctrines'. It is possible to imagine Reverend Ian Paisley drawing the nice distinction (for whatever good it may do) between abhorring Catholic errors and loving, or at least tolerating, Catholic individuals; indeed, Paisleyites are fond of saying how assiduous their hero is in pursuing the complaints of all his parliamentary constituents, 'Protestant and Catholic'. On the other hand, when Paisley says that the law must be impartial, that innocent men should not be locked up for life, 'even Roman Catholics', we may legitimately ask about the basis of such tolerance. Paisley's patriotism was never as eloquent as Cooke's:

Look at the town of Belfast. When I was a youth it was almost a village. But what a glorious sight does it now present! The masted grove within our harbour – our mighty warehouses teeming with the wealth of every clime – our giant manufactories lifting themselves on every side – our streets marching on, as it were, with such rapidity, that an absence of a few weeks makes us strangers in the outskirts of our town. And all this we owe to the Union. No, not all – for throned above our fair town, and looking serenely from our mountain's brow, I beheld the genii of Protestantism and Liberty, sitting inseparable in their power, while the genius of Industry which nightly reclines at their feet, starts with every morning in renovated might, and puts forth his energies, and showers down his blessings, on the fair and smiling lands of a Chichester, a Conway, and a Hill. Yes, we will guard the Union, as we will guard our liberties, and advance and secure the prosperity of our country.

There are at least three versions of this speech, but they all amount to the same thing, summed up in the concluding remark, 'Look at Belfast, and be a Repealer, if you can.' As Holmes notes, the *Northern Whig* had made the economic argument for the Union a few weeks before Cooke adopted it. It is as if the Belfast Protestants, in their affluence, felt themselves to have little in common with the poor in the rest of Ireland.

In 1841 Cooke was elected Moderator of the General Assembly, and continued his campaign against the Belfast Academical Institution. It was decided that the college's certificate was insufficient and that an Assembly committee should examine ordinands. To students worried about their qualifications, Cooke said his signature would be enough. He was less influential in other spheres. Despite his support of Sir Robert Peel, Cooke found the government unresponsive to his requests for help. For example, he could not persuade it to listen to the Church of Scotland's campaign for non-intrusion and against lay patronage. The Conservatives proved to be keen on conserving property rights. Cooke resisted a call for a special meeting on the issue.

He also asked Peel to help on the marriage question: a recent court case had made Presbyterian marriages illegal when one of the partners was of a different faith. An Act passed in 1842 protected marriages already solemnized, but said nothing about future ones. By the time the marriage problem was finally resolved, a year later, Peel had let down his loyal supporter yet again. The Prime Minister had listened to the lobbyings of both Cooke and Henry Montgomery over the still-live issue of Presbyterian property, and the resulting Dissenters' Chapels Bill came out for the Remonstrants.

In response to the government's conduct over problems such as the marriage question and the Church of Scotland's campaign, at the General Assembly of 1843 a resolution was proposed which recommended 'a more adequate representation of the principles and interests of Presbyterians in the Legislature of the country'. At this time Presbyterians made up about half of Protestant voters, but there was only one Irish Presbyterian MP. Cooke took violent exception to the resolution, and when a toned-down version was adopted he announced that he was leaving the Assembly and would not return until it was rescinded. This took four years.

As Porter admits, Cooke took the resolution personally. He had been used to representing Presbyterian interests himself within the Conservative Party (Porter claims he 'was its virtual head'); 'Dr Cooke was assailed by men who were not old enough to remember his great services.' It is ironic that one of his opponents, A.P. Goudy, was the grandson of James Porter of Greyabbey, who was executed in 1798 as an alleged United Irishman. Cooke had voted with the majority in the Synod in 1813 to reject the accuracy of a report about how James Porter's widow, Goudy's grandmother, had been excluded from the Synod widows' fund. Another opponent was incredulous at Cooke's behaviour: 'Who is this, that is so sensitively alive to any contamination of the church with politics?'

Although he stayed away from the Assembly in a pet for four years, Cooke remained influential. In 1847 the offending resolution was rescinded, narrowly, in a poorly attended debate, and he returned. He was appointed Professor of Sacred Rhetoric and Catechetics at the Faculty of Theology at Queen's College. He then set aside the Church's law, adopted to meet his objections in the Inst case, that a professor must resign his pastoral charge. He offered to forego his *regium donum* and stipend and remain in the May Street pulpit until a successor was found. Despite protests in the Belfast Presbytery and the General Assembly, he got away with it and, though he offered his resignation a year later, no successor was appointed for another twenty years.

He was well able to give up the wages of a minister for, though he was generous and gave freely to charity, his income from the *regium donum* agency, the professorship and his class fees was substantial and was boosted from time to time by 'presentations' from his congregation and his admirers. However, in 1849 he narrowly escaped dismissal from the *regium donum* post when it was revealed that an administrator in Dublin Castle had been embezzling from the fund for three years. Cooke appeared careless in allowing him to do so.

Cooke's involvement in the tenant right controversy showed yet again that his professed liberal tendencies were becoming submerged by the need to protect Protestantism. In 1847 the General Assembly called on the Lord Lieutenant to make legal and universal the Ulster Custom. This was the tradition by which Ulster farmers since the Plantation had had the right to fixity of tenure and the freedom to sell their interest in the farm – two of the three Fs sought in the tenant right campaign: the third F was fair rent. The Ulster Custom did not have the force of law, and the big landlords around Belfast, such as the marquises of Abercorn and Londonderry, and in Parliament Lord Castlereagh, were dismissive of the campaign, and enraged by the phenomenon of Presbyterian ministers and Catholic priests acting as spokesmen for their tenants.

In the Belfast Synod of 1850, Cooke shifted his ground. He was still for tenant right in principle, but against attacks on landlords. No doubt the thought of ministers and priests co-operating in political agitation, with its shades of '98, was alarming. The journalist James McKnight spoke about the campaign in terms that recalled the United Irishmen, if not their aim of separation: 'it may revive in Belfast a portion of that national spirit for which its people were at one time distinguished'. And if we thought that the Paisleyite vision of a global conspiracy between Moscow and the Vatican against Protestant Ulster is novel, Cooke was there first, when he rebuked some Presbyterian ministers for 'perfect communist interpretations' of tenant right.

There was a welling of anti-Catholic sentiment following the insensitive announcement by Cardinal Wiseman of the Vatican's new Hierarchy in England. In December 1850 Cooke held a public meeting in May Street to lambast

Wiseman and Catholicism. Once again the sectarian factor hampered what should have been a purely political movement. Henry Montgomery felt himself able to join Cooke at a dinner in Hillsborough given by the Marquis of Downshire's tenants, in which Cooke eulogized Downshire and Montgomery upheld the ties that bind landlord and tenant. In the 1852 general election Cooke supported Conservative candidates, attacked Presbyterian ministers who were involved in the tenant right campaign, and praised Lord Derby. This 'good, sound Protestant', before his conversion to Conservative ideas, had been responsible for introducing the National system of education.

The aggressive proselytizing that is characteristic of evangelicalism, of whatever denomination, is a constant feature of Belfast, but the 1850s were remarkable for it. Many evangelicals today look back nostalgically to the home missions and open-air preaching of that time. Ian Paisley has written one of several histories of the 1859 Revival, when fervour came to a head in a form of mass hysteria with, as Holmes puts it, men and women 'physically prostrated by a consciousness of sin' with 'an insatiable hunger for preaching and the experience of forgiveness'.

A preacher with a megaphone in Cornmarket or a gang of hymn-singers in Botanic Gardens can be merely irritating. (Why does no one complain about the noise?) But in the 1850s many of these enterprises were directed at Catholics, who often found them offensive. They were a reliable source of trouble, for instance in the summer of 1857. A Reverend Drew, who was fond of Orange songs, preached in Christ Church, between the Catholic Pound and the Protestant Sandy Row. He managed to provoke rioting, involving the hurling of cobblestones, which was only suppressed by military action. In response to the shooting of a young girl, Catholics formed gun clubs in Smithfield. In September, just back from a visit to England and perhaps not fully aware of the situation, Cooke got himself involved in another incident. He encouraged Reverend Hugh Hanna to defy the Parochial Town Mission, which had responded to a call by magistrates to cancel its series of open-air services. Following the inevitable riot, Cooke called on Hanna to wait 'for excited passions to cool and subside'.

Many Presbyterians had reservations about the 'quasi-prelatic' role Cooke adopted in his old age. He was elected Moderator of the General Assembly for a second time in 1862, and he had a habit of acting without the Assembly's knowledge or authority. In 1858 he escaped its censure for appointing army chaplains without informing the Assembly only because the two men who objected happened to die. He continued to attend political meetings, embarrassing though that was for the Church (following one 'Protestant and Conservative' demonstration in Botanic Gardens, for example, there was a riot), and he did so until old age prevented his voice being heard. He installed his son-in-law as Professor of Biblical Criticism in the Presbyterian College. He continued to lecture there himself, long after he should have retired. The favourite sermons he would reproduce at decreasing intervals became so familiar to his students that they were nicknamed 'the twelve apostles'. One student recalled the 'often fantastic and strange' interpretations he would come up with.

He probably was the most popular man in Ulster, or at least, he was very popular and well-loved by one section of the people. He never converted all Presbyterians to either his religious or his political beliefs: in his later years there were some Presbyterian churches where his arrival would cause a substantial section of the congregation to get up and leave. But he did as much as any individual to bring about the configuration of Ulster life that persists today. He encouraged the Orange Order, originally a rural body drawn from members of the Church of Ireland, and at a time when Orange parades were illegal, to take a place at the centre of events, even if he was never a zealous member like Drew. He consolidated the paternalistic nature of Unionist politics, which has always sought to bind the aristocracy and the working class. He promoted Protestantism as a political and sectarian bulwark against nationalism, republicanism and Catholicism. At the same time he emphasized the fissile nature of Ulster religion. He fostered that aggressive evangelicalism which clashes so disastrously and persistently with those from whom it differs, and which makes every aspect of life in a heterogeneous society a struggle.

Like Ian Paisley and most of the other loud scourges of popery in pulpits and on political platforms in Belfast ever since, Cooke would have rejected the description 'bigot': perhaps, in his mind, he genuinely loved Catholics, Arians and repealers. But he was perceived, by commentators who knew him personally, many of whom shared his deepest convictions, as a bigot and a bully, who enjoyed conquering his enemies purely for the sake of victory.

Henry Cooke's statue still looks up Wellington Place. His back is turned on the Royal Belfast Academical Institution which he tried so hard to strangle at birth. Perhaps he should have been turned round when it became 'Royal': no doubt William Drennan turned in his grave.

The monument is known universally as the Black Man, even though it is green, being weathered bronze. The site originally belonged to a statue that was really black, one commemorating the Earl of Belfast. This was Frederick Richard Chichester, a poet. At nineteen he gave the profits from his first musical composition to the relief of the Famine. He supported education for working men, and gave lectures on nineteenth-century poetry, which were published. He died in Naples in 1853, aged twenty-six. His statue was re-erected in the City Hall, where it can still be seen. He was also commemorated by the Chapel of the Resurrection, built in 1870, which was once in the grounds of Belfast Castle but is now separated from it by housing, disused, vandalized, and near a quarry. In *Belfast: an Illustrated Yearbook 1990*, Marcus Patton mentions the uncarved projecting stones that were intended to carry gargoyles, and says it is 'reminiscent of a Gothic film set'.

Coincidentally, its architect, Sir Charles Lanyon, proposed the motion in the town council for a committee to arrange Cooke's public funeral. All the academic, religious, civic and political bodies were represented; there were 154 carriages in the procession from Ormeau Park to Malone Cemetery, where the body was placed in a massive sarcophagus of polished granite resting on a granite pedestal. The Earl of Belfast's celebrity seems to have faded quickly: it seems unlikely that many citizens remember who the Black Man originally was, or why he is now green. Cooke altered his name twice before embarking on his carrer: no doubt he would have been delighted with this final change of name, to be mistaken, posthumously, for an aristocrat.

CHAPTER EIGHT

HARLAND AND THE PIRRIES

Contrary to all reasonable expectation, Belfast developed the largest shipbuilding business in the world, making the world's biggest ships. It provided Britain with the most advanced form of transport at a time when Britain ran an empire on which the sun never set, and ruled the waves between to boot. Belfast ships turned ocean travel into a luxurious and then a sybaritic pastime for millionaire businessmen, and a more tolerable ordeal for poor emigrants. Modern ideas of what a ship looks like and how it is built owe a lot to innovations first made on the Lagan.

This would have surprised an intelligent geographer or industrialist of the early nineteenth century, for there were few natural reasons for modern shipbuilding to flourish in Belfast rather than anywhere else. It is a phenomenon of Japanese proportions: a world-conquering industry sited in a country without any natural resource, to which all raw materials – up to two thirds the value of the finished product – must be imported.

Such would not have been the case in 1582, when Sir John Perrot reported to Whitehall that Belfast was 'the best and most convenient place in Ulster, for the establishment of shipbuilding'. The ships he had in mind were small and wooden, and the forests around the Lough had not yet been cleared. Nevertheless, Sir John Perrot looks rather more perspicacious now than he would have done for 250 years after his observation. Belfast was still a wild and dangerous place – dangerous to Englishmen, being outside the Pale. A few years previously, Holinshed had not thought Belfast sufficiently important to include amongst the seaports of Antrim and Down. By 1610 maps showed it as an unimportant village. By 1663 local merchants owned several ships, some of them built locally. There was a ketch of fifty tons, boats of thirty and forty tons, a barque of twenty-five tons, and eleven small trading vessels called 'gabbards'. Informal groups of ship's carpenters, who earned their living mostly from repairs, would occasionally get together to build a ship. Possibly their first notable ship was the 150-ton *Eagle's Wing*, which was intended to carry Presbyterians to America.

About this time Belfast was a 'layding place' or seat of customs, and no doubt there were problems with the smugglers around Belfast Lough, who used underground hiding places along the coast.

Like people from Easter Island to Brazil, the settlers who built the city completed the work of those they had replaced and cleared the forests. They left themselves with only disincentives towards constructing a great port and shipbuilding centre. The Lagan was unsuitable for boats of any size; it meandered lazily into an indeterminate merger with the sea amid expanses of wetland. That modern shipbuilding established itself is due to human factors: the prescience and persistence of a group of businessmen and public-spirited individuals; the family connections, intelligence and rigour of a group of capitalist adventurers and inventors; the charm and vision of a salesman; and the toughness and back-breaking toil of its workers. The moment of Belfast's ascendancy was entirely an act of will: the very ground on which the shipyard stands is man-made. Like the city as a whole, the industry was created by human hands, and provides the richest metaphor of the founders' idea of the world and of themselves.

In 1729 the Irish Parliament passed an 'Act for the cleansing of the Ports, Harbours and Rivers of the City of Cork, and of the Towns of Gallway, Sligoe, Drogheda and Belfast, and for erecting a Ballast-Office in the said City and each of the said Towns'. Belfast was growing, and its trade depended on its harbour facilities, but this legislation made little difference. In 1763 the Lagan Canal was built as far as Lisburn. Would the town look inward or outward? In 1785 a new Act created the 'Corporation for preserving and improving the Port and Harbour of Belfast'. This was the Ballast Board, of which Sam McTier, William Drennan's brother-in-law, was the first Ballast Master. It had wider powers, which allowed it to build 'ballast wharfs', and 'wet and dry docks for shipping'.

Local merchants invited William Ritchie to come to Belfast to explore the possibility of shipbuilding. He had started a yard in Ayrshire in 1775, working for Scots owners unable to buy from America because of the War of Independence. But work began to fall off in 1790, and he visited Belfast in March the next year in search of better prospects. These days he would have been enticed with an advance factory, a tax holiday and a government low-interest loan. In the late eighteenth century the Ballast Board, besides improvements already carried out – buoys and perches to assist navigation, and the leasing of land for quays – agreed to build a 'graving platform' on which boats could be careened for repair. At the time there were only six ship's carpenters in Belfast, working on a casual basis when jobs happened to turn up. So when William Ritchie returned in July with his brother Hugh, he brought with him ten men as well as tools and materials. He set up at the Old Lime Kiln dock, on the County Antrim side, where Corporation Street now is. The brothers' first ship, *Hibernian*, of 300 tons, was launched a year and four days later.

The business prospered and proliferated. The Ritchies expanded northwards along the sloblands and started building a new graving dock for the Ballast Board in 1796. Hugh started a new yard further north again, and when he died in 1807 he was replaced in the business by his eldest brother John, who had carried on building ships in Ayrshire. Alexander McLaine, also from Ayrshire, went into partnership with John in 1811. In 1812, William Ritchie & Co., and Ritchie & McLaine between them employed 'forty four journeymen carpenters, forty five apprentices, seven pairs of sawyers, twelve blacksmiths and several joiners'; William Ritchie also noted 'the weekly wages about £120'.

In 1818 William Ritchie launched an experimental sixty-ton schooner called *New System*, which was built to show an innovation in design. The *Belfast News-Letter* reported: 'She is constructed without frame timber, beams or knees, and without any metal below water, except a few bolts in her keel and rudder brace.'

Despite such progressive attitudes, Belfast was not in the forefront of early developments. The first successful steam boat, *Comet*, was built on the Clyde in 1812, and the first to be launched in Ireland, *City of Cork*, was built at Passage, County Cork, four years later. Ritchie & McLaine launched their first steam boat, *Belfast*, in 1819. It was 200 tons, and had two seventy-horsepower engines built by Coates & Young's Lagan Foundry (a maker of textile machinery, which quickly became Ireland's leading marine engine maker). Although iron ships were being built on the Thames, the Mersey and the Tyne and Wear, the Lagan's first iron ship, *Countess of Caledon*, which Coates & Young built in 1838, was the only example built on the river for some time.

By then another Scot, a former employee of William Ritchie, had bought his business and renamed it Charles Connell & Sons, whilst John Ritchie had bequeathed his business at Pilot Street to his son-in-law, Alexander McLaine. The Ballast Board had built a second graving dock in 1826, and there was a third yard, Kirwan & McCune, launching into the river at the newly constructed Dunbar's Dock further upstream. An old man and later a boy, who were to help transform all this, would have been a familiar sight on the river banks, docks and quays: their habit was to stroll along and see what was happening, no doubt as the old seadog told his grandson about his adventures, and filled him with a love of the sea and ships.

The grandfather was Captain William Pirrie, who was born at Wigton in Scotland in 1780. He was not apprenticed, but he became an experienced sailor on the Atlantic, and took out American citizenship. He worked for the American Consul at Malaga, and his ships traded with Spain and its colonies in the Americas during the Peninsular War. He was captured by the French, his cargo being contraband, and was held for twelve months, but eventually escaped in an open boat to England. In 1820 he arrived in Belfast, where he set up as a merchant and shipowner, though he may also have represented the coastal shipping interests of his father, William Perrie, or Pirrie, senior, of Port William. Herbert Jefferson's hagiographical *Viscount Pirrie of Belfast* is uncharacteristically frank about the Captain: he was 'a man who meant to keep company with a class that could assist him in business pursuits; he always aimed high'.

The Captain's son, James, emigrated to Quebec, where he married Eliza Swan in 1844. She was the daughter of Alexander Montgomery of Dundesart, County Antrim, and the sister of Reverend Henry Montgomery, the leader of the Non-subscribing Presbyterians. James worked as a merchant in North America and died of cholera in New York in 1849. His widow returned to Conlig with their two children, Eliza, and William James (though only 'William' appears on the boy's Quebec birth certificate), who was born on 24 May 1847.

By this time the Captain had become a leading figure in the life of Belfast, though this was due to his real achievements rather than to any bent for social climbing. If he was always keen for self-improvement, he was also determined that the young town should improve itself. His agitations for improvements to the channel led to his nomination to the Ballast Board in 1827. He was made a life member, though he put himself up for re-election annually.

The Board adopted a plan originally commissioned in 1829–30 which proposed that a straight channel be cut in the river. This would be done in two stages and maintained by the use of a new invention, the steam dredger. The harbour was to be deepened and private docks on the County Antrim side were to be purchased by the board for use as public docks, while new quays were proposed in the centre of town. The parliamentary Bill to allow this was opposed by the Marquis of Donegall, who wanted more money in compensation. But thanks to Captain Pirrie agreement was reached. In 1839 William Dargan, who had built the Ulster Canal, took over the project. Spoil from the new channel was dumped on the County Down side of the river to form an island of seventeen acres, which was at first known as Dargan's Island. Captain Pirrie opened the first cut in 1841.

The project – and Belfast shipbuilding – might have ended there, for by 1845 the board had bought all the private docks and quays, including the shipyards of Charles Connell & Sons, Thompson & McCune (successors to Kirwan & McCune) and part of Alexander McLaine & Sons. The improvements envisaged would have meant that only the last named would have had any – albeit restricted – access to the river, yet the board would not allow Dargan's Island to be rented. In 1847 the seventeen members of the Ballast Board became the Harbour Commissioners, with new powers to manage the harbour. Again it was Captain Pirrie who pushed through the second half of the project, despite the indifference of his fellow commissioners. He opened the second cut, the Victoria Channel, on 10 July 1849 by pouring a bottle of whiskey into it. Dargan's Island had become Queen's Island in March, in anticipation of a visit from Queen Victoria in August.

By this time the island had been put to use. There was a pond on the east side in which 2,000 logs of ship's timber could be seasoned. A pleasure garden was laid out, with a crystal palace, a ferry service from County Antrim, a bathing pool, a zoo, and a row of cannon for firing salutes. A 'patent slip' allowed ships of up to 1,000 tons to be hauled out of the water on a cradle. Thompson & Kirwan moved to Queen's Island to be beside the slip. Connell's had begun to concentrate on repairs.

In 1852 iron ships represented less than one fifth of all tonnage built in the United Kingdom, but this was changing rapidly. Again Captain Pirrie forced the pace. He chaired a committee to investigate the prospects for iron shipbuilding and persuaded the Harbour Commissioners to support a plan for a yard on Queen's Island. The idea was originally that of Thomas Nugent Gladstone, who had set up the Belfast Iron Works in 1851 with fellow Liverpudlian Robert Pace. Although their Eliza Street works had 'a forest of tall and graceful chimney stalks, cylindrical in shape, and symmetrical in architectural elegance', it had been built on borrowed money in the vain hope that coal and ironstone would be found in the area. The pair only lasted till 1853, when they handed over the business to Robert Hickson, also from Liverpool. Hickson inherited the shipbuilding plan too and, following work by the commissioners, by 1854 he was installed on Queen's Island and had built his first wooden sailing ship, *Silistria*, of 1,289 tons.

Hickson had sacked his manager before the launch, so it was in answer to an advertisement that Edward James Harland arrived to take over. Harland's father was a general practitioner in Scarborough, of which he was three times mayor. Dr Harland was an amateur inventor and shared his mechanical aptitude with his wife. He patented a road-going steam carriage in 1827, and experimented with electricity and organic fertilizers. He was a friend of George Stephenson, and sent his son to be an apprentice at the age of fifteen at Robert Stephenson & Co. of Newcastle upon Tyne. Edward was inventive too: in 1850 he designed and made a working model of an improved lifeboat. When he completed his apprenticeship, business was slack. He resigned and went off to London to see the Great Exhibition. He stayed in London for two months.

The Harlands were connected by marriage with the Schwabes, a family of Hamburg merchants who, like others, had left Germany in the 1820s for the more liberal trading climate of Britain. The Schwabes were originally Jewish, but had converted to Lutheranism in 1819. They in turn were related to the Wolffs, who were also from Hamburg. Gustav Christian Schwabe traded in textiles with the Far East and had various shipping interests, including a junior partnership in John Bibby & Sons of Liverpool. When Bibby's moved into iron screw steamships, Schwabe involved his relative, E.J. Harland, in their choices, and this led to his employment at J. & G. Thomson on the Clyde. He took over as head draughtsman there, then went on to Thomas Toward's on the Tyne, where he was left in almost sole charge. Nevertheless, prospects looked better on the Lagan.

When he arrived in 1854, aged twenty-three, he clearly felt that he had to impose his personality on Hickson's yard. The iron from Eliza Street was poor, wages were high and workmanship was slipshod. Harland cut wages and demanded better work. He forbade smoking, and the penalty for disobedience was dismissal. He stalked the yard with a piece of chalk and an ivory rule. He would examine the work and, when he found a mistake, would draw a circle round it in chalk. There was an immediate strike, to which he responded by bringing blackleg workmen over from the Clyde. The Scots suffered much intimidation, and most decided to go home again, but Harland prevailed. Some trace the prevalence of Scottish managers for many years afterwards at Queen's Island to this initial strike.

Harland had only been at the yard for a few months when Hickson's business collapsed, and Harland had to keep it going with his own money. Hickson lost the ironworks to his creditors but was allowed to keep the shipyard. As if this was not bad enough, the sacked manager whom Harland had succeeded, J. Jordan, acquired Thompson & Kirwan's yard on the County Antrim shore and took on men who had been antagonized by Harland's harsh new regime. In response to a suggestion that he might reasonably quit at this point, Harland said, 'Having mounted a restive horse, I shall ride him into the stable.'

The ship which had been on the slips when he arrived, *Khersonese* (1,273 tons), was finally launched on 5 October 1855. Harland had had one bit of good luck when William Houston, the head foreman at Toward's on the Tyne, along with several leading hands, arrived in Belfast following the death of Thomas Toward. But there was a last-minute hitch. The *Khersonese* stuck on the slipway, and Harland had to discover and quickly remedy the cause before its great weight could cause the ship to sink into the ground.

His cool assessment of the orders on hand at the height of the turmoil was proved correct, and the firm survived. In 1857 Harland took on Gustav Schwabe's twenty-two-year-old nephew, Gustav Wilhelm Wolff, as personal assistant. Wolff had left Hamburg in 1849 to attend Liverpool College and pursue a career in engineering. People grew up quickly in those days: at the age of twenty, Wolff had represented the famous Manchester engineering firm Joseph Whitworth & Co. at the Paris Exhibition. He took charge of the drawing office, and Harland sent him to sea on a Bibby vessel to learn about ships.

In the same year Harland began to look for land on which to build a yard of his own. Significantly, he looked to the Mersey, first on the Liverpool and then on the Birkenhead side, but he was unsuccessful. In 1858 the economy declined and Hickson was left with an unfinished ship under construction, which he attempted to complete at his own expense. Eventually he had to offer the yard to Harland for £5,000. Edward James Harland & Co. opened for business on 1 November 1858 and immediately received a big order from Bibby's for three iron screw steamers of 1,500 tons each, no doubt via uncle Schwabe.

The ships used a number of new ideas. One was for screws which could be raised to reduce drag when the ship was running before the wind. Another innovation was a new form of deck invented and patented by Harland. This used Portland cement instead of chocks of wood to fill the spaces between the frames, and the iron plates were covered with cement and tiles. The point was to overcome the problem of the different behaviours of wood and iron under changing temperature and moisture. This method was adopted elsewhere. The Bibby ships were successful and led to more orders.

Harland, resourceful as ever, believed that he could safely make ships that were longer, without increasing the beam. The iron deck had the effect of turning the entire hull into a box girder of great strength. On Merseyside, Harland's rivals called these long thin ships 'Bibby coffins', partly because of their shape and partly because they looked as though they would break their backs. But Harland's theory proved correct. He also gave them perpendicular stems and flat bottoms, so that more cargo and passengers could be accommodated. The square bilges gave rise to another nickname, 'Belfast bottom'. Ships have changed enormously since then, but perhaps Harland would not find the modern oil tanker a complete surprise.

In the second batch of Bibby ships the masts and rigging were unusual, and they had steam winches and braces, which reduced the size of the crew. The engines used a development which made them less liable to salt corrosion and saved fuel. Harland had been making ships on his own account for only four or five years, but already he was at the leading edge of technical change.

His method of dealing with customers was also important to the quality of the work done in the yard, the adventurous design of the ships, and the ability of the yard to attract business. It may have its origin in the family relationships that Harland and Woff had with the owners of important shipping lines. The shipbuilder undertook to provide the finished ship, having put the best available workmanship and materials into it, in return for a commission on the finished product – what an arms manufacturer might call a 'cost-plus contract'. The advantage was that time and money could be saved on the plans, and modifications could be incorporated at any stage without interruption. This arrangement called for a continuous, close relationship between the parties, and a lot of mutual trust.

In 1861 Gustav Wolff became a partner, and the firm subsequently became Harland & Wolff. He stood in for Harland when the latter was away chasing orders. Wolff also had engineering skills and managed the yard. But not the least of his qualifications must have been the capital he brought with him. His personal contribution was only £500, but uncle Gustav and Wolff's mother, Fanny, loaned the partners about £12,000 on generous terms. Another of his talents was versifying:

> You may talk of your Edinburgh and the beauties of Perth,
> And all the large cities famed on the earth,
> But give me my house, though it be in a garret,
> In the pleasant surroundings of Ballymacarrett.

This must be spoken with a German accent, which Wolff never lost.

At the age of fifty-eight Wolff began to spend less time at the yard and entered politics. He was MP for East Belfast from 1892 to 1910, and was returned unopposed in all but his first election. Perhaps the accent explains his nickname at Westminster: he was called Teutonic, after one of his ships; Harland was in the Commons at the same time and was known by the name of the sister ship, Majestic. Wolff retired from shipbuilding in 1908, and he died in 1913.

He recorded his pastimes as shooting and fishing. His London home was in Kensington Palace Gardens, or 'Millionaire's Row', as it is still known. Altogether, Gustav Wolff seems to have been determined to appear to posterity as a somewhat droll, comfortable, clubbable sort of chap. He is chiefly remembered for his self-depreciating remark during a speech: 'Mr Chairman, Sir Edward Harland builds the ships for our firm; Mr Pirrie makes the speeches; and, as for me, I smoke the cigars for the firm.' David Hammond's excellent book *Steel Chest, Nail in the Boot and the Barking Dog*, which transcribes interviews with current and retired shipyard workers, records the joke as it is remembered still by the men in the yard. It is only the final phrase that is remembered, and it is misattributed to Edward Harland.

The man who built the ships was effective and successful. But he does not seem as comfortable or clubbable, and in some lights he acquires a tinge of the eccentric professor, striding about the yard with his ivory rule and his bit of chalk, sniffing out illicit smokers with his fabled sense of smell, jotting down bright ideas on scraps of paper. He had rather definite ideas about clothes, and indeed would design his own. According to Jefferson, 'His bootmakers had not a comfortable time.' Harland was particularly proud of his design for shirts. He wore shirts of the best linen, but he had them cut to his own pattern. He disliked a large gusset under the sleeve. Also, the back of the collar was lower than the front, because he had a short neck; the button was behind rather than in front. In 1894 he wrote a letter to Walter Wilson, explaining his theories, and enclosing an old shirt for reference. He is supposed to have returned a dozen new shirts to the maker because they were half an inch longer than he had specified. Perhaps he used his ivory rule to measure them.

From 1875 to 1887 Harland was Chairman of the Harbour Commissioners, he was Mayor of Belfast in 1885 and 1886, and MP for North Belfast, unopposed, from 1887 until his death in 1895. But Jefferson claims he found the peculiarities of local politics wholly unnecessary 'miserable torments'. Harland was in no doubt where the secret of success lay: he felt there was no reason why the whole of Ireland could not build ships like Belfast, given enterprise, hard work and 'an environment of true patriotism'.

From the start the partners did everything right – they built better, more advanced ships and they reinvested their profits. They also had the great advantage of family connections amongst the shipping lines. Even so, hard work, patriotism, and wealthy relations, were nearly not enough. They also needed luck. The shipping industry was no less sensitive to the fluctuations of the world economy a century and a half ago than it is today. Events like the American Civil

War could present opportunities as well as the more obvious problems: luckily, the Confederate states needed fast ships to run the Union blockade. Gaining the approval of the Admiralty nearly proved disastrous: their first navy ship was built at a serious loss. Gustav Schwabe was helpful yet again when he introduced Thomas Henry Ismay to the firm: Ismay had just bought the bankrupt White Star line with Schwabe's assistance, and he took a ship off their hands that they had been forced to finish at their own expense.

Another problem was the development of the harbour facilities. The Harbour Commissioners, the Shipwrights Society and Harland & Wolff contended for a couple of years in a row about where to site a new graving dock. Even the election of February 1864, in which the yard faction prevailed, did not settle the matter. As they were to do at fairly regular intervals when in conflict with the authorities, or troubled by political controversy or workforce discontent, Harland & Wolff threatened to move to Liverpool if the dock was not built on the County Down side. The commissioners at last agreed, building the Hamilton Graving Dock and the Abercorn Basin on the south side of Queen's Island, though they also built a floating dock on the County Antrim side (the Dufferin and Spencer Docks).

A large body of Catholic navvies was assembled from other parts of Ireland to build the new docks. Tensions between them and the overwhelmingly Protestant workforce of the yard broke in August 1864, when the navvies returned from a trip to Dublin to attend the unveiling of a statue to Daniel O'Connell. At this time the Party Processions Act was in force, banning Orange marches. Provoked by the return of the navvies, the loyalists burned O'Connell in effigy. Serious rioting broke out, and shipwrights from all the Belfast yards were involved in looting and stealing guns, though the army intervened to protect St Peter's Procathedral. Next day the shipwrights attacked the navvies, who had to flee from their work and swim for safety or run off across the mud. Then they demanded that Catholics working in the yard – they were few in number – should be sacked on the grounds that they were informing against fellow workers who had been rioting. Harland announced that if any Catholics were forced out, the yard would be closed until they returned. Fortunately heavy rain cooled tempers and the rioting stopped.

Religious problems in the workforce recurred. For example, in 1872, during the tension surrounding the Home Rule debates which led to rioting in the town, five hundred men left work early and fought a battle with police. The partners tried to protect their Catholic workers from intimidation, but Catholics were being forced out of their homes in Protestant areas, such as Ballymacarrett, from which the Harland & Wolff workforce was largely drawn.

The 'miserable torments' of Irish politics brought yet another crisis which nearly proved terminal. There was a general slump in orders, and skilled men were emigrating. Gladstone had taken office for the third time in February 1886 with the intention of granting Home Rule. Harland, as Mayor, was one of the main organizers of the campaign against it. This was the occasion on which Lord Randolph Churchill told an Ulster Hall audience, 'Ulster will fight; Ulster will be right.' Harland & Wolff threatened to move to the Clyde if Home Rule was granted, though secret plans had already been made to move to the Mersey. Rioting continued even after the defeat of the Bill and the collapse of the government. Yard men regularly rampaged through the town equipped with 'Queen's Island confetti' (bolts and small pieces of metal called 'rovings'). Harland was criticized for failing to act as decisively against sectarianism as in 1864. Of the 3,000 men at the yard 225 had been Catholics. By 1887, only seventy-seven Catholics remained. It may be that the partners felt the firm's position was too weak and uncertain for them to credibly coerce their workforce, which in any case was slipping away.

As Mayor in 1885, Harland had spent £18,000 of his own money on a visit by the Prince and Princess of Wales to open Donegall Quay and a new graving dock alongside MacIlwaine & McColl's. When he stepped down as Mayor, Harland was offended to receive only a knighthood rather than a peerage, the usual reward for loyal mayors. This was seen as a concession to Home Rule opinion and Parnell. Harland became a Unionist MP, and within the year had been offered and had accepted a baronetcy. He bought a house next door to Schwabe who, like Wolff, also lived on Millionaire's Row.

Although early expansion of the firm was financed (apart from family loans) by the reinvestment of profits, both Harland and Wolff began to look outside the business to invest the wealth they had acquired. Harland bought two farms at Ardoyne, Wolff became a partner in the new Belfast Rope Works, which went on to become the largest ropemaker in the world. This connection incidentally allowed the shipyard to obtain sailcloth and rigging at cheap rates – another incentive when wooing customers. It provided jobs for many wives and daughters of shipyard men. Harland's chairmanship of the Harbour Commissioners, though useful to the yard, was time-consuming. They also invested in businesses like the Oceanic Steam Navigation Co., which ran the White Star line. Both Harland and Wolff eased themselves gradually into the background and, while they did not formally retire for some time, they handed over the running of the business to new partners.

'Gentlemen apprentices' were taken on at this period to learn a trade from the ground up, with a view to becoming managers. The first two gentlemen apprentices at Hickson's yard had been Walter H. Wilson and his brother. Walter was responsible for the design of most of the early ships, and came up with a number of inventions which were adopted generally.

The third gentleman apprentice at the yard was William James Pirrie. His grandfather, the sea captain, had forced Belfast, apparently against its will, to become a port which the biggest ships could use, and had formed the group of pilots. Captain Pirrie died in 1858, the year Harland bought out Hickson. In the same year young William Pirrie went, aged eleven, to the Royal Belfast Academical Institution, the school which William Drennan had helped to found, and which provided an education for a number of Harland & Wolff's key men. He went to school equipped with a compendium of maxims and rules gathered by his widowed mother. He kept the book for the rest of his life, and took it with him on all his travels. Some of the sentiments sound as if they would have been useful to a shipbuilder:

> *You have your own way to make. It depends on your exertions whether you starve or not.*
> *Bishop of Cumberland: 'It is better to wear out than to rust out.'*

Others, however, seem of more general application:

> *Civility costs nothing and buys everything.*
> *No company or good company.*

Mrs Pirrie might have found them on a calendar, except that tear-off calendars with mottoes were not invented until later in the century, in Belfast, by the printers Marcus Ward & Co.

Thus equipped with the wisdom of ages, Pirrie got through four years of school and signed on with Harland & Wolff in 1862. His mother allowed him to take lodgings in east Belfast, near the yard. The two bank clerks who lodged in the same house objected to his workman's clothes: they left, and he stayed. The landlady must have liked him. It is said that he had a rapport with the workers: even among the shipyard men of today it is Pirrie who is remembered as the great star, the magnate with the common touch.

In 1874, at the age of twenty-seven, Pirrie was made a partner, with the Wilson brothers. Wolff and Harland had developed outside interests, and Pirrie's influence grew. He had a background in building ships, but his talent was as a salesman.

He had already begun to travel everywhere that ships went. His purpose was to study the ships on which he travelled, as well as to look at the ports they had to use. One lucrative result was a relationship with the Union-Castle line. Pirrie had seen that at Durban, South Africa, big ships had to stand offshore because of a bar, and transfer passengers and cargo to smaller boats. Harland & Wolff built steamers for the Union line which, though they were 400 feet long, had a draft shallow enough to get over the bar. Such ships were also ordered by the Belfast-based Castle line, and the Union-Castle line was eventually formed.

After visiting the Pullman works in 1872, Pirrie promoted what he called 'almost American' methods in Belfast. He felt that European factories tried to produce too great a range of different things. On visits to places like Boston and

Buenos Aires he encouraged harbour improvements and cheaper loading and unloading. Apart from the general benefits of increased sea traffic, Harland & Wolff, as the makers of bigger and bigger ships, stood to gain if more ports could accommodate them. Pirrie encouraged the development of Portland, Maine, which he thought could take the winter trade of Montreal when it was icebound and link up with the Grand Trunk Railroad. He also called for the development of railways in Argentina; many years later Harland & Wolff was to make diesel locomotives for South America.

In 1879 Pirrie married his first cousin, Margaret Montgomery Carlisle. Her father was head of the English department at Inst from 1861 to 1884. (Because of the democratic impulses of founders like William Drennan, Inst for many years did not have a single principal, but autonomous heads of department.) Two of her brothers set up the Blue Star line in London, another became managing director of Harland & Wolff. Pirrie would bring his work home and she would share it with him. It is said that he invited people for dinner so that his wife could run her eye over them.

Her husband became a viscount, but is familiarly referred to as 'Pirrie'; she tends to be known in the books as Lady Pirrie. Perhaps she liked to aim high in society: although their acquaintance included the Kaiser as well as a selection of domestic dukes and baronets, they never established their footing sufficiently firmly on the social ladder for their own satisfaction. The pair of them would frequently walk 'in procession' around the yard, and these events are still remembered by old workers with apparent awe. Lady Pirrie would no doubt have worn her jewels and selected a striking gown and one of her notoriously unfashionable hats. They always had a man following behind with coats, in case of rain.

Besides the interest she took in the business, Lady Pirrie also concerned herself with the welfare of the men, asking after wives and families on her tours of inspection. Michael Moss and John R. Hume, in their impressive *Shipbuilders to the World*, suggest that it was thanks to her that Harland & Wolff bought an ambulance to take injured men to hospital. Further, they suggest that the dangerous nature of the trade was one of the reasons that Belfast, like Glasgow, gained a high reputation in medicine. Other remedies were more *ad hoc*: according to Jefferson, Pirrie was 'most dextrous with the blade of a knife in removing grit from a worker's eye'.

When 'the daughter of a prominent manufacturer' caught fever and died while a patient in the Frederick Street Dispensary and Fever Hospital, the monied classes felt something had to be done. As Lord Mayor of Belfast in 1896, Pirrie started a campaign to build a modern hospital. He set up a fund to which the shipyard gave £5,000 and the Pirries themselves another £5,000. Thanks largely to Lady Pirrie, £100,000 was raised, but the cost turned out to be £111,000, at which, legend has it, Pirrie immediately wrote out a cheque for the missing £11,000. The Royal Victoria Hospital was so called in honour of the Silver

9. Henry Cooke. Frontispiece to *The Life and Times of Henry Cooke, D.D., LL.D.* by J.L. Porter (*John Murray, London, 1871*).

10. *Above* The 'Black Squad': men given hard, dirty work, here repairing the salvaged liner *China*, 1898. (*Harland & Wolff Collection, Ulster Folk and Transport Museum*)

11a. *Opposite above* Titanic leaving Belfast, 2 April 1912. (*Harland & Wolff Collection, Ulster Folk and Transport Museum*)

11b. *Opposite below* Partners. Left to right: G.W. Wolff, W.H. Wilson, W.J. Pirrie, E.J. Harland. (*Harland & Wolff Collection, Ulster Folk and Transport Museum*)

12. *Above* Viscount and Lady Pirrie, he as an Irish Privy Councillor, at Ormiston House on their way to the opening of the Northern Ireland Parliament, 1921. (*Harland & Wolff Collection, Ulster Folk and Transport Museum*)

13a. *Opposite above* York Street Mill: warping. (*W.A. Green Collection, Ulster Folk and Transport Museum*)

13b. *Opposite below* Beetling engine. (*W.A. Green Collection, Ulster Folk and Transport Museum*)

15. *Above* Bomb at Smithfield. (*Pacemaker*)

14a. *Opposite above* Prime Minister Terence O'Neill meets Taoiseach Jack Lynch at Stormont, December 1967. (*Pacemaker*)

14b. *Opposite below* City Hall, November 1985, rally against the Anglo-Irish agreement. Ian Paisley and Peter Robinson second and third from left. (*Pacemaker*)

16b. *Above McArt's Fort. (Northern Ireland Tourist Board)*

16a. *Right Cave Hill Road. (W.A. Green Collection, Ulster Folk and Transport Museum)*

Jubilee. Despite its origins, it has never confined itself to treating the quality.

Grandeur and luxury became increasingly important in shipping as firms such as Thomas Ismay's White Star line competed for North Atlantic passenger traffic. Harland & Wolff maintained a close personal collaboration with the Ismays and built larger and more opulent liners for them. Passengers were accommodated amidships, away from noisy propellors and in the most stable part of the vessel. Interior decoration was based on Pirrie's observations of hotels on his foreign trips. As the ships got huger and conquered the oceans, the company grew and conquered the industrial world, and Pirrie too became grander and grander.

To begin with, though, he was a super-salesman rather than the Shah of shipping. He was a bright-eyed little man with a brisk manner and, evidently, all the charm in the world. Wilson and Pirrie took over more and more of the burden of running the company. Walter Wilson, an amateur painter and orchid-grower, was shy, happier with technical problems than meeting people, but Pirrie was gregarious, at least when there was a tangible profit to be made. It was his ability to get on with people that allowed the company to grow as it did. His knack for inveigling shipowners into giving him business was legendary, as in the tale about the dazed Liverpool owner who said, 'Pirrie has just persuaded me to order a ship and I don't know what the deuce I'll do with it.'

But there were other reasons for his sales figures. Pirrie took the established method of striking a deal over a ship a stage further. Rather than rely on personal relationships, family contacts and a network of business connections to bring in orders, Pirrie formed something of a freemasonry of shipping. Once a customer had a relationship with the company, Pirrie would suggest that the two sides could give each other preferential treatment: in return for a steady flow of orders, and cash advances in preference to long-dated bills, Harland & Wolff would build the ships to the highest standard and at low cost. An army of clerks was employed to draw up detailed accounts of expenditure stage by stage, so that the owner was sure he was being treated fairly. When the finished ship was delivered, an agreed commission – the company's profit – was added on to the cost. Another valuable perk was that a berth was kept available at Belfast for favoured owners, so that repairs, for example, could be started without delay. This group of favoured owners is usually referred to as the 'commission club', but it is doubtful if anyone except Pirrie knew exactly who was in it and what all the terms of membership were.

The system depended on trust between the two sides, and Pirrie's personality must have been an important factor there. It was also a risky strategy, for it worked best with high-value ships – the great liners like *Oceanic*, *Majestic* and *Teutonic* with which White Star dominated the North Atlantic – and also it depended on Pirrie's ability to attract a large number of orders. The commission system itself was not unusual, and has been cited as one of the reasons why British yards in general – for example on the Tyne – were unable to compete in the twentieth century with the Japanese: in hard times shipyards compete with each other for lower and lower prices, while owners prefer the certainty of a fixed price.

When two managers from J. & G. Thomson on the Clyde made a tour of inspection at Queen's Island in 1890, they were mystified as to how Harland & Wolff could produce cheap ships and get so many good orders with working methods that were so wasteful and inefficient. They were surprised, for example, to see timber worked by hand rather than machine, and large stockpiles of wood being stored unnecessarily. But Pirrie believed that productivity was sometimes less vital than production.

Although conditions were tremendously tough, Pirrie seemed able to charm his workforce as well as everyone else. Harland & Wolff paid slightly higher wages than other yards and on many occasions were able to remain aloof as disputes disturbed the rest of the industry. Pirrie's tendency was to conciliate rather than confront, and he preferred to leave problems of demarcation, for example, to be sorted out between unions rather than decided by management. In the nationwide lockout of 1898 Harland & Wolff, on the crest of success, stayed open, for Pirrie believed in plant-by-plant rather than national settlements. He granted a shorter working day in return for a system of three shifts in the American fashion, made possible by newly installed electric lights.

He was an iron disciplinarian, like Harland, and demanded high standards of workmanship. His visits to the yard were traumatic for all concerned. Yet he paid relatively well and left the workforce to its own devices to a surprising extent. The system appeared ramshackle and costly to the visiting managers, but they would have been unaware of the existence of the commission club. Perhaps the secrecy with which he operated, the apparent sleight of hand with which he seemed to pull orders out of his hat, accreted around his name until he became a figure larger than life, endowed with magical powers. Old yard men, as David Hammond records, still remember Pirrie's ability to find work for them and their ancestors. In one song, he replaces even the good lord Jesus:

> There's not a friend like the good Lord Pirrie,
> Four-nought-one, four-nought-one.
> He bought a house in the heart of Surrey,
> Four-nought-one, four-nought-one.
> He knows all about our struggles,
> He'll get us work till the day is done.

401 was the number of the *Titanic*.

Sometimes charisma derives from the reputation for possessing charisma; the cultivation of a magical aura gives one power over imaginations, but there are drawbacks to secrecy and the need to astonish. Some were to have a disastrous effect on the company; perhaps others had a more personal cost. However, there were more substantial reasons for Pirrie's success than personality. He had been learning the business since the age of fifteen. Increasingly important as the yard grew, he had a passion for numbers. He could tell exactly what was going on in the yard by looking at the accounts. He could juggle with huge sums of money, buying and selling stocks in a never-ending series of deals that are mystifying to the layman. On one occasion it appeared to the popular press that Pirrie had sold the British domination of world trade to the Americans, at the height of Britain's power as a global empire and industrial giant.

In the late 1890s his commission club was put under strain: a long-established customer, Frederick Leyland & Co., formed the Wilson-Leyland line, building its own ships at the Furness Withy yard to compete in the North Atlantic passenger trade. Pirrie tried to resurrect a plan originally devised in 1891 by his old friend Albert Ballin, of the Hamburg-Amerika line. This was for a North Atlantic conference, or cartel, which would control trade and manage fares. The great expansion in the North Atlantic had led to overcapacity amongst the better boats during the winter.

Pirrie's initial attempts failed. Then the American financier J. Pierpoint Morgan began buying up members of Harland & Wolff's commission club. His plan was to create a huge transport conglomerate involving shipping and railways, so that he could dominate transport from Europe to the Pacific. Pirrie acted for him, entertaining Ballin, White Star and Norddeutscher Lloyd at his London home with lavish hospitality. (One guest remarked, 'His domestic arrangements seem to point to great riches, even measured by London standards.') He persuaded them to form International Mercantile Marine (IMM). When the scheme was announced in 1902 there were squeals of alarm and outrage. At a time when Britain and Germany were competing to expand their navies, Pirrie seemed to have facilitated the takeover of private shipping by a cartel of Americans and German Jews, as it was put. Less obvious was what he had achieved for the Belfast shipyard: he had bought into a huge transport conglomerate, all of whose members agreed to give any orders for ships or heavy repairs to be done in the United Kingdom to Harland & Wolff on a commission basis.

IMM failed to absorb Cunard, which with assistance from the British government immediately ordered two big liners at another yard. IMM's share issue was disastrous. Pirrie was interrogated by the Select Committee on Steamship Subsidies but he proved difficult to pin down: under pressure, his usual tactic was to talk freely, overwhelming his questioner with words. Pirrie was seen as an unpatriotic wheeler-dealer. The Pirries' ambitions in London society were not helped, no doubt, though they were destined always to be thwarted, for whatever reason: perhaps their showy, *nouveau riche* style was one problem; perhaps his strong Belfast accent, which he never lost, was another. But Pirrie's own aim was achieved: that of keeping Harland & Wolff in business. Of the thirteen ships under construction in 1901, all but one had been ordered by companies in the syndicate.

Within two years IMM began cancelling orders. But Pirrie continued looking elsewhere for business and investing at Queen's Island. Sometimes the yard was kept going by building at below cost. In 1903 he initiated Owen Philipps into the mysteries of his commission club: Harland & Wolff would provide a monthly statement of the cost plus a 5 per cent profit, Philipps's Royal Mail Steam Packet Co. would pay cash or bills at three, four and six months. The other old customers not in IMM also continued to provide orders.

From about the time of the IMM deal, something seemed to snap in Pirrie. Walter H. Wilson retired in 1901 to grow his orchids, John Bailey, the company's first and so far only accountant, died in 1902. Pirrie removed all private ledgers to his home in London. He demanded copies of all letters sent out from Belfast. He had always been secretive, but from now on an impenetrable mist settled over Harland & Wolff.

In 1902, contrary to his confident expectations, Pirrie was passed over as the Unionist candidate for South Belfast. The Conservative Association preferred Charles Dunbar-Buller to Pirrie, who was a Liberal. In the event, Dunbar-Buller was beaten by a bigoted shipyard worker, Thomas Sloan, who evangelized in the platers' shed at lunchtime and inveighed against popery and the 'higher' aspects of the Church of Ireland. Pirrie persisted in his liberalism, a family tradition both for him and his wife, and one which was no doubt encouraged by Owen Philipps. Although his wife always had a personal antipathy towards him, Philipps became Pirrie's closest associate: he was an Anglo-Catholic and a Home Ruler, and had the connections in London high society that the Pirries lacked. In the 1906 election campaign Pirrie financed Liberal candidates in Ulster, and when the Liberal government took office he got his reward and was made a peer.

He began to act in a more lordly way. In 1907 he reconstructed the management of Harland & Wolff, moving its head office to 1a Cockspur Street in central London, just round the corner from Whitehall and Admiralty Arch. His office day was curious. Rather than sit at a desk, he preferred to lie on a chaise longue, with papers scattered about him. He had a favourite secretary, Iris Edmiston, who went with him wherever he went. She would provide a detailed dossier on whomever he was to interview. He started work at nine in the morning. Lady Pirrie would be driven in a Rolls-Royce from their house in Belgrave Square (now the Spanish Embassy) and arrive at six. They would finish off the day's work together, then she would take him home, at seven, eight or nine in the evening.

Rather than appoint any successors or replace Gustav Wolff as a principal, Pirrie overlooked his Tory relations on the board in favour of more amenable types. He called the committee of managers he created 'my splendid men', but they worked in the dark. Only two people besides Pirrie were allowed access to the private ledgers. Frequently the annual reports of profit and loss were cooked – in a way that was legal at the time. Embarrassing evidence of the real financial state of the company was concealed from shareholders and, presumably, his own board. Large sums were carried forward from year to year or buried in unspecified 'reserves'.

All the time Pirrie was doing deals with shipping lines and suppliers, buying and selling shares on a huge scale. On the surface this looks like the demented hyperactivity of the shopaholic, or it could have been a struggle to keep the business buoyant. By 1907 Pirrie was unable to invest in the new technology of turbines; the company was also threatened by a new cartel of forgemasters, which might have controlled prices of castings. But Pirrie merged Harland & Wolff with John Brown & Co., in one swoop gaining access to that company's knowledge of turbines and ensuring his supply of heavy forgings and castings.

In 1909 he bought his 'house in the heart of Surrey', Witley Court near Godalming, along with 2,800 acres. It had belonged to a crooked company promoter, Whitaker Wright, and Pirrie paid what was thought to be a bargain price, £200,000. It had an observatory, a ballroom, a music room, a private theatre and a palm house with a mosaic floor, Ionic columns and a barrel-vaulted roof of glass. There were three lakes, under one of which was a glass dome reached by an underground corridor. There were model dairy and poultry farms, a piggery and a flock of white turkeys. Jefferson says his homes were as luxurious as possible 'to please his guests' and 'as homages to his wife'. Lady Pirrie hated Witley Court.

The parallel between Pirrie's homes and Pirrie's ships is irresistible. White Star's *Olympic* and *Titanic* were to be floating Witley Courts. These were intended to be the biggest and the most luxurious ships ever, and Harland & Wolff was to build them side by side. It would be a coup impossible to ignore: on behalf of Britannia, Belfast ruled the waves; Queen's Island men could take on the world and beat it, just as Pirrie could operate on the world stage, organizing and dealing, charming himself into the position of being one of the most powerful men of the industrial age.

In order to build the two giant ships, new docks and new gantries had first to be built. A celebrated London company of interior decorators was bought to ensure the fittings were done properly. Orders for other ships had to be subcontracted to other yards. On 31 May 1911 *Olympic* sailed on her maiden voyage and *Titanic* was launched.

J. Bruce Ismay of the White Star line had inherited plans for four great ships on his father's death in 1899. When *Celtic* was launched in 1901 it was the first ship bigger than Isambard Kingdom Brunel's paddle steamer *Great Eastern*, launched forty years previously. This had been regarded as a wonder when it was being built, from 1854 to 1858, at Millwall, but it had had a fairly brief and ignominious career. It took £60,000 and three months merely to launch, and after acting as, amongst other things, a troopship and cable layer, it was scrapped in 1889. Pirrie, however, believed that *Great Eastern* had been before its time. When it had been built there were no docks big enough to take it. His preferred design was different: rather than *Great Eastern*'s hollow bow and fine ends, Harland & Wolff built ships which were long and of moderate beam, with the main body well fore and aft.

With White Star's help, Pirrie outshone even Isambard Kingdom Brunel, the man with the tallest hat and the biggest cigar in the Industrial Revolution.

Following the botched launch of IMM and the expansion of German shipping, Cunard received government aid to reassert British mastery of the North Atlantic with *Lusitania* and *Mauretania* (1907). The biggest of the White Star Big Four had been *Adriatic*, at 25,541 tons and 709 feet long. The Cunarders were each 790 feet long and used the new steam turbine. Pirrie is supposed to have suggested outdoing them during an after-dinner chat with Bruce Ismay in 1907. They would build not two, but three giant liners, each half as big again as the Cunarders. In the White Star tradition, they would sell tickets on comfort, elegance and safety, rather than speed. They were to use a new system combining reciprocating and turbine engines, which proved economical in *Laurentic* (1909).

The story of the *Titanic* is one of the myths that Belfast has given the film-makers, playwrights and poets of the world. Some aspects of it are more mythical than others. For example, John P. Eaton and Charles A. Haas, in *Titanic: Destination Disaster*, tell the tale of the hull number, 390904. It is true that some fanciful yard man, or, more likely, some ingenious journalist, saw that this, read mirror fashion, with screwed-up eyes and a bit of imagination, could be read as 'NO POPE'. However, Eaton and Haas go on, 'in the hearts of the pious, working-class Catholic employees in Belfast, there was deep indignation', and the number 'spelled doom for the vessel'. This hilarious conclusion misses the point: 'NO POPE', if it was noticed at all, would have been a lucky omen for the pious, but not predominantly Catholic, employees.

The legend of the workers trapped inside the hull by the speed of construction – tappings could be heard at night – is also supposed to have meant doom. Yet this does not ring true either. Queen's Island men are more likely to boast of their hard, hazardous work than to cower in superstitious dread. The tale of the ghostly tappings is a good yarn, typical of the yard's folklore – a fantastical story that satirizes the speed of work required and incidentally demonstrates the toughness of the men. In fact *Titanic* was a lucky ship, while it was being built. At the time there was a rule of thumb that there would be one death per £100,000 spent. Only two workers died building *Titanic*, which was better than average. Stewart Parker used the story of the ghost workers in his play *The Iceberg*.

The loss of the *Titanic* on its maiden voyage makes such a good story, with such a variety of unmistakable 'morals' – hubris, Nature's revenge, the decline of capitalism or empire, British phlegm – that some of the many who have adapted the story have been unable to resist embroidering it (quite unnecessarily), or reading even more significance into coincidences than is present already. So that while the disaster could never be anything but lamentable, there is a faint air of the ludicrous hanging around aspects of the story.

The story of the after-dinner plot by Pirrie and Ismay, for example, sounds like two schoolboys saying, 'Anything Cunard can do, we can do better.' Commentators have discovered curious facts like the 'prophetic' novel of 1898, *The Wreck of the Titan* by Morgan Robertson, or like the *Titanic* passenger, William T. Stead, who had written short stories, one about a liner sunk by ice, another about a shipwreck in which passengers had drowned because of a lack of lifeboats. Or there were Violet Jessop, a stewardess, and John Priest, a fireman: both were on *Olympic* when it collided, soon after launching, with HMS *Hawke* (one unforeseen drawback of such huge ships was that they tended to attract other bodies towards them when under way in confined spaces); both escaped from the *Titanic*; both escaped from *Britannic*, the third of the White Star's great ships, when it was sunk in the Aegean during World War One. John Priest went on to survive the sinkings of the *Alcantara* and the *Donegal* during the same war. According to legend, he had to retire from the sea because no one would sail with him after all that.

What did those passengers have in their heads, what stereotype were they trying to fulfill, when they shouted 'Be British! Women and children first!' and refused to get into the lifeboats? When lifeboat four was launched and, after an hour's wait, seamen cranked open the windows to let passengers board it, John Jacob Astor helped his nineteen-year-old wife, whom he had married seven months before, into the lifeboat. But then he declined to join her, lit a cigarette and nonchalantly waved her goodbye, despite the fact that the lifeboat left the ship only two-thirds full.

The *Titanic* disaster was not due to fate or to an offence against the gods, but to bad luck, human stupidity, laziness and disorganization. There was room on board for 2,435 passengers and 860 crew, totalling 3,295. On the maiden voyage there were 2,228 people. Yet the lifeboat capacity was only 1,176. The Board of Trade, which based its regulations on the volume of a ship, required lifeboats for only 980. *Titanic* had four collapsible boats surplus to requirements, each designed for forty-nine. Even so, some of the lifeboats left nearly empty. Although it took the ship more than two hours to sink and there was apparent calm for most of that time, there seems to have been utter, though unflappable confusion in the disembarkation. On the port side, the elderly New York millionaire Isidor Strauss refused to leave the ship until all women and children were safe. His wife got out of lifeboat eight and stayed with him: they drowned together. Eaton and Haas say that on the starboard side, one of the emergency cutters, with seating for thirty-five, was setting off with five passengers and seven crew aboard, because no one else was about. One of the first-class passengers aboard suggested that they should not go back once the boat had sunk to pick up survivors from the water in case they were swamped. Later her husband, a knight, is supposed to have presented each of the seven crewmen with a cheque for £5 'to replace lost kit'.

Bruce Ismay was on the maiden voyages of both *Olympic* – whose beds he found too soft – and *Titanic*. Interestingly, it is the survivor, Ismay, who attracted Derek Mahon: his poem 'Bruce Ismay's Soliloquy' portrays the shipowner's long, apparently sad and lonely life after the disaster in the house he bought in the west of Ireland. It is a poem which expresses the guilt of the exile, as well as of the survivor. Thomas Andrews, Harland & Wolff's chief designer and Pirrie's nephew, who had inherited the design of *Titanic*, died like a hero: he was last seen throwing deckchairs to people in the water. Seven other men from Queen's Island also died.

Pirrie had just had a prostate operation, a chancy business in 1912 – the newspapers carried bulletins of his progress – otherwise he might have been on board. But for a sixty-five-year-old it was an *annus terribilis*, as it was for Belfast: he had been lucky to get through a serious operation; his company's greatest achievement had destroyed itself, killing 1,513 people in the process, including his nephew; and his political activities were continuing at a time when the situation in Ireland, and Ulster especially, was deteriorating. Earlier in the year Pirrie had presided at the Home Rule meeting in Celtic Park (it had been hurriedly changed from the Ulster Hall) at which Winston Churchill and John Redmond had spoken; afterwards, at Larne Harbour, he had been pelted with rotten eggs and flour and called a traitor and a turncoat. Guns were being smuggled in for the Ulster Volunteers. The next time he was seen in public after the *Titanic* disaster, his hair had turned snowy white and he suddenly looked old.

Following the inquiry into the *Titanic*, regulations regarding lifeboats were changed, and an ice patrol was begun in the North Atlantic. It was also suggested that the ship would have survived if the watertight bulkheads had been continued to the first continuous deck, which was thirty feet above water level. As it was, so many watertight compartments had been breached by the long gash down the side of the ship that water spilled over from one to another even though they were eleven feet above water level. Edward Wilding, Andrews' successor as chief designer, designed and had patented several new safety features, including methods for keeping doors watertight, lowering lifeboats and holding bulkhead doors open in an emergency. *Olympic* returned to Belfast to have an inner skin fitted and her bulkheads heightened and strengthened.

The news of the sinking shared the front pages of the papers with the third Home Rule Bill, which promised trouble among the Harland & Wolff workforce however much Pirrie was in favour of it. The company was getting into increasing debt, and Pirrie sold a majority shareholding to John Brown. However, he remained in charge, and told Owen Philipps (though he seems to have told few others) that he was to succeed him at the head of Harland & Wolff.

The outbreak of war appeared to provide some respite, financially and politically. The Queen's Island managers decided, contrary to common practice, to complete their outstanding orders and to retain their skilled workforce. Pirrie ruled that the men were to be rested on alternate weekends, and their pay and conditions were kept above the wartime average. As a result there was little 'dilution' by unskilled workers, and Harland & Wolff had a much better strike record during the war than its competitors. Pirrie, temporarily relieved of overdraft worries, expanded in the three ports of Liverpool, Southampton and Glasgow.

The company now had seven works.

The first of its orders for the Navy was to build a series of decoy boats – merchant vessels made to look like warships so that the Germans would mistake the true position of the fleet. This dummy squadron was commanded by Commodore Herbert Haddock. They built monitors, and diversified in 1917 into making aeroplanes; Pirrie and George Cuming bought Aldergrove farm to provide an extra airfield for deliveries of planes.

All orders for merchant shipping were suspended during World War One so that every effort could be put into government orders, but little was achieved. By April 1917 German submarines had sunk 555,066 tons of shipping, but only 69,711 tons had been produced. When Sir Eric Geddis replaced Sir Edward Carson as First Lord of the Admiralty in July 1917, he appointed Pirrie as Controller General of Merchant Shipbuilding. Pirrie inherited the disappointing 1916 scheme of standardization and rather than scrapping it, imposed it rigorously: only twelve designs of merchant ships were to be used, and only one type was to be built in each yard. He synchronized the making of engines and hulls, and reduced the stockpiling of steel. His methods reduced the length of time it took to fit out a ship once launched: from January to October he halved the tonnage 'in the water', that is, launched but awaiting completion. Instead of expanding the shipyards, he increased productivity. He involved unions and management in monitoring the work, and he relied on accurate information, gleaned from frequent visits to yards and studying accounts, when making decisions.

Under his direction, the shipyards achieved great things. Output went up fifty per cent in the last eight months of the war. Of 1,534,100 tons completed, Harland & Wolff made by far the biggest contribution, with 201,070 tons. Workman, Clark, Belfast's other yard, was the third busiest, with 64,893 tons. Indeed, Workman, Clark managed to launch a ship, fit its engines and have it ready for sea within four days. The Admiralty had spent £28 million on three National Shipyards, where German prisoners were to build forty-one standard ships. At the end of the war they had nothing whatever to show for their money.

On the day the Armistice was signed, Pirrie ordered his own department to be demobilized. Possibly he feared nationalization or government interference in the industry. In any case, he and Philipps were apprehensive about prospects: Harland & Wolff had overextended itself during the war and there was also the question of whether new orders could be found to replace Government orders. A few days later Pirrie issued a call for a continuation of the wartime spirit: it would take an equally desperate effort if prosperity was to be achieved in the peace. In 1919 Philipps was still worrying how his company could re-establish itself. Pirrie must have sighed with relief when Royal Mail and P & O decided to take over all 137 standard ships then under construction. Of these, thirty-six were in Harland & Wolff, occupying every available berth. The political situation was also worrying: the Easter Rising in 1916 had pre-empted Home Rule for Ireland, which had been delayed for the duration of the war. All, including the aims of Pirrie and Philipps, had changed. Pirrie now favoured Partition. He did not think Harland & Wolff could survive outside the United Kingdom.

Serious strikes began at the shipyard in January 1919. These spread and brought the city to a standstill. The yard was still under the Ministry of Munitions, so the managers had little room for manoeuvre. Some union representatives happened to meet Pirrie on the Larne–Stranraer ferry: still Controller of Merchant Shipbuilding, Pirrie was able to negotiate with them. They were suspicious of one of their own leaders, the militant socialist Jack O'Hagan, and, under threat of military intervention, agreed to go back to the forty-seven-hour week they had had before the war, rather than hold out for forty-four.

Pirrie ordered new machinery to compensate for the productivity lost. He also embarked on a spree of expansion as orders began to flood in. He extended the yard in Belfast, rebuilt two yards on the Clyde, began a diesel engine works at Finnieston and Britain's largest iron foundry at Govan. He took over the Scottish steelmakers Colville's, and formed the British Mexican Petroleum Co. to ensure supplies of diesel oil. (He had been convinced that diesels were the power of the future while recovering from his prostate operation on a Baltic cruise.) In 1920 he bought another engine works at Scotstoun because Finnieston could not produce enough.

Yet Harland & Wolff was getting deeper in debt all the time. When Pirrie called a crisis meeting and halted all capital expenditure except on the Clyde foundry, it may have been due to a slump in shipbuilding, in realization that he had overextended himself, or in response to the political situation. The IRA campaign was raging, and the Black and Tans were responding brutally. Rioting in Derry spread to Belfast in June 1920 and in July Workman, Clark men marched through Harland & Wolff calling for the expulsion of all Catholics and Communists. Many Catholics were forced to leave and it was only after Partition in 1921, and with the strengthening of the Harbour Police, that 'good' (non-republican, or non-socialist) Catholics were allowed to return. Pirrie became a Senator in the Northern Ireland Parliament.

Debt problems were eased when Pirrie's favoured customers deposited large sums of money with the firm. The shipbuilding slump continued despite Lloyd George's attempts to reflate the economy. With two relatives in the Cabinet, Pirrie was well placed to benefit from the Northern Ireland Loans Guarantee Act of 1922, which helped him build repair facilities at Tilbury: Harland & Wolff was to own eleven sites at Tilbury alone. But Pirrie's strategy did not suit the times. He depended on being able to find a steady stream of orders for big, high-value ships from customers he had spent a lifetime cultivating. It did not matter that overheads in Belfast were higher than elsewhere, and prices and profits lower, so long as the orders kept rolling in. Now orders were few, and an increasing number were on fixed-price terms, which did not suit the 'Belfast practice' of concentrating on workmanship rather than economy. The expansion plans on the Clyde ran into the sand. Harland & Wolff owed £13 million, a sum guaranteed, somewhat nervously, by the P & O Banking Corporation. When they enquired at the firm's bankers, the Midland Bank admitted that it had not been allowed to see Harland & Wolff's balance sheet, but that it had every confidence in Lord Pirrie.

At the end of 1923 there was a premonition of disaster. In his increasingly autocratic way, Pirrie had ruled that only he and the owner were to decide on the basic design of each new ship. His decision would be conveyed to a centralized design department under Wilding in Belfast. No one was told under what terms ships were being built, and designers were forbidden to contact the owners except through Pirrie. Andrew Weir had ordered twelve ships to be built at Govan. Wilding, believing that these orders were on the usual commission basis, discussed modifications to the designs with the owners, which they accepted. These involved more expense, which Harland & Wolff were unable to charge for, as Pirrie had arranged a fixed price. When Pirrie found out, he summoned Wilding to London. The unfortunate designer broke down, and Pirrie suspended him for twelve months without allowing him to return to his office. He had his desk broken into in order to discover what else Wilding had been doing, but Wilding, fearing the worst, had cleared it before he left for London.

In 1924, failing to learn the lesson, Pirrie reorganized the system of design so that virtually he alone was to design up to twenty ships a year. The managing directors were not to be involved until a later stage, and so would have no way of estimating costs and prices. It sounds like the ultimate *folie de grandeur*: as if one sick old man could not only find orders but also do the work of an entire design department for a vast enterprise scattered all over the United Kingdom. But in a sense the reorganization, like his annual balance sheets, was window-dressing: despite his promises that orders were on their way from unspecified clients, Pirrie knew that very little, if any, design work would have to be done for some time. His salesman's charm had finally run out, and there were no more rabbits to be pulled out of hats.

He prepared for a trip to South America with apprehension. He asked a friend for reassurance that it was a good idea, and he signed his will before he left. He set sail with Lady Pirrie, a private secretary and a personal physician on board the *Ardanza* in March 1924. When they reached Buenos Aires they decided to go on rather than go back because the trip was doing their health good. No doubt Pirrie was enjoying mapping all the harbours they came to with his blue pencil. They rounded Cape Horn and reached Valparaiso, where they embarked on the *Ebro*, going north. Pirrie caught a chill and developed double pneumonia. Passing through the Panama Canal, which had been opened in June 1920, Pirrie insisted on being taken on deck to see it. He died at 11.30 p.m. on 7 June 1924, twelve hours' sailing time from Havana. The ship he died on, the *Ebro*, had been built by Workman, Clark. His embalmed body was taken across the Atlantic on board the *Olympic*, and he was buried in Belfast City Cemetery on 23 June 1924, sixty-two years to the day after his arrival at Harland & Wolff.

He had been, as the eulogies said, the 'Napoleon of Industry', yet he had little to show in the end – or rather little but show. His will was as fictional as his annual reports, for when he died he personally owed the bank £325,000, and was committed to buying back £473,260 worth of Harland & Wolff shares from the Colville family. The shares he owned provided no income. Owen Philipps, who had become a Tory and a peer, Baron Kylsant, went to some trouble to arrange an annuity for Lady Pirrie by making a collection from old associates. This was despite her unwavering hostility towards him and her attempts to prevent him replacing her husband at the head of the company. When, on the *Olympic*, she had invited Lord Inverforth (formerly Andrew Weir) to take over, she had been unaware that Royal Mail had controlled the company since 1919. Philipps immediately began a frantic scramble to conceal the full, horrible truth of the balance sheets and order book, and save the company.

Pirrie was a strange mixture of the charmer and the autocrat – though perhaps not so strange: it is not difficult to think of public figures in Ulster today who would fit that description. Pirrie, and his wife, were clearly kind-hearted: they sent Christmas presents to their managers and she would knit them woolly sweaters to keep them warm on their voyages. They employed their domestic staff at Witley Court, on their frequent absences, in making pyjamas, which they would present to visiting managers to take back and distribute in Belfast. If they had had children they would probably have been doting parents. Yet Pirrie was also unthinkingly cruel, quite capable of ordering someone to accompany him on a transatlantic trip at a few hours' notice. He was 'sentimental, and entirely without pity', 'often most dangerous when apparently most cordial'. A civil servant working for Pirrie during World War One was worried when summoned to his office. But the interview was most pleasant and he came away reassured. It was only over lunch, some time later, that he realized he had been given the sack.

Pirrie loved dressing up in uniforms, in the white feathers of the Privy Councillor or in the military uniform of the Controller of Merchant Shipbuilding, complete with spurs and sword. He cultivated the rich and famous – a visit to Witley Court was like a flick through Debrett's or *Who's Who* – yet he never lost his Belfast accent. He would descend on the yard like royalty for tours of inspection, equipped with three dispatch boxes, one for Harland & Wolff, one for Stormont, and one for the Royal Victoria Hospital. Yet when he began his career he had a rapport with and respect for the workers: he wore his dirty overalls with pride in his lodging house in Ballymacarrett. He was always able to make deals with the workforce while other shipyards were out on strike.

It is revealing that commentators take pains to explain Pirrie's political views, as if it was inconceivable that a capitalist tycoon could also be a Liberal and a

Home Ruler. Jefferson goes so far as to suggest that he only supported Home Rule out of pique at being overlooked as a Unionist candidate. Yet he was overlooked because he was already a Liberal. Both Pirrie and his wife came from Presbyterian, politically progressive backgrounds; a line can be traced through Lady Pirrie and her father to Inst, the school founded by the friends of Drennan that was anathema to the more conservative wing of Presbyterianism. Pirrie was an admirer of American methods, and seems to have had an American, rather than a British, attitude to wealth and ostentation. His grandfather was an American citizen.

Even when his politics suffered a sea change after 1916, it is arguable that Pirrie stayed truer to his principles than the Unionists, for Partition meant Home Rule, not rule from London. He was consistent in wanting Ireland – though we could justifiably substitute 'Belfast' – to have less to do with Westminster, without breaking the link altogether. It is easier to understand Pirrie's political choices by looking at his background and by remembering that all he did was with the company in mind. He had an honourably non-sectarian record as Lord Mayor of Belfast: it is usually thought worthy of note that his final official function was at a Roman Catholic bazaar; more important, perhaps, he ensured that when the council was expanded Nationalists and Labour should each have a guaranteed number of seats on committees – a proposal that would be novel to the Official and Democratic Unionists who run the council today.

Reports by those meeting him are usually written in tones of surprise. He was bright and loquacious, persuasive and quick. He always carried his mother's book of aphorisms about, and always followed her advice to work hard and succeed by his own exertions. He was a good shot, he liked Shakespeare and biographies, but he never read novels, and he couldn't bear romantic comedy. He could fall asleep in a chair and wake up in ten minutes. His hands were tiny, so that Lady Pirrie always stipulated that wherever they travelled the servants were to pack a special small set of knives and forks. He is remembered even now in the folklore of the shipyard workers as a great man. Even that was a business strategy he stumbled into through personal inclination: despite the homely gifts of woolly sweaters and pyjamas, he expected his managers, 'my splendid men', to live and to work in surroundings of splendour. If he liked dressing up and showing off he knew it was useful when seeking orders and persuading other industrialists to co-operate with him. The life of the childless Pirries, in Belgrave Square or in the big house in the heart of Surrey that Lady Pirrie detested, was a performance, and only Pirrie himself knew how far the performance diverged from reality: for all their entertaining, which was almost exclusively for business purposes, it sounds a lonely life. The pomp and the wheeler-dealing were for the good of the yard back in Belfast. Whatever excitement he felt when he went in his overalls at the age of fifteen to start work at Queen's Island can only be guessed at.

131

CHAPTER NINE

QUEEN'S ISLAND AND LINENOPOLIS

Belfast still has a shipbuilding industry, but only just. In the 1880s Britain made half the ships in the world, and Belfast had a lion's share; now Britain makes one in every fifty. Although Harland & Wolff is the largest construction yard in Europe, and despite continuing achievements, such as the *Seaquest* oil platform, the Belfast shipyard is more often in the news as a financial headache for government than as a thriving business. But its two giant cranes are yellow arches visible from almost any high ground in Belfast, and loom over the east as if to remind the little streets of what created them.

Arguably the shipyard's influence on Belfast extends even further. Harland and Pirrie repeatedly threatened to remove the business from the Lagan to, variously, Dublin, Liverpool or Glasgow, in response to what they saw as political threats or lack of support from the city authorities. The yard was a major reason for, or at least obvious evidence of, the difference between Belfast and the rest of Ireland. If its owners were convinced that it could only thrive as part of Britain, many others were too: Harland & Wolff came to be seen as one reason why Belfast and its hinterland could never break the Union with Britain. In William Conor's painting *The Launch*, three workers watch a ship going down a slipway under gantries. It is the men who dominate the composition, but the prow carries a small, yet conspicuously situated Union Jack.

At one point between 35,000 and 40,000 men were employed at building ships here. Between 1880 and 1925 the population of the city doubled from 200,000 to 400,000: one in every ten people was a Queen's Island man. Shipbuilding dominated the city in every sense, aurally and visually. The riveters' hammers rang over Ballymacarrett and across the lough, and must have done so for more than a century: Thackeray noticed the 'hammers clanging' in 1842. In *From the Jungle of Belfast* Denis Ireland describes 'the thunder of riveting flung across the river' and how 'In the dark of winter afternoons the red-hot rivets flew through the air like fire-flies'. The landmarks were not the cheerfully bright yellow cranes of today but black gantries and cranes like a company of mantises praying at the mystery of pupation, while steel ships took shape within their cocoons of staging.

Louis MacNeice locates his birthplace using what seem the obvious reference points, 'between the mountain and the gantries'. Elsewhere, his description of

Belfast cites the hammers that 'clang murderously on the girders' while for him 'Like crucifixes the gantries stand'. His poems' perception of the inhuman, symbolic landmark provides terms which crystallize thought, terms with which, once we are given them, we think about our own place. 'Belfast' is emotionally true about the driven intensity, the hive-like industry and the disastrous, blood-soaked religiosity of the city that, by visual pun or synecdoche, the shipyard represents.

Tommy Patten, a shipyard worker who became Lord Mayor of Belfast, tells in *Steel Chest . . .* how the yard, for him and his neighbours in the shadow of the gantries and in the din of the hammers, was inevitable: there was never any doubt that it meant his adult employment. So many people worked there that it would have been more difficult to find a Belfast family that was not linked in some way with shipbuilding than one which was.

The character of Belfast determined that of the yard: the character of the yard must have determined that of Belfast to a significant extent. If so, Belfast has been formed in a crucible of toil and suffering and hard-won achievement. By all accounts, including their own, the Queen's Island men are cheerful, energetic, hard-working, boisterous, fun-loving: 'rough diamonds' and 'the salt of the earth' are the most familiar clichés. The spectacle in the city centre as masses of workers for both Harland & Wolff and Shorts, the aircraft factory, caught the eastbound trams, was frequently used to characterize the Queen's Island men. The Shorts workers would be smartly dressed, in collar and tie, and would form orderly queues; the shipyard men wore dunchers and boiler suits, and when their tram came they would all rush it at once, swarming over it and hanging on to every available surface, inside and out, like refugees on a train in India.

If they were hard-working, they also needed to be simply hard. There is a particular shipyard humour that is very strong on practical jokes, tall stories and derisive nicknames, which suggests a certain degree of casual cruelty, aggression and in-group solidarity. 'Nail in the Boot', for example, got his name because a missing toe gave him a slight limp. 'Forty Watts' wasn't too bright. 'Wire Nail' was a tall, thin man with a big flat cap. One of the kinder practical jokes concerned a man who came in drunk one morning. He made it up the side of the ship, but fell into a deep sleep on three planks, high up on the staging. Somebody came along and nailed his clothes to the planks, then got a crane to lower him, attached like Gulliver to the planks, to the ground.

The shipwrights, who hew wood with the footadze, trace their craft, in the Masonic fashion, back to Noah building the ark. They would tell a new apprentice that he must learn to strike the wood in the right place with his eyes closed: somebody would remove the lad's cap, pretending to replace it but in fact putting his cap on the wood, so that when he finished wielding the adze and opened his eyes he would find his cap in shreds. He had likely bought a new cap to start work in. Such initiations suggest the sense of humour, the secret knowledge, and the teaching by example that are suggestive of the ancient mysteries, or masteries, of medieval crafts.

It would help in the feeling of specialness and comradeship that the work was something they could be proud of. At different periods men would emigrate near and far and find that Harland & Wolff's reputation for good engineering had preceded them. When American ships came in for repair during World War Two, they were obviously built to an inferior standard.

Robert Bell's short story 'Yesterday's Da' captures precisely the moment when a young man is initiated into the world of his father, and the dawning understanding and belonging that can engender. It is a rite of passage as meaningful as that of a Masai youth, though one increasingly rare as old patterns of employment break down. The story is also aware of the communal and familial nature of the yard. As in many industries throughout Northern Ireland, the common way to get a job was through relatives already working there: a man would put in a word for his son or nephew. It meant that the older men could look after the younger ones, help them along and also, no doubt, occasionally keep them straight. It would also have strengthened the bonding between the male members of households, in that they shared a life quite separate from their womenfolk. To some extent the continuing discrepancy in the distribution of jobs between Catholics and Protestants is a by-product of this: while there is active religious discrimination, the fact that people in Northern Ireland, more than anywhere else in Britain, get their jobs through personal contact tends to reinforce any imbalance in a company's workforce.

Responsibility for the work and its organization was devolved quite far down. This could even mean that riveters, on strict piecework, would break into the yard on a Sunday to set up their jobs for the coming week, so that they would not waste time in preparation on Monday morning. The men were left to their own devices in many other ways. It is relatively recent, for example, for protective clothing or footwear to be provided: in Pirrie's day you came to work in your own clothes and often provided your own tools as well. Much of the work was outdoors, high up overlooking the water, yet there was no heating. The ground itself was wet and muddy, having come from the bed of the lough. There was no water for drinking or showering. Men would gather the black glowter – tallow and soap – that was used for greasing the slips, and heat up water in a tin in order to clean themselves. There was no tea break, so when brewing up they had to post sentinels to warn of approaching foremen. If the men were happy-go-lucky, the provisions for them by the management in the old days seem haphazard.

In the Main Yard workers had to bribe the crane drivers to lift their materials: the crane drivers were so poorly paid that they demanded 'blood' money before they would lift things. This was supportable by large gangs of men, but single workmen could not afford to pay, and so had to struggle up the ladders carrying whatever equipment and materials they needed. No doubt the casualty figures of men falling off the staging were not helped by such practices. *Steel Chest . . .* records several instances of industrial injury – missing fingers, blood-poisoning from burns – for which the compensation was meagre or indeed judged unnecessary: the solicitors employed by the workers appear to have been remarkably restrained in the sums they thought appropriate. Compensation for industrial deafness is a very recent innovation: nowadays ear mufflers are provided.

In bad times you got a job at an event reminiscent of the old hiring fairs, or of the casual dock labour scheme condemned in the film *On the Waterfront*. Men would form a 'market'; out of thirty or forty, only three or four might get a 'start'. The foreman would pick a journeyman, and the journeyman would pick a helper. The word 'journeyman', worker for a day, recalls the time of the ship's carpenters, before there were any organized yards on the Lagan.

While the workmen admired figures such as Pirrie for qualities like toughness, aggression, self-assertion, smartness, they also feared their bosses, with good reason. For all the boisterousness, when a manager walked by, every head went down. The terms of the contract on either side were conditional: as with other forms of Ulster loyalism, the fervour of sentimental attachment coincided with hard-headed self-interest.

The system could mean that the men had the freedom to feel that they were sometimes beating the system. The 'homer', the object made in work for use or sale at home, was a legendary phenomenon: many brass pokers must stand even today at firesides in front rooms across the city. Tins of battleship-grey paint decorated homes during the second war. At one time, Queen's Island men were said to form the bulk of the audience at cinema matinée performances. And during the slump of the thirties, when there was no work, those who could not be sacked might find a quiet corner for sunbathing, or borrow a boat and row across to the entertainments of York Street.

The shipyard covers a huge area, and at one time people could get up to all sorts of things. You could fish for mackerel, with string and silver paper, or catch pigeons on the beams of cranes, and roast them on a spit if you were feeling particularly hungry. The shipyard provided a livelihood, and friends, and the opportunity to feel satisfaction in difficult or skilful work well done, something which may be getting rarer. It also provided endless fun: as one of Hammond's interviewees says, 'You'd be afraid to take a day off in case you missed the antics.' At the same time it was exposed, uncomfortable, dangerous, unhealthy, heavy labour on a scale that dwarfed the individual. Charlie Witherspoon's account of the dread of working between the double skins of a hull is very vivid: you felt 'as if you were in some ghost city. Especially if you were working at night, there was just the odd clang of a hammer, coming from far, far away, and you felt absolutely isolated.'

To describe the yard workers as industrious, aggressively charming, unpretentious, insouciant (and indeed long-suffering in a way that might seem unhealthy), is to describe Belfast. Yet however important it has been, shipbuilding is only one aspect of the city and its character. There are animus and anima in the industries which determined the shape and the sort of Belfast. On the right-hand side is engineering: now, the aircraft factory is more important than Harland & Wolff, but the shipyard remains, as do other toolmakers and engineering firms. Once – until the slight boom after the end of World War Two finally declined – that was balanced by a left-hand side dominated by textiles: for fifty years, from the 1870s to the 1920s, Belfast was the largest producer of linen in the world. This was at a time when it was also the largest producer of ships and of rope.

Cotton spinning began in the Clifton Street Poor House in 1778. By the turn of the century, a decade after the introduction of steam power, cotton was Belfast's biggest industry. It was organized much more efficiently than linen, which was still largely an adjunct of farming. It thrived until Britain removed protective tariffs from Irish cotton in 1824. Thomas Mulholland had one of the few cotton mills in Belfast, and when it burned down in 1818 he decided to rebuild it as a flax spinning mill. In 1861 there were thirty-two mills spinning flax in Belfast and only two spinning cotton. Supplies of cotton were disrupted for the next four years by the American Civil War, further encouraging the switch to linen. The last cotton mill in Ireland, at Springfield, closed in 1919.

Linen took a long time to become fully mechanized. By 1850 only two firms used power looms for weaving. Nevertheless, though most accounts say that weaving was the last aspect to be mechanized, hackling was still done by hand into the 1920s, when the 'iron man' began to replace flesh and blood. Three quarters of the spinning mill workers were women, but hackling was done by men who were regarded as the elite of the mill, doing a skilled job which it took up to seven years to master. At a time when a farm labourer earned ten or twelve shillings per week, a hackler could make four or five times as much. Many saved their money and bought small shops which their wives, the 'hacklers' ladies', managed. The hackler went to work wearing collar and tie (which would be removed in the mill) and waistcoat. His apron was of white linen, and he wore a cap, or in summer a paper hat, at work.

The fibre came to the hacklers retted, dried and scutched, like long, flaxen hair which they would comb through metal brushes. The hacklers' room had no noisy machinery, so they could talk to each other if permitted by management. Often a 'reader' would report the day's newspaper stories to the others. They were regarded as wits, and were given to riddles and nicknames as well as the universal practical jokes. When left alone, they might have a session of step dancing. But it was dry work: the air was filled with stir and pouce, fluff and dust from the flax. They chewed tobacco to keep their throats moist, and traditionally favoured strong liquor, rum and whiskey. The dust caused chest and eye diseases. Roughers dealt with dirtier flax, and so suffered more. This trade was one of the few in the industry to be unionized: many men were helped to emigrate to America at the start of this century. In her valuable study, *Picking Up the Linen Threads*, Betty Messenger says that these aristocrats of the mill are now quite forgotten in Belfast.

Large numbers of children worked in the spinning rooms until 1901, when the legal starting age was raised to twelve years. School had been made compulsory up to the age of thirteen, but many children began working on alternate days at twelve, and even younger children continued to come in, with forged birth certificates. When the bobbins on a frame needed to be changed the doffing mistress would blow her whistle and the gang of young doffers would come to help unload the machine and set it up again. They would rush from one end of the room to another in response to the whistle, for fifty-three hours a week.

It took two or more years for a girl to become a spinner tending her own 'stand', which would normally be between two double-sided frames, and dealing with one side of each. Spinners took pride in the tools of their trade, the chopper and picker, which were worn on a plaited cord around the waist and displayed on the apron. This array of tools could be dangerous, for sometimes they got entangled in the machinery and pulled the worker into the frame. At the turn of the century mill workers were regarded as poorly paid, though they earned more than farm labourers or domestic servants. The bobbins of rove were drawn through troughs of very hot water before they were wound onto bobbins, so the spinning room was hot, damp and dirty.

The spinners needed dexterity, skill and good eyesight to deal with broken ends of rove, which could become entangled in the machinery. Broken ends were joined together by stopping the flyer and rubbing the two ends together between the palms with a distinctive slapping and flexing motion: this was laying up the ends.

The spinning mill was a multistorey building, whereas the weaving factory usually had to be on the flat, since the looms were reciprocating rather than rotary machines. The factory had a serrated 'north-light roof' whose windows would be whitewashed in summer. Equally distinctive were the imposing, square, red-brick mills with their tall chimneys. Factory workers regarded themselves as rather better than mill workers: their jobs were cleaner, and the weavers were on piecework, besides having the chance of learning highly skilled crafts.

In Belfast, women mainly had the jobs of warping, winding and weaving, but this was not the case in the country areas. The low wages of handloom weavers helped delay the introduction of power looms until after the Famine of 1846–7. The first steam loom did not appear in Belfast until 1843, in Linenhall Street. By 1870 there were more than 15,000 power looms in Ulster, and Belfast's half-century as the linen capital of the world had begun.

Like the spinners, the weavers took pride in their work and the tools and particular skills it involved. The heddle hook, used to draw in the broken ends of the warp, was carried in the mouth, the small pair of weaver's scissors in the palm of the hand. Weavers were said to be inseparable from their scissors, which they could hold even whilst using both hands to do something else. The ripper could be plain or elaborate, the best examples having brass handles made by the men in the factory. The 'weaver's knot' was a special, very flat knot which it took much time to learn. The weaver 'kissed the shuttle' when she sucked the weft thread through the eye of the shuttle, when a new pirn bobbin was started. Betty Messenger notes that the weaver's kiss is idiomatic for something weak: flaking paint is 'strong as a weaver's kiss'.

Even with the Jacquard looms, which created patterns automatically, weaving required concentration, patience and craftsmanship. It could be fiddly to repair broken warps, to find the appropriate mail in the heddle, then draw the end through the right dent in the comb-like reed, and to join the ends as unobtrusively as possible. The weaver took her work to the cloth passer, who would fine her for any mistakes.

The looms were crowded in, and the noise was deafening, so weavers became adept at communicating by sign language or lip-reading. Humidity was kept high, especially for finer cloth. It must have been desperately tiring work. Indeed, it is said that the current revival in demand for linen for fashionable clothes and in newly developed mixed fabrics has not been fully exploited because of people's reluctance to go back to that sort of work. Betty Messenger takes pains to stress that conditions have been improved, and that the popular idea of life in mill and factory – now often more of a memory – is strikingly different from that of the workers themselves, who were cheerful and liked their jobs.

Occupational diseases were rife. The symptoms of mill fever make it sound like a general allergy to the heat, oily humidity and general busyness of the spinning room. Foot rot would result from going barefoot in the wet, warm conditions. Yet it was commonly thought that wet-spinning gave you a clear complexion and a 'fine big head of hair' and was a sovereign cure for a weak chest.

The divisions of the industry are celebrated by its songs: different trades within the mill or the factory would have poked fun at each other in song even though they very often relied on each other not to make the job more difficult than it need be. The reelers, for example, who transferred the yarn onto large wheels and who were supposed to have the best job in the mill, depended on the spinners for a steady supply of good bobbins, but there was a certain amount of rivalry between the two:

> Never marry a reeler
> For you wouldn't know her pay
> But marry a good old spinner
> With her belly wet all day.

As well as stressing the positive attitude of the women and girls to their work, Messenger also stresses the camaraderie within the various trades. The doffers were younger and full of song, and would march down the streets arm in arm singing and laughing. The weavers were often older women working in a very noisy environment on piecework, so that they had less opportunity or inclination for singing and mischief-making. But they had self-respect. The starched white apron was the badge of a superior job, as were the weaver's scissors.

From the weaving factory the grey cloth or brown linen was taken for bleaching and washing, and finishing. All over Ulster, but particularly in the Lagan Valley on the way into Belfast, the bleach greens used to be as extraordinary a part of the landscape as the great mills and factories: long lines of linen cloth lay across the grass like white carpets. Finally the cloth was washed, cleaned and polished at the washmill, the rub mill and the beetling mill.

For a crucial, formative period, Belfast was given over to two products, linen and ships, to the clang of hammer on steel and the busy clatter and odd poetry of the linen process. Shipbuilding, situated on man-made land as if it wanted to get as near the open sea as possible, used imported materials. Linen used an indigenous plant; it started not at the water's edge but inland, by streams. The yard's material is mineral, hard, huge and heavy: the mills and factories worked with an organic material that was fine and tiny. One required great strength, the other dexterity. One was outdoors; the other took place indoors, in a hell of intricate machinery, heat, humidity and fluff. One was male, mostly Protestant, and a symbol of the Union or 'Britishness'. Linen was much more mixed. Depending on the location of mill or factory, there was a varying ratio of denominations. Men and boys did some jobs on the periphery, while women and girls did the spinning and weaving.

Shipbuilding had a culture of *machismo*. You needed strength, stamina, courage to deal with huge steel structures, to handle red-hot metal, to keep a clear head hundreds of feet up in the air or lost in the bowels of a ship. You had to be equal to the tricks of your comrades, the demands of your bosses, and the cons of the hucksters who haunted the yard. You had to be a master of your craft, able to make something out of a lump of intractable metal or wood so that it was strong and would fit. The culture of linen was communal and sexy. A high proportion of the workforce consisted of young girls, aged thirteen and upwards, who were naturally interested in boys. At least one section of the industry spent a lot of time singing, often songs about marriage and sexual relations which might be improvised on traditional models by collective effort.

> A for Barney,
> B for Ross,
> Oh, but I love Barney Ross.
> All the world will never, never know
> The love I have for the band-tier-o.

By contrast, what has been collected from the folklore of the shipyard is more often a McGonaglesque ballad or a parody, as in the mock hymn to Pirrie, concerning work rather than love. Both industries had a variety of customs to do with the initiation of apprentices, involving sending them for a 'bucket of steam', a 'rubber hammer', a 'tin of striped paint', or a 'left-handed saw', but there appears to be a larger stock of rituals and traditions in the linen industry. Perhaps children and young teenagers were more given to devising rituals; in any case, the variety of them seemed to disappear as the age of the workers was raised. Many Hallowe'en traditions had to do with finding out the name of your future husband, by reading tealeaves, by brushing the pass or walkway and leaving the broom to see which boy walked by, or with a widow's key in a Bible open at the Book of Ruth. One tradition unique to the Belfast linen industry was the lighting-up party: in the days when artificial lighting was provided only in winter and gas fittings or, later, bulbs had to be put up beforehand, the workers would celebrate with singing and dancing, and food and drink bought in communally.

'Shawlie' and 'millie' could be terms of abuse. The girls would come out of work in shawls over dirty clothes and with dirty legs, barefoot. In the Belfast fashion, their humour could be aggressive and outspoken, and they formed themselves into raucous crowds. Yet even the censorious classes who deplored their vulgarity might retain a sneaking affection for the spectacle of the mill girls. Their petticoats were full and made of 'Newtownards strip', a heavy fabric in thin stripes of contrasting colours such as black and red, or light and dark blue. They might wear overskirts to and from work. Their underwear was often made out of bleached flour sacks. Gradually the habit of wearing coats and shoes filtered from the more genteel trades to the spinners and doffers.

The girls were remarkable for their singing. One of the few examples of industrial unrest recorded by Messenger was a dispute in 1912. Amongst other grievances were new regulations forbidding singing, laughing and talking at work. James Connolly, then working for the Irish Transport and General Workers' Union in the north, could not help the girls with the main problems, but he advised them 'not to go back in ones and twos, but to gather outside the mills and all go in in a body; to go in singing'.

William Conor and Denis Ireland provide contrasting attitudes to the linen industry. Both were Presbyterians, but there are few other resemblances. Conor more often painted mill girls than shipyard men and he has made the figure of the smiling woman in a shawl almost archetypal of a Belfast working class, and an attitude towards it, that has disappeared. Denis Ireland belonged to a family of linen merchants and manufacturers, and worked in the business himself, although his attitude to it, like his attitude to Belfast as a whole, was by no means one of sunny, unquestioning acceptance: he was more likely to refer to the 'black regiments of factory chimneys' than to eulogize industrial folklore or the urban picturesque. The two men may not have been far apart politically: Conor had an optimistic interest in the dignity of working people, and he Gaelicized his name, from Connor, in the style of the Celtic Revival. But for Denis Ireland, a self-proclaimed radical Presbyterian conscious of the United Irishmen tradition, there was a feeling of exploitation which, from Conor's perspective, as from the shawlies' themselves, seems irrelevant.

In *The Irish Sketch Book* Thackeray tends to the Conor attitude:

> *A fine night-exhibition in the town is that of the huge spinning-mills which surround it, and of which the thousand windows are lighted up at nightfall, and may be seen from almost all quarters of the city.*

It sounds like the home of Vulcan himself, with the glitter of red-hot rivets, Denis Ireland's fireflies, and the great mills with their lit-up windows. Thackeray's description of the work is equally vivid, but somewhat vague:

> *there are nearly five hundred girls employed in it [Mulholland's mill]. They work in huge long chambers, lighted by numbers of windows, hot with steam, buzzing and humming with hundreds of thousands of whirling wheels that all take their motion from a steam-engine which lives apart in a hot cast-iron temple of its own, from which it communicates with the innumerable machines that the five hundred girls preside over. They have seemingly but to take away the work when done – the enormous monster in the cast-iron room does it all. He cards the flax, and combs it, and spins it, and beats it, and twists it; the five hundred girls stand by to feed him, or take the material from him, when he has had his will of it. There is something frightful in the vastness as in the minuteness of his power. Every thread writhes and twirls as the steam-fate orders it, – every thread, of which it would take a hundred to make the thickness of a hair.*

Conor would have concurred with Thackeray's observations on the girls themselves and, no doubt, with his general conclusions:

> *I have seldom, I think, seen more good looks than amongst the young women employed in this place. They work for twelve hours daily, in rooms of which the heat is intolerable to a stranger; but in spite of it they look gay, stout, and healthy; nor were their forms much concealed by the very simple clothes they wear while in the mill.*
>
> *The stranger will be struck by the good looks not only of these spinsters, but of almost all the young women in the streets. I never saw a town where so many women are to be met – so many and so pretty: with and without bonnets, with good figures, in neat homely shawls and dresses; the grisettes of Belfast are among the handsomest ornaments of it, and as good, no doubt, and irreproachable in morals as their sisters in the rest of Ireland.*

Thackeray includes one of his own sketches of a pretty, black-haired girl in the mill. He shows no interest whatever in the machine she was working at.

The vestiges of the linen trade survive as tenuously as shipbuilding in Belfast today. Thackeray's account of his visit to what might well have been the first of the steam-powered mills could be about a world as remote as that of the handloom weavers. In *Rhyming Weavers* John Hewitt collected the verses those men composed as they sat at the looms in their cottages: James Campbell of Ballynure, for example, 'kept an inkhorn and paper with reach' for 'the principal part of his stanzas was composed at the loom'. Their poems were printed, mainly in Belfast, in pamphlet form, from about the middle of the eighteenth century until the trade died out and, like the books of John Clare, were sold by subscription, though usually only two hundred copies at a time. One of these poets, Alexander McKenzie, sold two hundred pounds' worth of his *Poems and Songs*. He bought a fishing boat and a cottage, but the boat was wrecked and he was evicted in 1812.

The handloom weavers were descended from the Scots planted in County Down by Hamilton and Montgomery and in Antrim by the Earl of Antrim. Hugh Porter of County Down wrote in 1813:

> . . . in the style appears
> The accent o' my early years,
> Which is nor Scotch or English either,
> But part o' both mix'd up thegither;
> Yet is the sort my neighbours use,
> Who think shoon prettier than shoes.

By 1844, the year Robert Huddleston's *A Collection of Poems and Songs on Rural Subjects* was published, this sort of weaver was dying out. Messenger records distant memories of the tramp hacklers, men who drifted from place to place, getting work for a while or, if none was available, setting off again after the other hacklers had taken a whip-round to send them on their way; perhaps some old weavers led such an itinerant life, others emigrated or gave up the loom and concentrated on farming. In 'The Lammas Fair' Huddleston gives a vital, vivid picture of a Belfast custom which is now as defunct as the trade of the man who wrote it. Nowadays 'Lammas Fair' means The Ould Lammas Fair in Ballycastle, so it is not only the language of this remarkable poem that is surprising to the modern reader.

> In Smithfield as I toddled through,
>   The dread uproar was deavin';
> Wi' tinsel'd frock, an' painted brow,
>   The pappit show seemed lievin'.
> A bulk o' fo'k aroun' was clad,
>   O' a' kin's you could mention;
> Tae see aul' Jerry wi' the wig,
>   An' miter'd frocks a' dancin',
>   For pense that day.

Wi' tassel'd caps an' gleamin' blades,
  Wi' fifein' an wi' drummin';
The red coat boys now on parade,
  They shake the grun they're gaun on:
An' clout the sheepskin yet extends,
  An' wheeper's louder blawin';
Till after them ful' mony wend,
  An' some's up tae them jawin',
    Right glib that day.

The music quats – the serjeant cries,
  Big bounty don't resist it;
A jug o' punch boys, don't despise,
  A soger's life's the best o't.
An' see how many blackguard rogues,
  An' strappin' billies listenin';
Wi' courage bauld charm'd ower their sads,
  An' cagy shillin's fistin',
    Wha'll rue't some day.

There sits a tinker wi' his tins,
  A turner wi' his ladles;
A gleg tongu'd spunkie's cryin' spoons,
  Anither's at her fables.
Billowre! a singer's come tae han',
  The crowd is geather'd roun' her;
A pick-pocket them slips amang,
  His booty there to plun'er
    Wi' craft that day.

There is Dickensian or Jonsonian vivacity in Huddleston's Smithfield, with its sharp-tongued spoon seller, the puppet show, the pickpocket, and the recruiting sergeant offering the King's shilling. One link with such scenes was destroyed when the old Smithfield secondhand market, an Ulster souk as seedy and unexpected as any browser or bargain-hunter could wish for, was first burnt down, then rebuilt as a mean little square of unattractive shops, then finally brushed away in a huge redevelopment scheme to provide malls for nineties shoppers.

Linen and ships made Belfast utterly different from any other place in Ireland, and perhaps helped alter the political fate of the whole island. Like industries everywhere, they quickened change: the past Huddleston worked in and wrote about was swept away, but by 1950 both ships and linen were themselves in decline, and overtaken in economic importance by engineering. The local flair for metallurgy is reflected from time to time when police discover caches of home-made machineguns.

When the postwar linen boom petered out, the Unionist government tried to promote a switch to synthetic fibres. There have been other, less permanent industries, brought by multinationals or rogue entrepreneurs lured in with government aid. When Ravi Tikkoo popped up, ready to 'save the shipyard', it was appropriate that his notion – since it seemed to be only a notion – for the most amazing ever luxury cruise liner was called the *Ultimate Dream.*

Other dreams included the Learfan, an attempt to carry out the last design of the man who gave us the Lear Jet executive aeroplane. It foundered when it failed to pass safety standards: it had two engines, but only one propeller. Then there was John Zachary De Lorean, given £80 million to make a fibreglass car with a stainless steel skin and gullwing doors (which occasionally trapped people inside). He was a plausible, likeable fellow, the sort of wayward genius whose promises of jobs have proved irresistible in Belfast. People seem to like him in America too: he persuaded the jury in his trial that the FBI had entrapped him in a massive drugs deal.

There are other, nobler failures in Belfast industry. John Boyd Dunlop, for example, the Scottish vet who, when in Belfast in 1889, perfected the pneumatic tyre and caused the eclipse of the penny-farthing bicycle. He was soon bought out of the business that still bears his name. Harry Ferguson invented the tractor, which has changed the face of the earth. He went into partnership with Henry Ford when he failed to find financial backing for it locally. Ford's grandson tried to repudiate the handshake agreement in 1947, but was forced to pay compensation.

De Lorean could be the nadir of Belfast's industrial pride. Just down the road from the failed car factory, where government intervention died a death, is the site of one of the greatest triumphs for state aid, the birthplace of Belfast's linen industry. Hilden – just a halt on the railway line, a village in the Lagan Valley between Belfast and Lisburn – still has a centre for research into the fabric. At the end of the seventeenth century, it was where Louis Crommelin laid the basis for an industry of world importance.

Samuel-Louis Crommelin (he later dropped the 'Samuel') was born in 1652 in Picardy to a wealthy family of landowners and flax growers. They were Protestants, but Louis converted to Catholicism in 1683. This did not help his family after the revocation of the Edict of Nantes two years later: their business suffered like that of other French Protestants. When Louis reconverted to Protestantism, his property was seized and his buildings were torn down. He fled to Amsterdam, where he went into banking.

William III, the new Dutch king of England, asked Crommelin to investigate the colony of French Huguenots who had settled in the Lagan Valley around Lisburn, and to study ways of promoting linen manufacture in Ireland. In 1696 the English had encouraged such Protestant immigration, as well as making imports of Irish hemp and flax into England duty-free. In 1698 King William had set out his plan to protect England from Irish competition in wool, but to allow Ireland to develop linen.

Crommelin arrived in autumn 1698, reported to the Treasury a few months later, and was appointed 'overseer of the royal linen manufacture of Ireland' at £200 a year. The scheme was granted £10,000, and provision was made for a French minister, Charles Lavalade, to look after the spiritual needs of the Huguenots.

Crommelin thought the spinning wheel he found in use in Ireland was better than those of other countries, but he employed craftsmen to make improvements. He bought looms from Flanders and Holland, and paid a premium of £5 for looms which were kept going. The finest reed-maker in Cambrai, the home of cambric, was brought in. The Huguenots trained locals in weaving, and Dutchmen were imported to teach the growing and bleaching of flax. Louis Crommelin died in 1727, and the only trace of his name in Belfast is Ulsterized, in the Crumlin Road. But he bequeathed an industry.

The beetling engine appeared just after the arrival of the Huguenots. Some say it derived from machines used in the Scots and Ulster paper and oil mills, but Bardon says it almost certainly came from Holland: 'The first one in Ireland was at Drumbo in 1735, managed by "a genuine Hollander".' Like the washmill, a Newton's Cradle of great wooden hammers which thump the fabric, and the rub mill, in which marble or lignum vitae plates rub ropes of cloth like a pair of hands, the beetling engine is huge and wooden, like a giant's toy. It is an outsize Pan pipes in which birchwood beetles of railway sleeper proportions are raised and let fall, one after another, to pound the linen, closing the web and making it shiny. This gives the characteristic sheen of the best linen and the sword-blade glister of damask (the weaving of which was later mechanized by another French invention, the Jacquard loom).

What Crommelin gave the industry was quality: before him, good linen and cambric had to be imported from the Continent; after Louis Crommelin, the best linen was Irish. In 'The Ballad of William Bloat' it becomes Nemesis: in his 'mean abode on the Shankill Road' William Bloat cuts his wife's throat then, in a fit of remorse, decides to hang himself with a sheet. His wife recovers, he doesn't:

> For the razor blade was German made,
> But the sheet was Belfast linen.

Despite this popular ballad, linen has to do with the celebration of marriage. The female principle of Belfast's industrial past survives as the coming-together of Irish, French, Dutch, Scots and English.

CHAPTER TEN

WHO THEN IS IT THAT DISLIKES BELFAST?

It was some time ago very much the fashion to abuse this unfortunate town, and indeed this propensity still continues amongst the very vile and ignorant, who always take their cue from those above them, and who are incapable of speaking at all without a prompter. Now, as there is perhaps no spot on earth where better morals, more decent conduct, more real virtue, or more of the light of reason prevails, it is curious to weigh the accusers against the accused.

Who then is it that dislikes Belfast?

A gang of corrupt courtiers, who build their fortunes upon the ignorance, vice, degradation and religious disunion of this country – they dislike Belfast!

A gang of prostitute and base mercenaries, dependent upon those courtiers, who raise themselves to their favour by all manner of villainy, such as persuading simple people to perjure themselves at elections by laughing at conscience and integrity as a State joke – they dislike Belfast!

A gang of dissolute Bishops, who enjoy a great portion of the lands of the country and a great share in the legislature of it, who, instead of taking any tender or affectionate interest in the welfare of the poor, are no further known to them than as they corrupt them by their example or oppress them by their avarice – they and their clergy hate Belfast! There are several laudable exceptions here.

The whole gang of tax-gatherers, pensioners and sycophants – cry out against Belfast!

The gentlemen of the standing army, whose duty it is to think, speak, and act as they are commanded, even when their own lives are in question, and who are often slaughtered before they are quite fattened – they swear most bloodily that they'll burn Belfast!!!

Booby Squires, who are dupes of subtle courtiers, and who have not sagacity to see that by making common cause with them they are running headlong into the consequence of their vices, 'Lives and fortune men' and 'Protestant ascendancy boys' – they are contemptible enough to spit their little venom at Belfast!

Guzzling corporations, jealous of their absurd monopolies and mock dignity – they drink damnation to Belfast!!!

Old, idle, card-playing tabbies, who complain that the mob have raised the price of chair-hire and butcher's meat – they are at a loss to account for the wicked

disturbances in Belfast!
And the disinterested tribe of the law – take no fees for railing against Belfast!

It seems that there has never been a shortage of people with strong adverse opinions about the city. To the *Northern Star*'s list of 1794, the critic Edna Longley could add the gentlemen of the standing army of Irish poets and novelists. She gathers the adjectives used by three Belfast writers, Michael McLaverty, Louis MacNeice and Brian Moore, to describe their town: *desolate, hard, cold, melancholy, lurid, run-down, provincial, grey, black, ugly, dull, dead.*

It is disturbing, what with one thing and another, how frequently such distaste turns into a desire for wholesale destruction. In *The Emperor of Ice-Cream*, two of Brian Moore's characters playfully extend the wartime Blitz to demolish, in their imaginations, the city's landmarks. If its most celebrated and most absent practising novelist can disown his home town in an early book, it comes as little surprise to remember that the poet John Hewitt was also half in love with an apocalyptic future.

Hewitt left Belfast for Coventry when he was passed over as Curator at the Ulster Museum because, he believed, of his politics. On the boat to England he thought of suicide. Yet he returned to live a long and increasingly honoured retirement. His straightforward verses, with their simple rhythms, made him a widely read and fondly regarded figure. In the changed atmosphere of the 1980s, despite his continuing socialism, Belfast City Council gave him the Freedom of the city, the first time it had honoured a poet.

It is true, however, that when the award was proposed the Unionists had to be told who John Hewitt was. It seems unlikely that many of them rushed across to the Linen Hall Library to consult his *Collected Poems*. If they had, they would have found that, in earlier work at least, the poet would have had little regret to have found Belfast replaced by nettles crowning 'mounds of rust' and its factory chimneys tumbled. Britta Olinder notes how Hewitt began by turning away from the city to the landscape 'because men disappoint me', to a countryside – the Glens of Antrim – in which he was a stranger. The 'problem' of Belfast, its constant confrontation of the individual with its morally and politically insupportable nature, may have encouraged its writers to make apocalypse a favourite theme. Yet, as Olinder points out, later in life Hewitt came to regret the passing-away of the old town he grew up in, which increasingly became associated with a personal history.

In verse and prose Belfast is often treated as a challenge, as the embodiment of the paradox of Irish life, or as the arena of its most problematic and unrewarding struggle. Derek Mahon associates Belfast with responsibility: in 'Afterlives' he explicitly says that to understand and commit oneself to the life of the city is to grow up and to learn the meaning of home: it is merely a middle-class fantasy to imagine that one's civilized, non-sectarian ideals make one morally superior. By removing oneself from the place one avoids complicity and compromise, but one also opts for dreams instead of the possibility of effective action. The city changes, for example visually, because of bombs, so that it becomes unrecognizable and inexplicable to the exile. Louis McNeice, as Longley points out, was one of the group of writers who first made the modern city a resonant subject in poetry, so it is interesting that for him Belfast was the first city. Although Birmingham was where he confronted the general social and political implications of urban life, the poet himself was aware, as Longley notes in her study of MacNeice, that images imprinted on the young mind are those the writer instinctively turns to: a garden is always his childhood garden, with the hedge that was periodically cut to reveal the headstones of the graveyard attached to his father's church.

For Seamus Heaney, Belfast is also a challenge, but one that is not, as Longley implies, confidently met. It is striking, she says, that his response to the suffering and injustice he finds there is 'the paralysis of faculties', a weariness, an inability to say the adequate thing, and a feeling that the light of reason, as lit by the United Irishmen, is decisively put out. Good poets are able, of course, to make good poems out of dumbness, but the contrast is suggestive. Unlike Hewitt, Heaney did not have to leave home to find rural subjects. Heaney's mentor, Michael McLaverty, was born in Monaghan and, although he has made his life in the city, his approach to it in his work has been from afar. In *Call My Brother Back* the protagonist comes from Rathlin Island to Belfast in the early decades of this century. The lapsarian title of another novel, *Lost Fields*, along with its nationalist reverberations, suggests the movement of these novels. The city, the capital of the newly devised Unionist state, is seen from a Catholic and a nationalist viewpoint as a sinful place.

Edna Longley records her relief when in the novels of Forrest Reid and Janet McNeill the city is merely a backdrop to the action. Film-makers too are susceptible to focusing on the setting rather than their ostensible subject. In an enterprising experiment, the young novelist Robert Wilson, author of *Ripley Bogle*, was given a small video camera and allowed to make a film for the BBC about his return home to Belfast. The resulting 'Video Diary' is chaotic, self-indulgent and perhaps naive in its readiness to offer solutions, but also immediate and authentic. Once again the city is a major protagonist (at one point personified in pretty girls seen in the street) which presents the hero with a choice involving many things – career, personal safety, one's own sometimes painful past, above all morality and personal identity. Does one not feel disgust for a place where people are routinely murdered, where Reginald Maudling's 'acceptable level of violence' is only kept within bounds by an often clumsily counter-productive army? Do the peculiar immoralities of the city – its sectarian bigotry, its social injustice, its still-strong philistinism – not impugn one's own identity, when one elects to make the place home? At the end of World War Two Hewitt wrote that it was only recently that even moderately sensitive minds could 'endure and remain'. Many writers, after 1945, found it difficult to endure and remain.

Brian Barton's book *The Blitz* treats not only the Luftwaffe raids which killed eleven hundred people and damaged over half Belfast's housing, but also the appalling poverty exposed in a city that had begun the century full of confidence. He also corrects two myths. One was that the bombing encouraged people to put sectarianism aside: however, when Bill Rolston, reviewing the book, asks what scale of war would be needed to dispel sectarianism, he misses the point, that war does not dispel sectarianism. The other myth was that Belfast 'did its bit' for Britain: the bombs severely damaged the shipyard's capacity, while the aircraft factory had very low productivity throughout the war. As with that other loyalist myth, the Somme, the facts do not agree: more people from the South than the North fought for Britain in World War One.

From the end of World War Two comes *Odd Man Out*, the film which established Carol Reed as an important director. Based on F.L. Green's novel, it was released in 1947. With a script by Green and R.C. Sherriff, it foreshadows Reed's most celebrated film, *The Third Man*: both deal with an anti-hero trying to escape justice; both show his nocturnal flight through a vividly portrayed city in symbolic and expressionistic terms. If *The Third Man* has the more romantic elements, *Odd Man Out* is arguably richer and more complex.

Once again Belfast becomes a character in a study of moral choice, ethics and the clash between political and religious purity on the one hand, and compromise and personal desire on the other. The film begins with a shot from an aeroplane flying over Belfast Lough, the docks and the Albert Clock. Important turns in the plot are associated with Belfast landmarks: the mill which is robbed by 'the organization'; the bomb shelter in which Johnny McQueen, the wounded gunman played by James Mason, hides; the Falls Road tram that is so overcrowded it has to stop, allowing one of the gang to be captured; the snug in the Crown Bar that allows Johnny to hide till closing time; also perhaps the derelict gentility of the ruin inhabited by the painter, Lukey, the internal features of which appear to be based on the Crescent; and, brooding over all, the Albert Clock.

Reed uses the children of the streets to add authenticity. And it is significant that what begins as a taut, apparently conventional thriller swiftly turns into something stranger and more ambitious as soon as its anti-hero goes outside, into the real world, as it were, signalled by location shots of Royal Avenue and Donegall Square: Johnny, just escaped from jail, suffers vertigo, a lack of clarity of vision, which ultimately causes his death and the death of the girl who loves him. The city, the film says, is bewildering, and in formal terms the city is presented as reality. It turns into a phantasmagoria – literally, at one point, for the dying man – at first of ordinary people to whom the gunman's story is irrelevant, and finally of grotesques, who see in him only their own interests reflected.

Robert Wilson and Glenn Patterson, another young Belfast novelist with whom he collaborated in making his film, echo F.L. Green and Carol Reed in talking about how bewildering Belfast is, with its normality, its tremendously likeable vitality, and its apparently inseparable horrors. The way in which these coexist without the discomfort one would expect seems at times indecent. Patterson admits that Belfast has been filmed over and over again. This is true, but only of the period since the present Troubles broke out. Before then, *Odd Man Out* was extremely unusual. Literature has some parallels: Edna Longley sees an unlocking of individual memories since 1969, and the growing self-confidence of non-metropolitan artists since the 1960s, encouraged by the Arts Council of Northern Ireland, has helped to make Belfast a familiar subject. At any one time there seems to be a large number of plays about Belfast and the 'Irish question' running in the London fringe theatre, few of them worth seeing.

One of the most powerful treatments of Belfast in literature, and arguably the most important poetry event in the 1980s, derives from the re-entry of Ciarán Carson into publishing. After his first poetry collection, *The New Estate*, Carson concentrated on playing and listening to traditional music, one of the glories of Ireland and of Belfast, where it is possible to hear music of the highest quality and integrity in a number of pubs and clubs across the city. If it were not a phrase fraught with so many overtones already explored by the poems themselves, one might be tempted to say that *The Irish For No* and *Belfast Confetti* have rewritten the map of Belfast.

Edna Longley distinguishes between those who see Belfast as their fault and those who see it as their fate. Belfast is Carson's fate. The city is a map of itself. Its layers represent history and paths not taken in history – there are maps which too optimistically include prospective developments, maps which show streets and areas that have disappeared, replaced by new developments already destined to disappear; they represent memory, like ghosts or layers of wallpaper; they represent the languages of those who have renamed and reclaimed streets and places, whether from Irish to English to Irish again, or graffiti on graffiti, saying, *This place is ours*, or *We were here*; they represent home and family, progressively discovered. Everything is itself and also a sign to be deconstructed, a visual or verbal pun that recalls another fragment of childhood, a news story, an historical event.

Carson is unlike Robert Wilson and almost every other Belfast writer in one way: brought up in the Catholic tradition, he writes about Belfast as his own city, an insider who has neither arrived from elsewhere nor gone into exile. Derek Mahon, from another tradition, talks of 'my own' people, but as someone who has left and is aware of his loss of 'home': there is never any doubt where Carson's home is. Michael Longley, the other outstanding resident poet of Belfast, draws on the different strategy of MacNeice, Yeats and Synge, who looked to the west of Ireland for some sort of authentic Irishness that might include them. John Montague has claimed, only half in jest, that he is the 'missing link' of Ulster

Catholic poetry with the Gaelic poets of the eighteenth century, and that, as a young man, there was no question of him going to Belfast to write poetry.

Carson is engaged in a process not dissimilar to that of the club of Australian exiles he celebrates in both poem and essay, who get together to talk about home and between themselves reconstruct, street by street, house by house, the Falls Road. Carson's evocation of Belfast, seen from the viewpoint of the Falls Road, is no less meticulous than that of the Woolongong exiles, or indeed of James Joyce's re-creation of Dublin in *Ulysses*. Such evocation implies loss: it is as if everyone is an exile in Belfast, not only the vast numbers forced to leave their homes when the Troubles erupted, but all who have simply grown up and remember a city that has changed beyond recognition in twenty years or so.

In Carson's 'Slate Street School' the children watch snow falling and are told that each snowflake is a soul released from Purgatory as it reaches the ground. It may not be straining a point to see the consciousness behind this treatment of Belfast as essentially Catholic. It inhabits and appears to relish an infinitely complex, and complicated, intellectual construct that seeks to account for, if not to explain, the world. Carson's attitude is open and contingent, but amongst the ashes of the burnt Smithfield he sees an elaborate key.

Carson shares the taste for the apocalyptic, but differs from Derek Mahon in seeming to inhabit the last days cosily, where Mahon's relish is puritanical. Carson celebrates the 'collapse' – a word which recurs – of the city. This is literally visible, in the lean of the Albert Clock or the sag of the Grand Central Hotel, now gone. But such things are the facts of postmodern life: Carson does not waste time drawing morals.

Like others he discusses or alludes to the unfailing topic of Belfast discourse, identity. One essay is precisely about questions of identity. 'Question Time' tells how he was stopped when cycling around the streets he grew up in, on the Falls Road: local vigilantes forced him to prove that he did come from the area as he claimed by answering a series of questions that amounted to a catechism of local history. In the poem 'Campaign' assassins are anxious to establish 'who exactly' their target is, but then decide to kill him because of 'what' he is.

What makes Carson's treatment of identity richer and more rewarding than most is that it discusses the question in far more precise terms, while allowing for the frustrations and the delights of imprecision. As Ciaran McKeown, one of the founders of the Peace People and an unfailingly fertile pacifist thinker, observes in Robert Wilson's 'Video Diary', there is a constant pressure in Belfast to identify and define precisely, to set one's thoughts against what prevails. Michael Longley says that in meeting people one is more alert and alive, one's antennae are more sensitive in Belfast than elsewhere. Carson's elaborations have an insane compulsiveness about them that could be claustrophobic, but he enriches our understanding of the city we share in the way he sifts the riches of his own recovered understanding. Identity, we realize, is infinitely more complicated, richer and more interesting than anything which could be represented by a flag. To imagine that calling oneself an Ulster Protestant, for example, is a definition of one's political views, social class, antecedents, or indeed religious beliefs is to ignore the past, and to engage in the strategic blurring of which Henry Cooke was guilty.

The Falls, the area in which Carson was brought up, is on the line of that ancient, perhaps pre-Celtic, track from the Black Mountain down the Falls Road, Divis Street and Castle Street that Estyn Evans sees as the line of Catholic penetration of the city in the nineteenth century. High Street, which runs on from Castle Street behind the Albert Clock, is funnel-shaped, wide and curving because it follows the course of the Farset River, now covered in, which once allowed ships into the town centre. Carson meditates on *Falls*, from the Irish *fál*, meaning *hedge*, *frontier*, or *thing enclosed*. There are new, man-made boundaries in Belfast, the 'peace line' walls to keep apart differing communities, but the Farset, further upstream, divides the ancient track of the Falls and the ancient track of the Shankill. So the Falls remains a frontier, and also perhaps a sort of enclosure, in the sense of ghetto. Carson also makes us think of 'the undiscovered country from whose bourne no traveller returns', which is death, but which can also be the dead, or the past. Carson's poems and essays are an act of appropriation by a native of the city, and perhaps hold out the hope that Belfast might be owned imaginatively by all its people at last.

At present it is held, but hardly owned, by Britain, although Unionist politicians might not agree. In the City Council chamber members of the Official Unionist Party (OUP) are still able to act as if they retain, as always, the divine right to rule, and seem to be working very hard to preserve their own complacency. They share out the chairmanships of committees amongst themselves and the members of the Democratic Unionist Party (DUP) and act without consultation, treating their opponents with contempt. The grandeur of their high-handed manner is not reflected by the solidity of their position or the range of their powers. To watch a council session is to see decency, whether on the Unionist or opposition benches, brought low by stubborn stupidity and meanness.

Most of the Official Unionists have dull suits, several look like middle-aged businessmen rather too fond of Ulster fries. Next to them are the Democratic Unionists, a curious mixture. A couple are in rather more flashy blue suits, one clutches a Bible before the meeting opens. Sammy Wilson, the star of the show, wears a leather jacket and an Ian Botham haircut and, in between jibes at the other parties, propounds Thatcherite policies on council spending.

Behind him sits Rhonda Paisley, the Big Man's daughter. It is touching to see the ancient Unionists treat her as their mascot: they seem to find it difficult to cope with the presence of an attractive young woman in their midst. As it is January, the first session of the year, she is opening Christmas cards they have sent her: she turns her big eyes upon them and smiles at each in turn. As the business goes on, individual Unionists nip over to sit beside Rhonda and exchange a few whispers. One old chap from the OUP benches brings her a boiled sweet, which Rhonda gracefully unwraps and pops into her mouth.

Opposite are Alliance, in tweed jackets and pullovers, or in suits, looking like teachers and lawyers. The Social Democratic and Labour Party (SDLP), at the other end of the opposition benches, are surprisingly smart: this is the Catholic middle class, who would not appear under-dressed in Surrey, looking more educated and polished than the slightly *nouveau* and proletarian DUP, or the hoplessly old-fashioned OUP. Between Alliance and the SDLP are the Sinn Féin councillors, a sinister bunch, ranging from an Irish-language enthusiast in a pullover to two men in shiny suits who are constantly raising their eyes and pulling faces, playing to the public gallery.

Each time a Sinn Féin councillor gets up to speak, the Unionists troop out of the chamber, while Sammy and Rhonda keep up a barracking to prevent them being heard: it is like the bizarre ritual of an unknown tribe engaged in a ceremony whose arcane rules have been elaborated over centuries to a pitch of futile formality. But it is hard to feel sympathy for the Sinn Féin members: their sneering manner and their carefully calculated air of menace speak of a contempt for rather more than the misgovernment of the city. When one vote is taken, on predictably sectarian lines, they look meaningfully at those who record votes against them. Most bizarre, most sickening, facing them is the widow of a man murdered by republicans. It would be fair to say that George Seawright was an offensive bigot, but it is something of a triumph for the human faith in political structures that his widow should be a councillor, that the council should operate at all, however poorly, under such circumstances. It is bewildering for the observer and, one suspects, for many of the participants too. How can one make sense of a city run like this? Despite the shouting and abuse and rage, almost everyone seems to be having fun.

The Unionists cling to what power is left them, but many functions have been taken away, for example by the Housing Executive, set up to avoid the sectarian allocation of housing by local councils. Belfast is not typical of the province, for in other places the parties co-operate to a surprising degree. But in Belfast the Unionists are like sleepwalkers who have not woken up to the fact that things must change, that much has already changed. For years the City Hall has had a banner announcing '*Belfast says No*'.

The town began as private property, and remained an asset of the Chichester family for two centuries. But their own folly liberated the city, just as the folly of the Unionists let the state of Northern Ireland slip out of their hands.

George Augustus, the second Marquis of Donegall, was born in 1769 and lived a dissolute life in St James's, London, and at Fisherwick in Staffordshire. His family had not lived in Belfast since the castle burned down in 1708. In 1795 he found himself in debtors' prison, but was extracted by Edward May, a moneylender and owner of a gambling house. George Augustus married Anna, May's daughter, in Marylebone. He succeeded to the title in 1799, and the Mays got their reward (later two of Anna's brothers became sovereigns of Belfast, and the Mays gave their name to streets in the town). George Augustus found that £30,000 per annum was not enough to live on, so he came to Belfast in 1802 to cut down on expenses. He owed something like a quarter of a million pounds, which W.A. Maguire estimates at more than fifteen million at current values. His first plan was to marry his son, the Lord of Belfast, to a daughter of the sixth Earl of Shaftesbury. This fell through in 1818 when it was revealed that George and Anna were not legally married. The Marquis managed to have the marriage law changed retrospectively, and in 1822 the Lord of Belfast married Harriet Butler, daughter of the Earl of Glengall.

However, the Marquis still needed £217,000 to pay off his debts. He arranged to sell perpetuity leases at the same or even lower rents in return for cash. Much of Belfast and his land in counties Antrim and Donegal was leased in this way. The result was that the control the first Marquis, an absentee, had exercized, which had obliged developers to build at a uniform height and in sound materials, was gone. Georgian Belfast, with the Lagan Canal and the elegant public buildings built at the landlord's expense, was overlaid by Victorian Belfast. Both marquises had been generous in giving land: the first for the Poor House and the White Linen Hall, the second for the Fever Hospital, the Gasworks and the Commercial Buildings. But the second Marquis was poor: although he gave the land for the Belfast Academical Institution and launched its building fund with a promise to donate £600, he never actually paid the money.

The second Marquis raised more than he needed from the sale of leases, but by the mid 1830s he was in trouble again. When he died in 1844 it was discovered that he had not paid off his debts at all, but spent the money, probably on political sweeteners, gambling, entertaining, and building houses at Ormeau and Doagh.

After the Famine, many estates fell into difficulties because tenants could not afford to pay rent. In 1847 an Encumbered Estates Court was set up to sort out such problems, selling land to pay off the debts of landowners. The Donegall estates were one of the first and largest it dealt with. Because most of the tenants already had perpetual leases at low rent, a large proportion of the estate had to be sold. By 1855 most of Belfast had changed hands, except for Ormeau and the park under the Cave Hill.

Two years later the third Marquis at last achieved an alliance with the Shaftesburys when his only surviving child, Harriet, married the heir of the seventh Earl of Shaftesbury. (W.A. Maguire tells us that Shaftesbury did not approve of her worldliness and lack of decorum.) In 1867 the Marquis and his second wife built a new Belfast Castle on the slopes of the Cave Hill. They abandoned Ormeau House, which fell into ruin and was eventually levelled.

Ormeau Park was leased by the council as Belfast's first public park.

They also built the Chapel of the Resurrection as a family mausoleum and to commemorate their only son, the young Earl of Belfast who had died in Naples aged twenty-five. But the chapel was never finished. The Shaftesburys inherited the Donegall estates, and performed openings and did charity work, but in 1934 they donated Belfast Castle and its grounds to the city.

The old order, of the city and the state, ended in débâcle. As Liam de Paor makes clear in *Divided Ulster*, written in 1970 with a bitterness sharpened by contemporaneity, the state of Northern Ireland was created, more or less, to provide a viable unit for the city and its surrounding Protestant areas. Two of the six counties separated from the rest of Ireland at Partition would not have had Unionist majorities, while the city of Derry was cut off from its natural hinterland in Donegal. Northern Ireland was created – against the will, it must be said, of many Unionists – *in extremis*, amidst bloodshed, but unjustly. It was under constant siege: the permanence of the Special Powers Act, with its provisions to allow arrest and detention without trial, and practically anything else the Minister for Home Affairs could think of, is the most eloquent testimony to its 'abnormality', if such a concept has any meaning. It was brought about, as de Paor points out, by acts of mutiny and revolution instigated by English Conservatives; it sought to sustain itself by dividing its own working class; it was run by a rich elite whose interests never coincided with those in whose name they claimed to rule.

None of this constitutes an argument for the depraved acts of revenge and spite that have been passed off as 'armed struggle' since 1969, or for acts of injustice in the name of 'justice'. But the current problems of Belfast have a different perspective when we remember the disaster of the twentieth century as a whole. Maybe Northern Ireland's greatest sin was to be so poor for so long: from 1925 to World War Two, one quarter of insured workers were unemployed; in some places there was for generations no tradition of male work. The rest of Ireland was desperately poor too: except for a brief period it was never able to sustain its population without massive emigration.

Robin Bryans's *Ulster: a Journey Through the Six Counties* optimistically records a fading 'NO SURRENDER' slogan on a wall: the early sixties, when he took his journey, was a period of hope, which was dashed by eagerness to repeat the evolutions of the past. Evil governments are not always run by evil people: we inherit social systems as we inherit our name, our colour of hair, our parents' beliefs; we start, not where we choose, but where we find ourselves, on the Falls Road or the Shankhill, on either side of the Farset, in Andersonstown or Ballymacarrett, on either side of the Lagan.

Captain Terence O'Neill was a descendant, we were often told at the time of his appointment as Prime Minister in 1963, of the High Kings of Ireland. (In fact the link is distant, for he comes from the O'Neills of Lower Clandeboye, not the

Tyrone O'Neills; he is more closely related to the Chichesters.) Despite his limitations, he did not seem an evil man. At the general election of February 1969 he said that Northern Ireland was at a crossroads. He wanted to reform it, against the will of much of the Unionist Party, which put up official candidates against those sympathetic to O'Neill.

He resigned two months later and was succeeded by Major James Chichester-Clark (military titles were very popular) who lasted a little under two years. When Brian Faulkner became Prime Minister old heads were shaken. People had got used to gentry running Stormont, now here was someone in trade! (Though the great James Craig had been the son of a whiskey millionaire.) No doubt the old hands were not surprised when Faulkner joined the power-sharing Executive in 1973, and when Northern Ireland was taken out of Unionist hands by direct rule.

If you pull one thread you tighten the tangle rather than undoing the knot. That is true of any town, no doubt, and the best and worst of life can be found anywhere. Could it be that what makes Belfast so invigorating is that the extremes are more hard-edged? There is a quality of the light that makes things stark and sharply focused, a side effect of the maritime winds perhaps, the salt in the air and the moisture enhancing those negative ions, damping out the static that makes things cling together.

Whatever it may be, there is occasional evidence of exhilaration amongst visitors and returners. Looked at a certain way, Belfast 'is a large and pretty town, all along the road you see an arm of the sea on your left, and on the right high, rocky mountains, whose tops are often hidden by the clouds, and at the bottom a very pleasant wood, full of simples of all sorts'. Thus wrote Gideon Bonnivert, a French solider who arrived in Belfast in the hot summer of 1689 to fight for William of Orange. From his description the 'mountains' sound lofty, more like Himalayas than the hills we know. But we also know they *are* grand and wonderful.

BIBLIOGRAPHY

The editions referred to are those consulted.

Adair, Patrick, A True Narrative of the Rise and Progress of the Presbyterian Church in Ireland, Belfast 1866.

Adamson, Ian, Bangor, Light of the World, Belfast 1987.

Adamson, Ian, The Cruthin, Belfast 1974.

Adamson, Ian, The Identity of Ulster, Belfast 1982.

Bardon, Jonathan, Belfast: an Illustrated History, Belfast 1982.

Barton, Brian, The Blitz, Belfast 1989.

Beckett, J.C., Belfast: the Origins and Growth of an Industrial City, London 1967.

Beckett, J.C., A Short History of Ireland, London 1973.

Beckett, J.C., 'Belfast to the End of the Eighteenth Century', in Beckett, Belfast: the Making of the City.

Beckett, J.C. (et al.) Belfast: the Making of the City, Belfast 1988

Bell, Robert, 'Yesterday's Da', in Blackstaff Book of Short Stories, Belfast 1988.

Benn, George, A History of the Town of Belfast from the Earliest Times to the Close of the Eighteenth Century, Belfast 1877.

Benn, George, A History of the Town of Belfast from 1799 till 1810, Belfast 1880.

Berresford Ellis, Peter, The Boyne Water, Belfast 1989.

Berresford Ellis, Peter, Hell or Connaught!, Belfast 1988.

Bossy, John, and Peter Jupp, Essays Presented to Michael Roberts, Belfast 1976.

Boyle, Emily, '"Linenopolis": the Rise of the Textile Industry in Belfast', in Beckett, Belfast: the Making of the City.

Brady, Ciaran (ed.), Worsted in the Game, Mullingar 1989.

Brett, C.E.B., Buildings of Belfast 1700–1914, Belfast 1985.

British Association, Belfast in its Regional Setting, Belfast 1952.

Brondsted, Johannes, The Vikings, Harmondsworth 1960.

Bryans, Robin, Ulster: a Journey Through the Six Counties, Belfast 1989.

Buchanan, R.H., and B.M. Walker (eds.), Province, City and People, Antrim 1987.

Calendar of the State Papers Relating to Ireland: 1598 January–1599 March, London 1895.

1599 April–1600 February, London 1899.

1600 March–October, London 1903.

1 November 1600–31 July 1601, London 1905.

1601–1603, London 1912.

Carr, Peter, *The Most Unpretending of Places*, Dundonald 1988.

Carson, Ciarán, *Belfast Confetti*, Dublin 1989.

Carson, Ciarán, *The Irish for No*, Dublin 1987.

Carson, Ciarán, *The New Estate*, Belfast 1976.

Chadwick, Nora, *The Celts*, Harmondsworth 1976.

Chart, D.A. (ed.), *The Drennan Letters 1776–1819*, Belfast 1931.

Chart, D.A. (ed.), *A Preliminary Survey of the Ancient Monuments of Northern Ireland*, Belfast 1940.

Clarkson, Leslie, 'The City and the Country', in Beckett, *Belfast: the Making of the City*.

Clifford, Brendan, *Belfast in the French Revolution*, Belfast 1989.

Clifford, Brendan, *Thomas Russell and Belfast*, Belfast 1988.

Daley, Mary Downing, *Irish Laws*, Belfast 1989.

Derricke, John, *The Image of Irelande with a Discovery of Woodkarne*, Belfast 1986 (first published 1581).

Downing, Taylor (ed.), *The Troubles*, London 1982.

Eaton, John P., and Charles A. Haas, *Titanic: Destination Disaster*, Wellingborough 1987.

Evans, E. Estyn, 'Belfast: the site and the city', *Ulster Journal of Archaeology 3rd series*, 7 (1944).

Evans, E. Estyn, 'The Site of Belfast', *Geography* 22 (1937).

Evans, E. Estyn, *Ulster: The Common Ground*, Mullingar, 1984.

Gantz, Jeffrey (trans.), *Early Irish Myths and Sagas*, Harmondsworth 1983.

Gerald of Wales, *The History and Topography of Ireland*, London 1982.

Gerald of Wales, *The Journey Through Wales; The Description of Wales*, London 1988.

Green, E.R.R., *The Lagan Valley 1800–50*, London 1944.

Hamilton, Gary, and Michael Hall, *Cúchulainn, Champion of Ulster*, Newtonabbey 1989.

Hammond, David, *Steel Chest, Nail in the Boot and the Barking Dog*, Belfast 1986.

Harmon, Maurice (ed.), *The Irish Writer and the City*, Gerrards Cross 1984.

Heaney, Seamus, *Selected Poems*, London 1980.

Heaney, Seamus, and Michael Longley, *An Upstairs Outlook*, Belfast 1989.

Herodotus, *The Histories*, Harmondsworth 1980.

Hewitt, John (ed.), *Rhyming Weavers*, Belfast 1974.

Hildesheimer, Wolfgang, *Mozart*, London 1982.

Hill, Rev. George, see Montgomery.

Holmes, R. Finlay, *Henry Cooke*, Belfast 1981.

Inglis, H.D., *A Journey Throughout Ireland During the Spring, Summer and Autumn of 1834*, London 1834.

Ireland, Denis, *From the Jungle of Belfast*, Belfast 1973.

Jefferson, Herbert, *Viscount Pirrie of Belfast*, Belfast 1948.

Joy, Henry, *Belfast Politics*, Belfast 1974.

Joy, Henry, *Historical Collections Relative to the Town of Belfast*, Belfast 1817.

Kinsella, Thomas (trans.), *The Táin*, Dublin 1979.

Leydon, Maurice (ed.), *Belfast City of Song*, Dingle 1989.

Longley, Edna, *Louis MacNeice: A Study*, London 1988.

Longley, Edna, 'The Writer and Belfast' in Maurice Harmon, *The Irish Writer and the City*, Gerrards Cross, 1984.

Longley, Michael, *Poems 1963–1983*, Edinburgh 1985.

Lydon, James, 'John de Courcy' in Ciaran Brady (ed.), *Worsted in the Game*.

Lynch, Martin, *The Interrogation of Ambrose Fogarty*, Belfast 1982.

Maguire, W.A., 'Lord Donegall and the Hearts of Steel', in *Irish Historical Studies* 21, 1978–9.

Maguire, W.A., 'Lords and Landlords – the Donegall Family', in Beckett, *Belfast: the Making of the City*.

Maguire, W.A. (ed.) *Kings in Conflict*, Belfast 1990.

McLaverty, Michael, *Call My Brother Back*, Dublin 1982.

McLaverty, Michael, *Lost Fields*, Dublin 1980.

MacNeice, Louis, *Collected Poems*, London 1966.

McNeill, Mary, *The Life and Times of Mary Ann McCracken*, Belfast 1988.

McNeill, T.E., *Anglo-Norman Ulster*, Edinburgh 1980.

Madden, R.R., *The United Irishmen, Their Lives and Times*, London 1858.

Mahon, Derek, *Poems 1962–1978*, London 1979.

Messenger, Betty, *Picking Up the Linen Threads*, Belfast 1980.

Millin, Shannon, *Sidelights on Belfast History*, Belfast 1932.

Moloney, Ed, and Andy Pollak, *Paisley*, Dublin 1986.

Montgomery, William, *The Montgomery Manuscripts (1603–1706)*, edited, with notes, by Rev. George Hill, Belfast 1869.

Moss, Michael, and John R. Hume, *Shipbuilders to the World*, Belfast 1986.

Neeson, Eoin, *Irish Myths and Legends* Books I and 2, Cork 1988.

O'Byrne, Cathal, *As I Roved Out*, Belfast 1982.

O'Faolain, Sean, *The Great O'Neill*, Cork 1982.

O'Faolain, Sean, *The Irish*, Harmondsworth 1969.

Olinder, Britta, 'John Hewitt's Belfast', in Maurice Harmon, *The Irish Writer and the City*.

Orel, H. (ed.), *Irish History and Culture*, Dublin 1979.

Owen, D.J., *History of Belfast*, Belfast 1921.

de Paor, Liam, *Divided Ulster*, Harmondsworth, 1977.

de Paor, Liam, *The Peoples of Ireland*, London 1986.

Parker, Stewart, *Three Plays for Ireland*, Birmingham 1989.

Patton, Marcus, *Belfast: An Illustrated Yearbook 1990*, Belfast 1989.

Public Records Office of Northern Ireland, 'The United Irishmen', *Education Facsimile Series*, 61–80, Belfast 1989.

'The '98 Rebellion', *Education Facsimile Series*, 81–100, Belfast 1989.

Porter, J.L., *The Life and Times of Henry Cooke*, London 1871.

Reid, James Seaton, *A History of the Presbyterian Church*, London 1853.

Smith, Robert Jerome, 'Irish Mythology', in Orel, *op. cit.*

Snyder, Henry L., 'From the Beginnings to the End of the Middle Ages', in Orel, *op. cit.*

Snyder, Henry L., 'From the Treaty of Limerick to the Union with Great Britain', in Orel, *op. cit.*

Stevenson, Noragh, *Belfast Before 1820*, Belfast 1967.

Stewart, A.T.Q., *The Narrow Ground*, London 1971.

Thackeray, William Makepeace, *The Irish Sketch-Book*, Belfast 1985.

Thompson, Sam, *Over the Bridge*, Dublin 1970.

Tone, Theobald Wolfe, *Autobiography*, London 1937.

Warren, W.L., 'John in Ireland, 1185', in John Bossy and Peter Jupp, *Essays Presented to Michael Roberts*.

Wilson Judith C., *Conor*, Belfast 1981.

INDEX